CONCEPTS
AND
METHODS
OF
SOCIAL WORK

PRENTICE-HALL SOCIOLOGY SERIES
Herbert Blumer, Editor

CONTRIBUTORS TO THIS VOLUME:

Genevieve Carter
Professor Emeritus,
School of Social Work,
University of Southern California

Walter A. Friedlander
Professor Emeritus of Social Welfare,
University of California

Gisela Konopka
Professor of Social Work,
University of Minnesota
Director, Youth Development and Research Center

Henry S. Maas
Professor, School of Social Work,
University of British Columbia

SECOND EDITION

CONCEPTS
AND
METHODS
OF
SOCIAL WORK

Walter A. Friedlander, editor

Professor Emeritus of Social Welfare
University of California at Berkeley

PRENTICE-HALL, INC., Englewood Cliffs, New Jersey

Library of Congress Cataloging in Publication Data

FRIEDLANDER, WALTER A.   ed.
   Concepts and methods of social work.

   (Prentice-Hall series in sociology)
   Includes bibliographies and index.
    1. Social service.   2. Social case work.
3. Social group work.   I. Title.
HV40.F74   1976   361   75-45164
ISBN 0-13-166488-3

© 1976, 1958 by Prentice-Hall, Inc., Englewood Cliffs, New Jersey

Printed in the United States of America

10   9   8   7   6   5   4   3   2   1

PRENTICE-HALL INTERNATIONAL, INC., *London*
PRENTICE-HALL OF AUSTRALIA PTY. LIMITED, *Sydney*
PRENTICE-HALL OF CANADA, LTD., *Toronto*
PRENTICE-HALL OF INDIA PRIVATE LIMITED, *New Delhi*
PRENTICE-HALL OF JAPAN, INC., *Tokyo*
PRENTICE-HALL OF SOUTHEAST ASIA PTE. LTD., *Singapore*

CONTENTS

Preface, ix

chapter one
Introduction: Generic Principles of Social Work   1
WALTER A. FRIEDLANDER
Objectives of Social Work   6
The Field of Social Work   9

chapter two
Social Work with Individuals and Families   13
HENRY S. MAAS

I. Some Fundamentals of Casework Practice   15
II. Exploring a Family's Adaptation to a Stressful Situation   21
   A. *The Coyle Family Case Record, 22*
   B. *Analysis of the Coyle Family Case Record, 31*

III. Basic Concepts Relevant to Casework Practice   39
    A. The Concept of a Social Role in Casework Practice Theory, 40
    B. The Concept of Mode of Adaptation in Casework Practice Theory, 53
    C. The Concept of Ego in Casework Practice Theory, 59
IV. Principles of Casework Practice   63
    A. General Principles of Casework Practice, 64
    B. Differential Principles of Casework Practice, 71
 V. The Place of Casework in Larger Contexts   78

Selected Bibliography   82
Social Work with Individuals and Families, 82
Knowledge Basic to Social Work Practice with Individuals and Families, 83

chapter three
The Method of Social Group Work   85
GISELA KONOPKA AND WALTER A. FRIEDLANDER

 I. Goals and Purpose of Social Group Work   85
    Values Underlying the Professional Use of the Group Work Method, 87
    Human Needs Served by Social Group Work, 88
    Group Work and Religious Prejudice Among Small Children, 93
    Human Capacities Strengthened by Social Group Work, 95
 II. Theory of the Social Group Work Method   99
    Application of the Scientific Method to Social Group Work, 99
    Theory of Individual Dynamics, 101
    Group Process, 103
    Summary of Theoretical Framework of Social Group Work, 106
    Fact Finding, 107
    Diagnosis and Treatment Plan (Assessment and Action), 111
    Treatment (Action), 114
III. Principles of Social Group Work in Practice   116
    The Group of Seizure Patients, 117
    Summary for the Group of Seizure Patients, 142
    Help with the Process of Decision Making, 142
    Balance of Self-Determination and Help, 143
    Recognition of Unexpressed Needs, 144
    Individualization in the Group Situation, 144
    Constructive Use of Limitations, 145
    Use of Program in Relation to Needs, 146
IV. The Group Worker as Teacher and Supervisor   150
 V. Group Work As A Part of Social Work and As A Part of Service to Humanity   154

Selected Bibliography   156

chapter four
Community Organization and Social Planning   158
GENEVIEVE W. CARTER

I. Introduction   158

II. A Developing and Changing Professional Practice   161
   A. Changing Concepts, 161
   B. Major Strategies or Approaches, 165

III. Components of Practice   174

IV. A Profile of Practice   197
   Planning for the Aged—A New Agency, 199
   An Integrated Services Demonstration, 206
   The Practitioner of Tomorrow, 212

   Selected Bibliography   214
   Interorganization Theory/Organizational Theory, 214
   Management (Technologies) P.A., 214
   Information Systems, 214
   Social Problems, 214
   Communication, 215
   Political Science, 215
   Social Change, 215

chapter five
Social Welfare Administration and Research   216
WALTER A. FRIEDLANDER

I. Generic Aspects of Social Work Practice   216

II. Techniques Facilitating Social Work Practice   219
   A. Social Welfare Administration, 219
   B. Social Work Research, 224

   Selected Bibliography   228
   Social Welfare Administration, 228
   Social Work Research, 228

Author Index, 233

Subject Index, 241

PREFACE

In the first edition of this book, the authors emphasized that social work concepts and methods are not static but are changing with new philosophies of social work and changing professional knowledge and skills. The three basic social work methods—social casework, social group work, and community work—still remain the essential functions of social workers, but a combination of the skills of the three methods is now more frequently required, and the borderlines between these methods have become more fluid.

There is a trend to a generic type of social work that goes beyond the three basic methods to include community work in social reform. Social workers must participate in broader endeavors to assist people in obtaining better opportunities and in achieving social justice. All three social work methods consider the social setting in which people live, but newly developed methods also aim at regulating "large-scale organizations" and their change. In social casework, the treatment may have to include the use of group work. The use of well-trained caseworkers might be limited to the function of social services that require professional skills, while simpler tasks may be performed by persons with less advanced preparation or, after short training periods, by social assistants recruited from the circle of welfare recipients. Community work may be either task oriented—for example, aimed at improving medical services by establishing a clinic or providing for undernourished children—or process oriented—for example, organizing client groups to determine the priorities of their needs, such as housing for disadvantaged groups, shelter for homeless families, and how to find resources in order to achieve necessary changes in local policies. Community work will help to strengthen the capacity of clients to make their own decisions about the priority of their needs and in this way will lead to more effective participation by clients in the processes that should help them. In the area of community organization that was operated mainly by private councils in 1958, numerous governmental agencies are now assuming major responsibilities, thus leading to a very different structure and practice in the field, with new concepts, goal, and functions, which are emphasized in this edition.

In the developing countries, community work in the form of "community development" often is directed toward increasing the local resources of the community to meet urgent needs—for example, digging wells for pure water or constructing roads with some technical help of experts. In general, community work does not deal with social pathology, or deviance, or delinquency, for which social casework and group work are still the main resources of change. Community work aims at the solution of conflicts in peaceful ways through compromise or mutual understanding, without disruption of vital community operations.[1]

---

[1]Eileen Younghusband, "Intercultural Aspects of Social Work," *Education for Social Work* 2, no. 1 (Spring 1966): 59–65; Elizabeth Wickenden, *Social Welfare in a Changing World* (Washington, D.C.: Department of Health, Education, and Welfare, 1965), p. vii; and John M. Romanshyn, *Social Welfare: Charity to Justice* (New York: Random House, 1971), p. 5.

CONCEPTS
AND
METHODS
OF
SOCIAL WORK

CHAPTER ONE

INTRODUCTION: GENERIC PRINCIPLES OF SOCIAL WORK

Walter A. Friedlander

The basic values of social work do not spring up like wild flowers by the wayside; they are, instead, rooted in the deep fertile beliefs that nourish civilizations. Our own civilization in the United States has grown up from beliefs in ethical and spiritual equality, freedom of individual development, free choice of opportunities, fair competition, a certain degree of personal independence, freedom of speech, and freedom of expression and communication. Our system of social sanctions is based upon mutual respect and concern for the rights of all. Social work is directed toward the realization and implementation of the ideals of democracy in our civilization.

We shall characterize as "generic" the principles that apply to the three primary types of social work: *social casework, social group work,* and *community organization.*[1] These generic principles are derived from the

---

[1] The authors discuss in this book the principal *methods* of social work, their *concepts,* and *principles* of practice. An earlier school of thought under the leadership of William I. Newstetter preferred the term "process of social work." See Werner W. Boehm, "The Terminology of Social Casework: An Attempt at Theoretical Clarification," *Social Service Review* 28, no. 4 (December 1954): 386. "Social work process" implies the interaction between client and social worker in interview, social diagnosis, and treatment; the interaction of the members of a group with one another and with the group workers; and the interaction in community organization between the various individuals and groups in the community.

1

goal of social work in our society, which is to prevent or at least to alleviate the socially and psychologically damaging effects of crisis situations and social injustice[2] and to remove barriers to the healthy development of individuals, groups, and communities.

The feelings, attitudes, orientation, and practices of social workers in the American culture are, at least in theory, inspired by the following democratic values:

1. *Conviction of the inherent worth, the integrity, and the dignity of the individual.*[3] This concept determines the approach of the caseworker to his client and their mutual relationship in the helping process. It is the basis for the changes achieved in the client's social conditions and in his attitude toward his personal problems. The same conviction determines the social group worker's role in providing for the individual member within the group the opportunity to establish a helpful relationship of belonging, of being a vital part of the entire group. The group worker's acceptance that each person in the group deserves full recognition, respect, attention, and consideration as the group develops its aims and activities plays a decisive role in the process.[4] In the area of community organization or "social intergroup work," the same concept fits the representatives of various groups and organizations in the community. The social worker as a community organizer respects individual members of the community as persons who offer thoughtful considerations, observations, and valuable recommendations. The worker developing social services for welfare and health aims to assist all members of a community in securing a better life, happiness, and satisfaction. The democratic ideal of the worth and dignity of the individual remains pivotal. The belief in human dignity represents also the motivating factor for social work research and social welfare administration, which are the secondary, or auxiliary, processes of social work.

2. The second generic principle is the conviction that the individual who is in economic, personal, or social need has *the right to determine himself what his needs are and how they should be met.* In the practice of social work, the individual in material or emotional need is entitled to retain his *right of self-determination.* His claim to exercise "self-help" is accepted as a human civil right. In social casework, no longer does the worker believe in performing all necessary steps for the client or in manipulating his

---

[2]Henry S. Maas and Martin Wolins, "Concepts and Methods in Social Work Research," in *New Directions in Social Work,* ed. Cora Kasius (New York: Harper, 1954), p. 215.

[3]Arline Johnson, "Development of Basic Methods of Social Work Practice and Education," *Social Work Journal* 36, no. 3 (July 1955): 104–14; and Harriett M. Bartlett, *The Common Base of Social Work Practice* (New York: National Association of Social Workers, 1970).

[4]Gisela Konopka, "The Generic and the Specific in Group Work Practice," *Social Work* 1, no. 1 (January 1956): 72–80.

affairs. He recognizes that the essential change in the client's economic and psychosocial conditions will take place only when the client is helped to help himself. The client will be able to overcome his problems to the degree that he assumes the role of solving for himself the crisis situation, although the support of the caseworker will prove to be an essential factor in his growing independence.[5]

The social worker believes that people are capable of changing their attitudes and behavior; he believes that techniques that will help people to change as they want to change can be communicated and learned. The client, shaken by economic failure, ill health, or emotional disturbance, may win back his self-respect and confidence when the caseworker guides him to his own acceptance of his problem and to his own decision to find a new way. The client's freedom of choice forestalls any frustrated, discouraged feeling that he is asking for help, that another person is interfering with his private life or managing his affairs. He regains confidence in himself when he recognizes his ability to find solutions for his problems and to decide on a way of following through.

Social work concepts and practice are strongly influenced by the rapid change of social and economic conditions in our present society, not only in the rich, developed countries, but also in the newly developing nations. Especially in the postindustrial countries of western civilization, this rapid change leads to questioning many earlier values, such as the principle of monogamy, marriage as the sole source of sexual relations, and the nuclear family, all of which are being challenged by new forms of marriage such as communal marriage and homosexual marriage. Although it is very doubtful whether some of these experimental relations lead to a more gratifying life, social workers need to be trained for the professional work of providing essential services in consulting all classes of society about the desirable solutions of conflicts and problems in personal relations, and social workers need to be prepared and trained for such professional work.[6]

In social group work, the principle of the right of the group to determine the goals, means, and objectives of its activities is respected

---

[5] Scott Briar and Henry Miller, *Problems and Issues in Social Casework* (New York: Columbia University Press, 1971); Florence Hollis, *Social Casework: The Psychosocial Approach, Encyclopedia of Social Work (1971)* [hereafter cited as *Encyclopedia (1971)*], pp. 1217–26; Helen Perlman, *Perspectives on Social Casework* (Philadelphia: Temple University Press, 1971); and William J. Reid and Laura Epstein, *Task Centered Casework* (New York: Columbia University Press, 1972).

[6] See Eleanor B. Sheldon and Wilbert E. Moore, *Indicators of Social Change* (New York: Russell Sage Foundation, 1971), pp. 180–98; Marvin B. Sussman, "Family, Kinship, and Bureaucracy," in *The Human Meaning of Social Change*, eds. Angus Campbell and Philip E. Converse (New York: Russell Sage Foundation, 1972); Jessie Bernard, *The Future of Marriage* (New York: World Publishing, 1972); and Edward R. Lowenstein, "Social Work in Postindustrial Society," *Social Work* 18, no. 6 (November 1973): 40–47.

by the social group worker. He or she has faith in a sound reaction of the group as a whole and of its members. The worker respects the group members' desire to find for themselves the aims and forms of their being and acting together. The social group worker's role permits him to assist when difficulties in the work of the group cannot be solved by the members of the group alone, when clarification of possibilities and methods of cooperation is needed, and when dissent, hostilities, and other problems of the group or of its individual members call for the worker's insight, knowledge, and experience. Although the tendency to form groups is widespread in many countries, the use of social group work for physical and spiritual growth, increased pleasure, and the cultural improvement of our environment is especially characteristic of our own country.[7] In social group work, the fact of being together and interacting is purposefully developed as a socially accepted, constructive goal in itself that permits creative, satisfactory activities.

In the practice of community organization, the social worker needs to respect fully the right of the community, its government, organizations, and groups, in deciding what action seems necessary and desirable in order to meet the welfare needs of the people. The investigation of the needs of the community, the assessment of priorities, the planning of health and welfare services, and the decisions about changes and expansion depend upon the social convictions of individuals and groups in the community who recognize the possibilities but see also the limits of local resources. Democratic philosophy proposes that the members of the community are equals in spite of their differences in wealth, education, status, faith, race, and occupation. For this reason, all groups of the community should be responsible for the common welfare. The social worker as community organizer will be able to strengthen the faith of such groups and individuals who are willing to undertake the mobilization of whatever new resources in the community may be required to meet essential social needs or to change inadequate services. But a worker will not succeed unless he is sensitive in recognizing what the community seeks for itself and fully respects the opinion of the members of the community and their sincere assessment of social needs and resources.[8]

[7]Gertrude Wilson and Gladys Ryland, *Social Group Work Practice* (Boston: Houghton Mifflin, 1949), pp. 17–20; Gisela Konopka, *Social Group Work: A Helping Process,* 2nd ed. (Englewood Cliffs, N.J.: Prentice-Hall, 1972), pp. 19–28; and William Schwartz and Serapio R. Zalba, eds., *The Practice of Group Work* (New York: Columbia University Press, 1971).

[8]Robert A. Nisbet, "Moral Values and Community," in *Perspectives on the American Community* (2nd ed.), ed. Roland L. Warren (Chicago: Rand McNally, 1972), pp. 85–93; Robert Morris and Martin Rein, "Emerging Patterns in Community Planning," in ibid., pp. 273–81; and Ralph M. Kramer, "Future of the Voluntary Service Organization," *Social Work* 18, no. 6 (November 1973): 59–69.

3. A third concept that is of decisive importance for social work in a democratic society is the *firm belief in equal opportunity for all, limited only by the individual's capacities.* Social work cannot adhere to racial, religious, or political prejudice without defeating its fundamental convictions of human dignity and self-determination. Social services must be available to all without distinction in religion, caste, or class. In social casework, the needs of the individual, whether financial, social, or emotional, must draw a really sympathetic, human understanding from the caseworker who attempts to help the client meet his needs within the framework of the resources of the community. The caseworker might help the client to regain his lost place in his family or occupation, to establish a satisfactory way of living with others, or to readjust in new ways when conflicts with family, friends, or society have led the client into trouble and unhappiness.

In social group work, this value proposition of democratic equality leads to the practice that the individual member who is joining a group, advised and supported by the social group worker, will find a sympathetic, friendly atmosphere of acceptance. The cooperation and confidence of the group eases the integration of the new member and stimulates his spiritual and emotional growth in a congenial atmosphere. But the group also expects the new member to cooperate with others in the functions and obligations of the group. In this way a new member is acquainted with cooperative behavior and is no longer solely concerned with his own well-being and pleasure but is also interested in the well-being of the other members and in the functioning and success of the group. He learns that giving to his utmost capacity is not only an obligation, but a joy.[9]

The social worker plays a vital role in conveying to the members of the group his sincere conviction of human equality of people of different race, religion, color, and class. He uses in his work with the group members his knowledge of sociology, civil rights, and education, as well as human behavior. The group worker enables the various types of groups with whom he is connected to cooperate. With the group worker's assistance, the program and activities of the different groups lead to a personal interaction of the group members that contributes both to their satisfaction and spiritual growth and to a constructive, enriching group life that is an asset to the community.

The community organizer is guided by his conviction of the human right to equal opportunities for meeting basic needs. He encourages the

[9]Henry S. Maas, "Evaluating the Individual Member of the Group," National Conference of Social Work, *Group Work and Community Organization,* 1953–54 (New York: Columbia University Press, 1954), pp. 42–43; and Gisela Konopka, *Social Group Work,* pp. 83–115.

leaders of the community to provide the necessary social services and facilities to procure opportunities for learning and to realize physical health, cultural growth, and pleasure for those individuals and groups for whom present conditions have not secured these means.

4. A fourth value common to all methods of social work is the conviction that man's individual rights to self-respect, dignity, self-determination, and equal opportunities are connected with his *social responsibilities toward himself, his family, and his society.* This conviction involves the challenge of creating a clearer understanding of a give-and-take relationship between our society and human beings as individuals, groups, and communities who receive assistance, support, advice, and opportunities for growth and for human happiness. Both the social caseworker and the social group worker have to show the individual and the group that full recognition of their own rights also requires insight into their obligations and limitations, and the acceptance of and respect for the needs and rights of others. In work with the individual as well as with the group, the social worker encourages and enables the achievement of desirable social goals. Both caseworker and group worker use their knowledge of human motivations and behavior, familiarity with the program of the group, and their relation to the individuals who form the group in order to develop an acceptance of social responsibility and a desirable interaction for the welfare of our society. In community organization, the social worker is fully aware that no program or action should injure health and welfare needs of other groups. He endeavors to maintain in the use of community resources a healthy balance between measures of preventive or curative care, facilities, and opportunities.

OBJECTIVES OF SOCIAL WORK

Within the framework of basic values that we have discussed, social work seeks to assist individuals, groups, and communities to reach the highest possible degree of social, mental, and physical well-being.[10] The methods that social work applies to achieve this goal differ from those of other professions, such as medicine, law, the ministry, nursing, and teaching, because social work operates in consideration of *all* social, economic, and psychological factors that influence the life of the individual, the family, the social group, and the community. The members of other service professions, although they assume the duty of promoting the well-being and respecting the confidence of the individual whom they serve, focus

[10]United Nations Economic and Social Council, *Training for Social Work: An International Survey* (1950), p. 10; and Harriett M. Bartlett, "Social Work Fields of Practice," *Encyclopedia (1971),* pp. 1478–81.

their services upon one specific aspect of the personal needs involved. Social work functions with the awareness of the dynamic interplay of personal, biological, and psychological elements with the socioeconomic forces of the environment in which human beings live. In his diagnosis and planning to find solutions for problems of social adjustment, the social worker cannot exclude any aspect of the life of the individuals with whom he works or any social condition that exists in the community where he operates.[11] This twofold approach of social work has been called "dualistic"—its aim is not only to help the *individual*, the *family*, and the *group of persons* in their social relationships, but it is also concerned with the improvement of general *social conditions* by raising health and economic standards, advocating better housing and working conditions, and supporting constructive social legislation.[12]

The forerunners of social work—poor relief and charities—provided meager relief of a palliative nature to the lowest class of society, the destitute and miserable. Traditionally, they gave financial aid for sustenance to the destitute, the blind and deaf-mute, the indigent, and the chronically ill. But social work today is losing its class character; its operations serve the betterment of all classes of the entire community. Social services increasingly assist people of all social levels, including individuals and families that are not economically dependent, and in a wide variety of social situations.

To perform this integrating function, social work uses the strengths of the individual and of the group, as well as the constructive forces of the environment. This task is achieved through social institutions, such as welfare agencies, schools, hospitals, clinics, employment services, churches, and the courts, which are the societal means of assisting people who face economic or social problems in meeting the demands of their environment or in their personal relations. Some of these problems, arising perhaps from age, mental illness, or physical conditions, are such that individuals are unable to manage their own affairs.

The goal of social work is to reconcile the well-being of the individuals with the welfare of society in which they live. This objective precludes that social work attempt to force the people with whom it works to accept destitution, deprivation, or humiliation as given facts or to adjust to conditions that are harmful, unjust, and depriving. Unlike early charity practice, modern social work no longer tries to make the client or the social group "acquiesce" in such conditions; rather, it attempts to help

---

[11]Ibid., p. 1480.

[12]Herbert Bisno, *The Philosophy of Social Work* (Washington, D.C.: Public Affairs Press, 1952), p. 72; and Arnulf M. Pins, "Changes in Social Work Education and Their Implications for Practice," *Social Work* 16, no. 2 (April 1971): 5–15.

clients get a clear insight that permits them first to face conditions as reality and then to try to improve them. At the same time, social work attempts to mobilize social forces to resolve those social and economic situations that lead to ill health, mental suffering, frustration, and asocial behavior.[13] In cases of conflict, social work helps individuals overcome the difficulties they encounter in the right use of the facilities their environment offers, explaining to them the community resources created for their benefit.[14]

Among these objectives there is the effort to help the indigent client and his family to obtain basic economic security through social insurance benefits, veterans' pensions, public assistance payments, or voluntary social agencies support. Aid can also be made available by utilizing other community resources for employment, medical care, psychiatric treatment, cultural and educational advancement, vocational guidance, training, and rehabilitation, as well as recreational opportunities. The integration of measures for financial assistance to people in economic distress requires careful consideration of individual psychological problems or health difficulties that may exercise pressure on the client and impair his normal development.[15]

As social work recognizes the multiplicity of causation of social problems, it is concerned both with giving personal help to clients in need of service and with measures that aim toward a change of the societal conditions that cause or contribute to human suffering and maladjustment. In working toward the social adjustment of the individual and of the group, social work needs to consider the cultural environment from which the individual clients or group members come. Clients' values may not be the same as those of the social worker or of the group that determines the policies of social work practice through its organizations. The objective of social work remains to help individuals and groups to find the best way of achieving goals without subduing anyone to conformity, unless a person's behavior and actions violate the well-being and rights of others. Unjust behavior and actions cannot be supported by social work. Based upon knowledge of the elements that determine human behavior, social work attempts to develop constructive forces in the individual and in the social group that enable them to build for themselves a fuller, more satisfactory life. Social work only assists people in solving their emotional, social, and economic problems by releasing their natural abilities and creative energies, but it also encourages clients'

[13]Arnold Gurin, "Social Planning and Community Organization," *Encyclopedia (1971),* p. 1334.

[14]Alfred J. Kahn, *Issues in American Social Work* (New York: Columbia University Press, 1959), pp. 3–38.

[15]Robert Perrucci and Marc Pilisuk, eds., *The Triple Revolution Emerging* (Boston: Little, Brown, 1971), pp. 319–29.

active participation in working toward their self-selected goals. These goals are not limited to the remedy of economic destitution or physical and mental disabilities, but rather include stimulation of full human growth and application of creative abilities that seem desirable for the fulfillment of man's potentialities and a sound development of our society. In this way, social work assists in realizing democratic principles and human rights, seeking to secure for all citizens a decent standard of living, social security, and the fulfillment of the universal human need for love, acceptance, recognition, and status.

THE FIELD OF SOCIAL WORK

Methods of social work are applied in a variety of settings that may be briefly indicated in this text. As we saw, the methods have in common as their immediate and main objective the direct enhancing of the well-being of individual members of our society, either alone, in groups, or in communities. The settings consist of: (1) services to disadvantaged individuals and groups, the sick, handicapped, destitute, dependent children and the aged, minority groups, and newcomers to communities; (2) services that provide protection to individuals and groups that are exposed to unusual hazards and hardships, such as disabled veterans; victims of natural disasters, epidemics, or war emergencies; families of servicemen; and (3) protective, cultural, and developmental services for children and youth, senior citizens, Indians on reservations, and isolated groups in need of community integration.

The major activities in the field of social work may be classified according to type of service, as follows:

PUBLIC ASSISTANCE. Social services to persons in financial need, including general assistance or indigent aid; categorical assistance of higher standards to the aged, blind, totally disabled, and dependent children; and institutional care for indigent aged, blind, and other handicapped persons who cannot live at home.[16]

SOCIAL INSURANCE. Services to provide insured workers, self-employed people, and their families with protection against the loss of income due to old age, unemployment, industrial accidents and occupational diseases, death of the family breadwinner, and against certain aspects of other illness through medical care, hospitalization, and rehabilitation.[17]

FAMILY SERVICES. Casework and counseling on personal and family

---

[16]Ida C. Marion et al., "Social Services," *Encyclopedia (1971)*, pp. 423–35.

[17]George Hoshino, "Money and Morality: Income Security and Personal Social Services," *Social Work* 16, no. 2 (April 1971): 16–24.

relations, marriage, health, economic and budget problems, special services to people away from home, travelers, migratory families, the Indians, recent immigrants, prisoners, and provision of legal aid.[18]

CHILD WELFARE SERVICES. Placement of children in foster care and children's institutions, day nurseries, and day-care centers; supervision of foster families and adoptions; protective services to prevent maladjustment and asocial behavior; infant and preschool children care, school social services, and child labor protection.

HEALTH AND MEDICAL SERVICES. Maternal and child health services, well-baby centers and dispensaries, child conferences, visiting nurse service, medical care for recipients of public assistance and the self-supporting "medically indigent"; financial and medical aid and rehabilitation to crippled children, blind and deaf, victims of such diseases as cancer, tuberculosis, infantile paralysis, heart disease, and cerebral palsy, under both public and private agency auspices.[19]

MENTAL HYGIENE SERVICES. Services in hospitals and sanatoriums for the mentally ill and the mentally retarded; vocational training; placing out and supervision of patients suffering from nervous diseases; rehabilitation services; preventive and therapeutic treatments, through child guidance clinics for children and through psychiatric out-patient departments of hospitals and mental hygiene clinics for adults.[20]

CORRECTIONAL SERVICES. Probation services in juvenile and criminal courts; diagnostic and treatment services; casework and group work in detention homes, prisons, penitentiaries, reformatories, and transition camps, assisting in the adjustment of offenders and in their preparation for return to community life; parole service for juvenile and adult offenders released from correctional institutions; community services for prevention of delinquency.[21]

YOUTH LEISURE-TIME SERVICES. Community and youth centers,

---

[18]For a critical view of family structures see Eric Gronseth, "The Familial Institution," in *American Society,* eds. Larry T. Reynolds and James M. Hensch (New York: David McKay, 1973), pp. 248–93; and Gwendolyn C. Gilbert, "Counseling Black Adolescent Parents," *Social Work* 19, no. 1 (January 1974): 88–95.

[19]Anselm M. Strauss, "Medical Ghettos," in *Poor Americans—How the White Poor Live,* eds. Marc Pilisuk and Phyllis Pilisuk (Chicago: Aldine, 1971), pp. 151–68; George E. Ehrlich, "Health Challenges of the Future," *Annals of the American Academy of Political and Social Science* 408 (July 1973): 70–80; Bertram S. Brown, "Mental Health in the Future: Politics, Science, Ethics and Values," ibid., pp. 62–69; David Mechanic, "Human Problems and the Organization of Health Care," ibid. 399 (January 1972): 1–11; and Mary W. Herman, "The Poor: Their Medical Needs and the Health Services Supplied Them," ibid., pp. 12–21.

[20]Herman D. Stein, "Social Work Manpower and Training," *Social Work Education Reporter* 20, no. 1 (December 1971–January 1972): 23–24; and David Mechanic, *Mental Health and Social Policy* (Englewood Cliffs, N.J.: Prentice-Hall, 1969).

[21]Gerald O'Connor, "Toward a New Policy in Adult Corrections," *Social Service Review* 46, no 4 (December 1972): 581–95.

settlement houses, neighborhood houses, and recreation facilities; service with boys' and girls' groups, the YMCA, the YWCA, the 4-H associations, children's clubs, Boy and Girl Scouts, and other youth organizations, summer and vacation camps, and cultural youth activities.

VETERANS' SERVICES. Casework and group work services to disabled veterans and war veterans in need of medical or psychiatric treatment in hospitals and clinics; casework with the families of veterans; vocational guidance and rehabilitation; educational aid; special employment services; priority in civil service positions and promotions, in public housing; loans for purchase of farms, homes, and business enterprises; compensations and pensions for disabled veterans and survivors.

EMPLOYMENT SERVICES. Placement of workers looking for jobs; assistance to industry and agriculture in finding qualified workers; vocational guidance; labor protection and safety education; services in vocational rehabilitation.

HOUSING SERVICES. Family and children services in public housing projects and new housing developments, particularly in industrial regions and for projects involving racial and ethnic minorities; special services for aged or chronically ill persons and families with numerous children, assistance in protection against exploitation, help in budgeting and economic management; loans under federal guarantee for home purchase or building; slum clearance and urban redevelopment.[22]

INTERNATIONAL SOCIAL SERVICES. In such agencies as the United Nations, the World Health Organization, the U.N. Technical Assistance Program, the United Nations Children's Fund, the International Council on Social Welfare, Pan-American Union, the International Red Cross Committee, the World Federation of Mental Health, International Social Service, the World YWCA, and World Association of Youth; or in national social agencies that operate in foreign countries, such as the Administration of International Development, the American Friends Service Committee, Church World Service, YMCA, Catholic Community Service Council, American Joint Jewish Distribution Committee, and Unitarian Service Committee, which require competence in community organization, planning, supervision, and social welfare administration and knowledge of foreign cultures and values.[23]

COMMUNITY WELFARE SERVICES. Planning, organizing, and financing social and health services through such organizations as Community

---

[22]Roland L. Warren, *Perspectives on the American Community*, 2nd ed. (Chicago: Rand McNally, 1972), pp. 252–72; and Robert E. Forman, *Black Ghettos, White Ghettos, and Slums* (Englewood Cliffs, N.J.: Prentice-Hall, 1972), pp. 13–38 and 103–43.

[23]For more details see Walter A. Friedlander, *International Social Welfare* (Englewood Cliffs, N.J.: Prentice-Hall, 1975).

Welfare Council, Planning Board, Community Chest, United Fund, and coordinating and neighborhood councils.[24]

The basic methods of social work that we analyze in this study—casework, social group work, and community organization—are applied by all groups that offer the types of services we have mentioned. The methods are not used only by those agencies that are organized primarily to provide these social work services, such as public welfare departments, family and children's agencies, adoption agencies, settlement houses, community centers, youth agencies, but also by organizations that combine services to people with other activities, such as the Salvation Army, the Red Cross, International Institutes and Immigrants Protective Leagues, and recreation commissions and park departments. Social work methods are also applied by organizations in which social work operates merely as an auxiliary division, as in hospitals, clinics, schools, vocational rehabilitation centers, juvenile and criminal courts, housing authorities, and research and health foundations. Finally, the method of community organization is the core function of agencies that are not rendered direct service to individuals and social groups but that are organized in order to assist in planning and financing social agencies in the community—for example, community welfare councils, community chests, and united fund-raising associations.[25]

Recently social work methods have also been used in settings outside these four categories of social agencies or related institutions. Industrial establishments, factories and mines, churches, mass recreation centers, consumer and producer cooperatives, and labor unions employ social workers in order to benefit from social work methods in the interest of their members, employees, or partners. In this development, casework, social group work, and community organization begin to affect many other organizations and institutions beyond the framework of the original social welfare agencies.

---

[24]Marc Pilisuk and Mehrene Larudee, *International Conflict and Social Policy* (Englewood Cliffs, N.J.: Prentice-Hall, 1972), pp. 192–98.

[25]Robert Perrucci and Marc Pilisuk, "Racism, Poverty and Inequality," in Perrucci and Pilisuk, eds., *The Triple Revolution Emerging*, pp. 319–422; Dorothy B. James, *Poverty, Politics and Change* (Englewood Cliffs, N.J.: Prentice-Hall 1972); Martin Greenberg, "A Concept of Community," *Social Work* 19, no. 1 (January 1974): 64–72; and Thomas P. Holland, "The Community: Organism or Arena," ibid., pp. 73–80.

CHAPTER TWO

SOCIAL WORK
WITH
INDIVIDUALS AND FAMILIES

Henry S. Maas

When a neighbor calls the Human Resources Office about two young children who are left alone repeatedly, for hours at a time, in the apartment upstairs—as in the Rodgers family, described below—should a social worker enter the situation? If so, for what purposes? And how—that is, doing what by way of intervention? These are appropriate starting questions for us to consider, because the "whys" and "hows" of direct social work intervention with individual persons and families are what this chapter is about.

You might argue that a social worker has no right to become directly involved in a family situation unless an invitation to do so is initiated by the persons concerned. Family life is a private affair, and what goes on within its boundaries concerns only its members. Or is this assumption not tenable under some circumstances? If parents want to keep a child out of school or refuse to allow the child health care or medical treatment, should such decisions be left up to the parents alone? Does a child have rights apart from his parents? What if a parent practices physically punitive discipline or at times completely loses control and seriously abuses a young child? What if the physical abuse involves a retarded adolescent? Or an adult spouse? Under such circumstances, the boundaries of family may be legally penetrated by agents of society or community members to protect the powerless. But before the need for protection arises, should entry be possible in order to correct a stressful family situation? To prevent it?

We are clearly into important ethical matters and specifically into issues of personal autonomy and accountability and social responsibility. We are into the attendant questions of when a human situation becomes a "problem" calling for societal action, who defines it as a "problem"— the persons involved or societal authorities—and how under varying definitions of a "problem" the boundaries between what is public and what is private may shift.

To pursue such complex issues at any length would be to delay our getting into the central matters of this chapter. There are some good discussions of these questions elsewhere.[1] In brief, legal and other governmental provisions have codified widely shared values about society's responsibilities to persons in positions of relative powerlessness—for example, young children, the infirm aged, and physically or mentally handicapped persons. Persons in such situations are often of special concern to social workers who provide direct services. But of course any one of us may become subject to stressful conditions, and anyone in an overwhelming or stressful situation may become powerless; therefore, any of us may become a person of concern to social work.

The "whys" or purposes of social work practice with individuals and families grow in part out of our human concern for persons in troubling or potentially troublesome or stressful conditions. The "whys" grow also in part out of our understanding of persons in difficult circumstances. Part of this chapter is therefore addressed to a consideration of various kinds of stressful situations and what we know of how people behave in response to them. In the broadest sense, it is clear that such people need help from some sources; if there were no social workers to provide help, there would very likely be other persons using another name providing the same kinds of assistance social workers offer, at any given time. I use the last phrase because what social workers do has changed considerably over time.

The "hows" or modes of direct social work practice with individuals and families are the other central theme of this chapter. The theoretical bases of such practice, like theories in related sciences, are constantly developing, with many problems awaiting further study. My aim in this

---

[1]For example, see Donald P. Warwick and Herbert C. Kelman, "Ethical Issues in Social Intervention," in *Processes and Phenomena of Social Change*, ed. Gerald Zaltman (New York: Wiley & Sons, 1973), pp. 377–417. The selected bibliography at the end of this chapter includes references that expand on many of the topics in this chapter.

chapter is to present as coherent a sense of some of the fundamental ideas on current practice as is possible within the limits of a basic text. I shall use traditional formulations where these are likely to be clear to the nonprofessional reader; some concepts I shall reformulate so that the reader can relate them to what he has learned in basic courses in psychology and the social sciences.

Section I of this chapter provides the reader with an introduction to some of the basic elements in practice with individuals and families today, starting with a brief description of Dee Rodgers and her children. Section II presents the case record of the Coyle family, giving a somewhat extended illustration of some of the concepts and principles touched upon in section I and developed more fully in sections III and IV. Section III deals with basic concepts needed to understand the behavior of persons in stressful situations. Section IV reviews some of the major principles of practice in social casework. Section V aims to integrate our understanding of the concepts and principles discussed in sections III and IV into larger frameworks. The chapter ends with a selected bibliography for the curious reader.

I. SOME FUNDAMENTALS OF CASEWORK PRACTICE

Much of casework practice today is short term (relatively few interviews) and clearly focused as to goals, of which both the client and the worker are well aware. Some of this practice is carried on in a crisis framework, at the sudden turning point in a person's life when there is both an overwhelming feeling of being unable to cope and an openness to changing one's previous way of life, which may have contributed to the crisis. This means that some social agencies have to be open and accessible to people almost all around the clock. It also means that workers have to be skilled in initiating rapid, concerned, and trusting relationships with clients, who may telephone in about their suicidal impulses or about a deserting husband's threat to his wife to run off with their child.

There are also, of course, many relatively long-term relationships with clients in agencies serving individuals and families. Sometimes these are essentially supportive relationships for persons who have marginal capacities for coping on their own—for example, physically or mentally handicapped persons who can manage outside of institutional facilities but periodically need help of one kind or another. Here the goal is not to effect change so much as to maintain an adequate level of independent living. Sometimes a relatively long-term relationship is developed in an effort to effect changes in a client's way of life that will not yield to short-term casework. The special conditions under which this route is followed are discussed in section IV of this chapter.

More typical of casework practice today, however, is the clearly focused and rather brief relationship like the one summarized below, which is aimed at helping the Rodgers family over a hurdle and starting a somewhat new set of life processes going, with the opportunity for Mrs. Rodgers to get in touch with the social worker again should need arise. To understand what occurs prior to, during, and subsequent to the period of social work intervention, we should have some understanding of persons' behavior in stressful circumstances, how they are likely to feel, and what meaning casework help might have for them then. The summary of the Rodgers family situation is presented in two columns, the one on the right being a commentary on the record.

RECORD (SUMMARY)

(1) Mrs. Dee Rodgers (Mrs. R.) was visited five times in response to an initial complaint by a neighbor that she was leaving her two preschool children, Annie, 18 months, and Joe, 2½ years, alone, locked in the apartment for half a day or more at a time. On my first visit she talked to me only through the half-opened door, the two children clinging to her skirt. She said her husband was away, the children were all right, and she wanted nothing to do with social workers. I said it was late in the day, she was probably busy making supper, and I should stop by tomorrow morning. The neighbor told me Mrs. R. had lived in the house only three or four months and seemed to have no friends.

(2) Since Mrs. Lake, in my single-parents Thursday-night group, lives right across the street, I told her that Mrs. R. was a newcomer who seemed to know no one in the neighborhood. Mrs. Lake phoned me early the next day, saying she had visited Mrs. R. and that Mrs. R. wanted to see me tomorrow.

(3) I found that Mrs. R. was indeed without friends in the city, having just moved here, she said, from Marysville. She felt unable to go out on the street with the two children and sometimes

COMMENTS

(1) Situations of child neglect are sometimes reported like this by a neighbor who does not feel comfortable speaking directly to the parent involved. Studies suggest that such parents are often uncommunicative with the people in their communities, are likely to move often, and seem both isolated and rootless. Since integration of persons with their community and its facilities is a prime purpose of social work, parents like Mrs. R. are high on the list of social work's "persons of concern" or "target populations."

(2) The principle of confidentiality, discussed in Section III, might lead one to question speaking to one client about another. Yet if neighborhood integration is desirable, involving Mrs. Lake this way might be justified. What do you think?

(3) To modify an attitude of anticipated rejection, a social worker may provide a client like Mrs. R. with experiences in community resources where she will be readily accepted, thus in-

just had to get away without them. Her husband had gone "up north" to log and periodically sent her money on which she managed adequately. Her only pastimes were sewing and watching TV. She knew nothing of the community, including the Canby Street Day Care Center. Moreover, her attitude about looking into such places was one of anticipated rejection.

dicating the inappropriateness of the client's attitude.

(4) Having arranged for us to visit the day care center when Mrs. R. expressed an interest in seeing it, I was nevertheless not too surprised when she failed to appear. When I visited her at home later that day, she said she had not been feeling well. On that visit she told me spontaneously about the small Indian village in which she'd grown up until age 10, then of the series of foster homes and finally group home for teenagers in which she'd lived until she married at age 16. I noticed that her approach to her children seemed somewhat screened by her preoccupations with herself; her expectations for their behavior seemed beyond their capacities at times, and at other times she seemed to treat them like dolls. We talked about young children and their needs and also about the difficulties of being a single parent with personal needs that young children could not fulfill.

(4) Note that the social worker does not inquire about the client's earlier years—there is no reason to do so—but that the client spontaneously, probably in response to the social worker's concern and nonretributive approach to the client's having failed to come to the day care center, tells the worker about her childhood and foster care experiences. Child-parent difficulties are often transmitted from one generation to the next; improving any situation like the R. family's is likely to have preventive value for the next generation. Satisfying a single parent's peer-relation needs may help make parenting more gratifying and appropriate.

(5) After a visit to the Canby Street Day Care Center, Mrs. R. put Joe's name on the waiting list for one morning a week. For Joe's required health checkup, I introduced Mrs. R. to the Bluevale Pediatric Clinic, which she used for Annie too. On my last visit, Joe was starting at Canby Street on a one-morning-a-week schedule, and Mrs. R. had joined a group of mothers who used the Center's sewing machine. They also bought some material collectively and exchanged clothing patterns. Mrs. R. remarked, "I have some girlfriends now." I left my agency telephone number in case she wanted to speak with me again.

(5) As Mrs. R. begins to use community resources, her ability to cope increases, and feelings of powerlessness and rejection may decrease. Her children may profit directly from these resources. The R. family ceases to be anonymous or invisible in the neighborhood; integration allows the family to give as well as receive.

Because of forces beyond one's control, anyone at some point in life may be unable to make a personally or socially satisfactory adaptation to an overwhelming or stressful situation. Under such circumstances, one may engage in behavior that one knows is not "right." Most probably, for example, a person like Mrs. Rodgers knows quite well about the physical, if not the psychological, dangers to young children who are left alone. But in a crisis situation, self-survival becomes paramount for some people, more important than their normal concerns for others, even for those who are close to them. In such a situation, a person may become unaware of much that is going on around him. Under stress, our awareness tends to become restricted. One may remain aware of little more than one's feelings of inability to cope. One may be aware of needing help, but the nature or source of such help is often not immediately apparent. If a person should deny to himself that he is in trouble, others in the community—for example, neighbors, teachers, or the police—may still see him as a person beset by "problems." "Problems" are needs not being adequately or acceptably met by the needs-meeting facilities of society. An imbalance is apparent in the person's relationships with his world.

This imbalance may originate in the person's current incapacities for using available community facilities or in the nonaccessibility or breakdown of the facilities themselves. The facilities are the family and our society's economic, educational, legal, medical, recreational, religious, and other social institutions. For an understanding of the general determinants of personal-social imbalances or stressful situations, we now have a variety of minitheories on human adaptation to stress. The unique constellation of determinants in any specific case of personal-social imbalance, if the imbalance is to be remedied, often calls for assessment by a team of professional people, of whom the social caseworker is one. Such assessment precedes the planning of appropriate action. Stressful situations are complex phenomena; casework with persons in such situations is often difficult and challenging.

People do not voluntarily move into situations of personal pain and anxiety or of social threat and discomfort. Rather, they find themselves there, unable to do or feel otherwise. Often they do not really want to change their situations, fearful of something worse arising. Research on human growth and development, with its biological, psychological, and social facets, has provided ample evidence that stressful situations may be an inherent part of growing up and growing older in our rapidly changed and unpredictable times. Under such conditions, the right to help through personal and social services provided by one's community is becoming universally recognized.

When a person comes to a social agency for professional help, he and the caseworker are in very different positions. The caseworker is employed by an agency with societally prescribed goals. The range of functions of the caseworker is defined by the agency. With the supports and limits of such role-definition, with a relevant knowledge of human behavior, and with skills in helping that are guided by the principles of casework practice, the caseworker enters the client-caseworker relationship.

The client, on the other hand, is a person under stress. He may be in a personally quite painful situation or in a culturally deviant and therefore socially threatening position. For example, an unemployed father in a period of high employment, a recently arrived immigrant having difficulty in learning a new way of life, a single parent like Dee Rodgers, and a delinquent adolescent are all in socially deviant roles, as judged by the norms of our dominant culture. Such persons may feel themselves to be under stress and in need of help. They may voluntarily come to a social agency for help. On the other hand, they may recognize no such feelings in themselves, but the caretakers of our culture may refer them to a social agency for help. In either type of situation, caseworkers find themselves face to face with persons in situations of stress and social deviation. In all these cases, personally or socially unsatisfying modes of adaptation are being employed by the clients, and personal-social imbalances are apparent.

In the casework method, client-caseworker relationships are the medium for modifying such imbalances. The forms and directions that client-caseworker relationships take vary with a variety of conditions. A major purpose of this chapter is to discuss what some of these conditions are and how they relate to the ways in which client-caseworker relationships are developed. From the outset, however, it must be clear that in each case, how the client perceives his situation and what the client himself wants and feels able to do about it—that is, the client's own goals and capacities—provide the caseworker with initial cues for the formulation of appropriate casework goals. Such goals, in turn, affect the caseworker's development of means instrumental to the realization of the goals. Generally, the caseworker tries to communicate acceptance and concern for the client. Upon casework goals, however, depend the depth and intensity of interactions in the client-caseworker relationship. The kinds of experiences related to the client's problem situation that are discussed, which the client may come to see in a different light as the relationship develops, also depend on these goals. Thus, the goals and the nature of the client-worker relationship are intimately interrelated.

Although it should be clear that specific goals in different cases involving similar problem situations may vary widely, the general or ideal goal of client-worker relationships may be stated in terms of our society's charges to its social agencies. This goal is to enable the client to enjoy, with some degree of permanency, more satisfying, effective, and acceptable experiences in the social situation in which he finds himself. This goal may be achieved through effecting changes in the client's environment or social living situation, through clarifying the client's possibly distorted perception of his living situation, and otherwise through strengthening his capacities for coping with his environment. Any or all of these approaches may be used to a greater or lesser degree in a given case. The desired outcome is that an effective dynamic balance between the person and his social world is at least partially restored.

In order for client-worker relationships to help clients move toward this goal, caseworkers must be able to use skillfully knowledge of human behavior in stressful situations. Such knowledge is to be found in psychological theories on the structure, development, and functioning of the ego and the ego's manifest expressions in personality. (See discussion of the concept of ego in section III of this chapter.) Such knowledge includes applicable theories on the social and cultural supports and barriers to human adaptation under stress. (See discussion of the concepts of social role and mode of adaptation in section III of this chapter.) Such knowledge should include some awareness of biological theories on normal growth, maturation, and homeostasis.[2]

Skilled in applying such knowledge, the caseworker is able, together with the client, to engage in the three interrelated procedures of assessment, goal-setting, and a variety of supportive or change inducing interventions (see sections II and IV). In the course of initially trying to understand the client in his situation, the caseworker is able to make tentative assessments of the client's current, relevant past, and possible future modes of adaptation to stressful situations and to related normal living situations. The caseworker and the client are able to consider possible adjustments or changes in the client's immediate physical and social world. In an on-going relationship, plans are continually reformulated, as the caseworker and the client engage in appropriate corrective action. These refinements may lead to modifications in goals and, consequently, in the means used to move toward them.

Because of the complexity of human behavior and professional helping relationships, and the sea of still unanswered questions about such relationships, the caseworker is not successful in reaching desired

___

[2]"Homeostasis" refers to the dynamic states of bodily equilibrium that living organisms must constantly maintain for survival. The concept of homeostasis is the purely biological equivalent of personal-social balance. The latter term is used in this chapter to designate the optimal effect of all processes aimed at intrapersonal and interpersonal, or social balances, as well as biochemical homeostasis. The pre–World War II studies of Walter B. Cannon on homeostasis, of Paul Weiss on adaptation, and of Ludwig von Bertalanffy on "system theory"—all biological research—led directly after World War II into behavioral science thinking called systems theories. These theories have influenced social work's approaches to families, larger groups, and collectivities as social systems.

goals with all clients. Part of the skill in the planning and execution of casework involves the setting of limited or partial goals. In the course of working toward these goals, the client's capacities for making constructive readaptations and for using to advantage changes in his social and physical situation are constantly assessed.

While working with clients, the caseworker always remains sensitively responsive to the client's cues about his goals and capacities and his feelings and attitudes. Caseworkers communicate their respect for and acceptance of the client as a person whose decisions about his living situation are almost always his own to make. Caseworkers are especially aware of their own values; their self-awareness serves as a guard against their imposing their value judgments upon the client in his decision making. At the same time, in order that the client make decisions with an eye to personal and social satisfactions in his subsequent living, caseworkers may help the client to see as clearly as possible and to modify apparently obstructing attitudes, feelings, and objective realities in the problem situation. The caseworker's interactions with a client are guided by the kinds of principles of casework practice merely alluded to in this paragraph. In section IV of this chapter, such principles are discussed in some detail.

Finally, it must be clear from the outset that at the heart of casework practice is the skilled, as well as informed, caseworker. Knowledge of theories of human behavior, of the structure and resources of community life, and of the principles of casework practice does not equip a person to practice casework any more than knowledge about the fundamentals of human anatomy, physiology, biochemistry, and pathology and about the principles of medical practice equips a person to practice medicine. On the socially sanctioned educational route to becoming a physician or caseworker, there is the all-important interne status. In social work education, the student spends approximately half of his years of study in actual practice with clients in the field. There, under the supervision of qualified practitioners in the profession, the student applies what he is learning about human behavior and the principles of casework practice, and he consciously develops and tests himself in relationships with clients. Obviously, no chapter on the fundamentals of casework practice theory can provide the reader with a substitute for such supervised experience and the sizable segment of knowledge underlying it.

II. EXPLORING A FAMILY'S ADAPTATION
TO A STRESSFUL SITUATION

In section I of this chapter, we introduced a number of ideas that are considered basic in social casework practice theory. Before examining the use of some of these ideas in a case, that of the Coyle family, let us review in outline the major ideas referred to in section I.

1. Stressful situations involve personally and/or socially unsatisfactory adaptations to problems that are often beyond the control of the persons enmeshed in them. Such situations may be observed as personal-social imbalances.
2. Our culture's acceptance of this assumption is manifest in our society's chartering and support of social agencies to help persons in stressful situations, despite opposition to this assumption in some segments of our society.
3. In some of these social agencies, the casework method is used, having client-worker relationships as its medium, the restoration of satisfying and effective personal-social balances in the clients' lives as its goal.
4. For the casework method to be effective, the caseworker must be able to use psychological, social, and biological conceptual tools skillfully for understanding human behavior in situations of stress and social deviation.
5. Similarly, in the procedures of assessment, goal setting, and other intervention modalities, the caseworker must be able to use skillfully the guiding principles of casework practice.
6. The skilled and informed caseworker is at the heart of casework practice.

In our examination of the casework record on the Coyle family and subsequently, we shall want to keep in mind the ideas of: (1) persons in stressful situations, (2) the social purposes of social agencies, (3) the client-worker relationship, (4) concepts for understanding human behavior, (5) principles of casework practice, and (6) the caseworker as the basic helping agent. These six items should help us organize our thinking about the changing situation in the Coyle family record, drawn from an agency in the field of public assistance.

A. The Coyle Family Case Record

The mother and children in the Coyle family are receiving financial assistance through a governmental agency in Putnam County. Mr. Joseph Coyle, aged forty-six, the husband and father, is at present at Long Pines, an honor camp connected with Poston Prison. Three years ago he was imprisoned on a morals charge involving a minor. Mr. Coyle is a plumber by trade and was an adequate wage-earner prior to his arrest.

At home are Mrs. Helen Coyle, thirty-two, and three children, Patrick, sixteen, Stephen, fifteen, and Katie, twelve. According to the record, Mrs. Coyle was last seen in December. (It is now July.) From the December and previous record entries, it seems that Mrs. Coyle is very defensive regarding her husband's conviction for sexual misbehavior with a local girl. Of the two boys in the family, Patrick, the older, is apparently more upset, quite concerned that his friends and acquaintances may learn of his father's imprisonment. Stephen shrugs off his concern. Katie is considered "still loyal."

Mrs. Morin, the new caseworker for the Coyle family, wrote in the record, prior to her first interview with Mrs. Coyle: "My questions concern the children's current adjustment, and specifically whether they have ever visited their father in prison; the possibilities of parole for Mr. Coyle; whether Mrs. Coyle has ever considered employment; and, particularly, what Mrs. Coyle has done about her own feelings in regard to her husband's offense, imprisonment, and separation."

Note that the caseworker has analyzed the family situation in terms of possible problem areas. These problem areas all fall within the province of services offered by the agency employing Mrs. Morin. In this agency, which is based on legislation on public assistance, policy statements on welfare services propose and delimit in a general way appropriate problems for agency services. Interpretation of welfare legislation helps also to define Mrs. Morin's role as caseworker. That role calls for "family-focused" casework with the following purposes: to help the family move closer to self-support, to improve parents' relationship with each other, to better parent-child relationships, to assist the family in becoming better integrated in the community, and to help the family through any confusion having to do with eligibility for public assistance.

The questions Mrs. Morin raises for inquiry all relate to self-support and parent-parent and parent-child relationships in the Coyle family. Concerned about the mother's and children's feelings and other reactions relevant to this situation, the caseworker wonders also about the family's future plans for self-support, either through the parole of Mr. Coyle or though substitutions for the economic functions he served and now carried on on a limited budget by the governmental agency.

Mrs. Morin approaches her first interview with Mrs. Coyle with goals for studying the persons in this stressful situation, their modes of adapting to the situation, and their potential for change. Can casework in this agency be of any help to the family in its current situation? If so, with what specific goals? Can any of the potential damage to the children and mother, threatened by this stressful situation, be alleviated through casework or other services, either in this agency or in other community resources that are available and acceptable to Mrs. Coyle?

Mrs. Morin's summarized record of her initial interviews with Mrs. Coyle is presented below, together with a commentary consisting of certain observations and inferences. Mrs. Coyle is referred to in these texts as Mrs. C., Mrs. Morin as CW (caseworker). Mrs. Morin's interactions and intentions as she recorded them are italicized so that the reader may see more clearly what the caseworker does and why. The observations and inferences are intended to provide further understanding of what guides the caseworker in the process of the interview.

Note that Mrs. Morin is simultaneously assessing and beginning to work with a client in a stressful situation through a developing client-worker relationship.

CASE RECORD	OBSERVATIONS AND INFERENCES
July 2: (1) *I arranged by letter for an office visit,* and Mrs. C. came in on the appointed day. I found Mrs. C. to be an attractive woman who seemed highly nervous during the interview and who relaxed her tension somewhat before the interview ended.	(1) Federal law requires an annual visit in cases like Mrs. C.'s, and other codes sanction as many other interviews as may be necessary. Mrs. C. does not postpone appointment but responds affirmatively to agency request. Initially anxious with CW, she seems able to use relationship with CW to become less anxious in this situation.
(2) *Mrs. C. and I spent some time getting acquainted so that she might feel free to discuss some of her concerns with me. Obviously her tension was somewhat related to having to tell her story to another person, and I dealt directly with this.*	(2) CW provides for initial development of client-worker relationship. In openly and acceptingly remarking about Mrs. C.'s discomfort in discussing her situation with CW (a stranger), CW gives Mrs. C. some evidence of CW's capacity to understand Mrs. C.'s feelings in the interview; thus CW may begin to become somewhat less a stranger to Mrs. C.
(3) During the interview we covered the following areas in some detail. Mrs. C. was able to discuss her feelings about her husband's imprisonment and then to deal in retrospect with the distance she felt she had come in accepting the separation and trying to make the best of it. She could see the relationship between her acceptance and that of the children, and she discussed in detail what she thought their adjustment had been.	(3) Mrs. C.'s description of changes in her feelings about her situation suggests that she has "ego strengths" (see section III) to help herself in this type of stressful situation. Her awareness of how her feelings affect her children's feelings about the situation indicates some understanding of parent-child relationships in her family. These are important cues for CW in considering possible further casework services for the C. family.
(4) Mrs. C. saw herself as having been completely thrown by the experience at first and talked of having closed herself in her house, literally, for about a year after her husband had gone to prison. She said she felt this was a measurement of her friends and acquaintances and that the friends she had left had really tested their friendship for her during this tedious period. Mrs. C. said that gradually she realized that hiding herself away was no answer and that, as she began to feel better about	(4) CW is aware that social withdrawal is frequently a psychologically adaptive behavior in situations of stress, and especially in response to the loss of a loved one (e.g., in mourning). Mrs. C. seems to have been protecting herself also from the possible disapproval of friends. In effect, she isolated herself as society had isolated her husband, as though his crime were hers. Is Mrs. C.'s attachment to Mr. C. an extremely close one? Nature of the husband-wife relationship is theoretically relevant to

her situation, she had had to face what it meant.

(5) *I helped her to sort out some of these feelings, some of which had not as yet been identified. We speculated on whether she really had faced the actual charges and whether she had made up her mind how she had felt about them.* Mrs. C. spoke with great loyalty about her husband and said they had had a good marriage. She said that because he was older than she, many people had implied that the marriage itself was probably a demonstration of his abnormal desires toward a younger woman. Mrs. C. said she was sickened by this kind of implication and that this, too, had been a most unhappy blow for her to face. Actually, she had come to some conclusion as to what her husband meant to her, and this helped to separate her feelings from the feelings of others around her.

the nature of the development of the children in the family.

(5) CW senses Mrs. C.'s strength and some still unclear feelings, perhaps not fully admitted into Mrs. C.'s own awareness because they seem so threatening and unacceptable to her (and to others?). Such feelings require energy for their control, energy that might otherwise go into more satisfying and effective adaptations to daily living. CW therefore tries to help Mrs. C. clarify these feelings. In the process, CW continues to accept Mrs. C. warmly as a person with these feelings—which Mrs. C. may expect others to reject her for having. To this extent, CW's support and clarification may provide a corrective experience for Mrs. C.

Note that CW begins with Mrs. C.'s feelings about her husband's offense, a phase of the situation Mrs. C. had previously avoided mentioning; she had talked only of her feelings about Mr. C.'s imprisonment and separation. This omission gives CW a cue that the offense may still be a troublesome area for Mrs. C. CW apparently feels this early client-worker relationship can support discussion of this painful topic or that Mrs. C. is able to back out of this discussion if she does not feel able to talk about it. CW therefore initiates the subject. Mrs. C. begins with a defense of her husband and their relationship, then expresses her "most unhappy" fears about the meaning to her of her husband's sexual behavior, ascribing this interpretation to "many people." Note that CW does not pursue this belief, by either further exploration or denial, with Mrs. C. at this time. CW probably continues to communicate her warm acceptance of Mrs. C., despite this "sickening" possibility.

(6) Mrs. C. said that the oldest boy, Pat, had the most trouble in facing his friends and acquaintances. He still found it hard to let any new person

(6) Mrs. C. is not so disturbed as to be unable to show a keen appreciation of differences in the reactions of her children to the situation. She does not dis-

know about his father and he rarely discussed it, even with people he knew were aware of the story. Mrs. C. felt this boy probably never would be able to accept the situation fully. She mentioned that Stephen, on the other hand, who has a quite different and more outgoing personality, shrugs off these experiences by saying that people will know anyway so why shouldn't he tell them. Katie is a particularly strong admirer of her father and is much attached to him. All the children had been to see Mr. C. after his wife had first visited to see the setting. At this point of the discussion, Mrs. C. said that Pat had gone to spend some part of the summer with his aunt, Mary Ellis (Mrs. C.'s sister), who lives in Ashville. The child looked forward to this vacation as it gave him an opportunity to be out of doors and to live rurally and, at this point, to rub elbows with his uncle, who served as a kind of father substitute for this period of time.

approve of Pat's leaving home for a visit with an uncle and aunt, a probably sound plan in view of Pat's reaction. In a parental relationship less sensitive to children's needs, a mother might require all to stay at home during a family crisis. Is Mrs. C., in other ways too, even under current stress, a quite effective mother?

(7) Pat had been much disappointed not to have his application accepted for apprenticeship in the shipyard. It was Pat's hope that he would be able to continue his education while earning his way. However, when the application was submitted it was returned saying that the application closing date had been June 1. Pat still plans to keep in touch with the Post Office in the event that openings reoccur.

Mrs. C. spoke also of having tried to sell cosmetics herself, as an attempt toward her own employment, and of her disappointment when she had little result from her sales. Mrs. C. added that her husband has remained active with the plumbers' union and has been promised employment the moment he leaves prison.

(7) Pat is apparently able to move in the direction of planning for self-support. But does his missing the closing application date indicate some current feelings of inadequacy about stepping out into a work role? Is Mrs. C.'s inability to move out on her own economically due only to her emotional upset, or to the feeling that her working would close off a position that her husband formerly occupied, as the wage earner in the family, and thus make more difficult his return? Is this an area in which clarification is needed, and may CW be of help? Note, however, that Mrs. C. gives no evidence of being motivated now to find work, nor does she give CW any cue that she wants help preparing herself for employment.

(8) Mrs. C. said her husband was transferred to Long Pines Camp on April 8. She said she has been able to visit him only about once a month, and

(8) In discussing her adaptation to Mr. C.'s imprisonment, Mrs. C. makes clear her efforts to visit her husband, her acceptance of help from friends in

that if she goes by public transportation (i.e., bus), the cost is $22.12 round trip for an adult. It is $11.06 for one-half fare for a child. The expense demands a great deal of scraping and managing for her to make even the one trip a month. On two occasions, she was helped by friends who offered her a ride to the prison.

Mrs. C.'s hopes were rising again regarding her husband's parole. He will be considered for parole in September or October. Mrs. C. asked whether this department could send a supportive letter at that time, saying what we know of the family circumstances. *I said that we could talk about that letter again when it was near that period and that I would be happy to send whatever letter reflected our contacts with her.*

this effort, and both her hopes and concern over the possibilities of Mr. C.'s parole this coming fall. Only at this point in the interview, toward its end, does she make any specific request for help, perhaps indirectly or covertly at first about the matter of money for bus fare to see her husband, and then specifically and openly for a letter that might help in their reunion. In addition to the manifest nature of this request, CW wonders whether Mrs. C. is indirectly asking for help concerning her relationship with Mr. C., but CW does not pursue this today. CW offers to send a letter contingent upon further evaluations in casework interviews.

Following the interview, CW writes in the record the note on "evaluation and plan."

EVALUATION AND PLAN: I feel that Mrs. C. and I managed to discuss a good deal about her feelings in regard to the present situation. I sense that she is still feeling pretty nervous and shaky about it, although from my perspective, as well as her own, she has made a great improvement over her original poor adjustment. I sense, too, that Mrs. C. is a good manager on a very strained budget. At this time I see no particular entree to further discussion with Mrs. C. on any specific area of adjustment. I feel she has stabilized her situation somewhat and that I will not invest casework time in intensive interviews, as there seems to be no immediate pressure for change on her part. I plan to see her again and will keep in touch with her by telephone, which we both understood when we terminated this interview.

Note: Mrs. C. is aware that her son's visits to his aunt are considered visits. He plans to spend part of his time at home as well as part in Ashville. Hence, I do not see that the budget is affected.

July 21 and August 24: (9) *On both these occasions I talked to Mrs. C. by telephone to inquire how things were going for her.* She reported mostly about the children, and during our last telephone conversation *we made an appointment for an office visit an August 28.*

(9) Having promised to write a letter in regard to the consideration "in September or October" of Mr. C.'s parole, CW believes this second interview, at the end of August, almost two months later, is needed. Certain questions from the first interview remain unanswered. (See questions in observations and inferences, items 7 and 8.)

August 28: (10) Mrs. C. came into the office as agreed. She looked most attractive and well poised. Many of her nervous mannerisms had disappeared, and she began by telling me how much better she felt than the last time she had seen me. She then went on to say that during the previous period she had had letters from her husband that seemed so depressed and upsetting that she had hardly known how to feel about them. She said that her husband apparently had begun to worry as to whether she might not be becoming interested in someone else. She said that her visits to him had had to be less frequent because of the distance, and she speculated that he had decided that this actually represented some disinterest on her part, though at the same time he knew intellectually why it was necessary for her to be sparing in the expenditure of money.

Mrs. C. was, at first, obviously upset over all of this and, as she put it, eventually she "got mad." As a result, she not only "told him off" in her letters but made a special visit to see him wherein she let him know exactly how he made her feel when he took the attitude he did. She said she was so incensed that she angrily related all of the times his hints and accusations had upset her, sparing no detail of any time during the past three years that she had felt this way. She said it had done a great deal for her to have spoken this way as it was a quite different attitude for her to take.

She said that he seemed dumbfounded at first, then completely reassured, and that she had not had the feeling since that he doubted her in any way.

We talked for a while as to what this kind of attitude might have meant to him as well as to her. Mrs. C. felt that maybe she had done some growing up and that she was in a more responsible and controlled position than she had ever felt herself to be in before. She said that she had also done some real sorting

(10) CW leaves the way open for Mrs. C. to initiate discussion of whatever aspect of the situation is of concern to her today. In the first interview, CW was initially more active in starting and guiding the interview and in providing evidence of her capacity to understand and not to disapprove of Mrs. C. Thus, there began a client-worker relationship in which Mrs. C.'s social defenses might be lowered and she could feel free to discuss, without fear of social reprisal, some unpleasant aspects of the family situation that were troubling her. Today Mrs. C. begins promptly and on her own to tell CW about Mr. C.'s questions about Mrs. C.'s fidelity.

One may speculate about how much CW's supportive relationship with Mrs. C. reinforced Mrs. C.'s own psychological strengths, which in turn enabled her to behave as she did with Mr. C. Among the "normal" modes of a wife's reactions to sexual behavior such as Mr. C.'s would be feelings of anger directed against him. Yet nowhere in the first interview did Mr. C. give any overt evidence of harboring any such feelings. One may infer from her description of how she initially closed herself in her house that she was probably at that time feeling quite depressed. Depression is often the outward expression of inner disguised, but intense, feelings of anger turned or misdirected against oneself. At this time, however, Mrs. C. apparently feels sufficiently secure and adequate to express openly her feelings of anger toward her husband. The extent to which CW's supportive relationship with Mrs. C. played a part in Mrs. C.'s apparently satisfying and effective response to Mr. C. is difficult to estimate.

Note that Mrs. C. reports that her expression of anger to Mr. C. had done "a great deal" for her and that it marked a real change in attitude for her. This was a new mode of adaptation for her, apparently based on and further developing her new sense of se-

out about her feelings regarding her husband and decided that whatever he represented or had done, at any event she felt he was the man for her, and this was why she was waiting for him and why she felt it was worth waiting. She said she had every belief still that he was innocent and that perhaps she wanted to believe this and would continue to do so. She commented that in a long marriage such as theirs, one got to know a person pretty well, and it was out of this kind of a background that she had placed her trust and belief. Mrs. C. spoke as one who had really sorted out many things. At the same time, she commented in retrospect on how hard it had been for her to handle her feelings in this way. *We could also see together that such a show of emotion must have been a most reassuring experience for Mr. C., representing as it did how much she cared and representing too the kind of reassurance of her love that perhaps reached him better than any of her former affectionate assurances.*

curity and of adequacy. With the recognition and expression of her long-inhibited feelings of anger, Mrs. C. is better able to look clearly at her marital relationship and at Mr. C. and to decide that she wants to keep them as part of her life.

To reinforce what Mrs. C. had learned about herself and the appropriate expression of anger, CW approves of Mrs. C.'s behavior in terms that express how beneficial this response probably was for Mr. C., too.

Note that this communication was a joint one, in which CW and Mrs. C. were in consensus.

In this entire situation, it is apparent that CW is concerned about Mrs. C. as a person trying to make a satisfying and effective adaptation to a stressful situation. Beyond this, however, we assume that Mrs. C.'s mode of adaptation affects the total C. family and especially the development of the three children. To this end, CW is engaged in "family-focused casework," aimed at improvement in parent-parent or parent-child relationships. We assume that improvement in parent-parent relationships—that is, the modification of Mrs. C.'s possibly overly dependent or "little girl" approach to Mr. C.—will help also in movement toward or achievement of self-support. May Mrs. C., feeling freer to express herself in her relations with Mr. C., be less likely to feel she is threatening their relationship if she obtains employment? Prior to this time, Mrs. C. was unsuccessful in this respect (see item 7, above).

(11) Mrs. C. asked whether I would send out a letter to the State Adult Authority, referring to Mr. C.'s consideration of parole. Mrs. C. said that minimum sentence for Mr. C.'s particular crime was one year and that inasmuch as he was imprisoned almost three years ago, he had more than served his minimum sentence. *We agreed together that my letter would touch*

(11) Following this reaffirmation of the positive client-worker relationship, Mrs. C. makes her request again for the letter. Had CW structured the opening of this interview by referring immediately to the letter, the important preceding content initiated by Mrs. C. might not have come up.

upon the family's financial situation as we knew it, and of what we had observed about Mrs. C.'s feelings toward her husband.

(12) Mrs. C. tells me that Mr. C. is automatically considered for parole around October of each year and that just before this period she finds her tension mounting and her nervousness increasing. *We speculated as to what would happen if the parole was not granted,* and she said she knew, more than she ever did before, that somehow she could take that kind of decision at the same time that she dreaded the idea of another period without him. Mrs. C. said the children were soon to start school and that their lives were settling down again somewhat, except for the impending decision about parole.

Inasmuch as she was particularly concerned over this present situation this day, we let most of our consideration concern itself with how she would handle her feelings whether or not her husband was granted parole. I felt we made some strides in this, and Mrs. C. commented that she felt much better for this kind of discussion. *I promised Mrs. C. a copy of the letter written to the State Adult Authority.*

(12) Assured of help in regard to the letter—a tangible service—Mrs. C. now spontaneously tells of her feelings in regard to the uncertainties of Mr. C.'s being paroled. CW's conversation does not pursue this statement as though Mrs. C. were ambivalent (see section III) about Mr. C.'s return—though perhaps Mrs. C. is as much concerned about adaptation to his coming home after three years' absence as about the prolongation of his absence. CW selects the latter possibility, related to more apparent stresses and the possible continuation of the C. family in the county program. Note that the discussion is preliminary to possible later consideration of Mrs. C.'s seeking employment, if Mr. C. is not paroled. See CW's final "Evaluation and Plan" for a more appropriate time to consider the family's self-support.

Note that CW promises to send a copy of the letter to Mrs. C., a further effort to keep the client-worker relationship an open and supportive one for Mrs. C.

EVALUATION AND PLAN: I feel that Mrs. C. is well on her way toward handling whatever she needs to face in terms of either her husband's return or continued imprisonment. I feel that Mrs. C. has a lot of personal resources upon which she can call to help her through the situation, and she quite obviously has matured through her experience in a constructive way. I am impressed with the difference in what she was able to discuss and her approach towards it between the interview I held with her in July and the one today. It is my opinion that this woman could respond very well to the kind of casework relationship that keeps her aware of her direction and helps her to reflect upon and examine her feelings so as to be better able to cope with them. Actually, Mrs. C. is prepared to do much of this for herself, having passed the crisis point when she was floundering in emotions and beset to the point of almost complete inaction. I feel that, having passed the tension point of the parole period, Mrs. C. could actually consider what it means to her to remain unemployed, as well as to face whatever reality there may be in continued separation from her husband.

B. Analysis of the Coyle Family Case Record

Let us now reconsider the Coyle family case record somewhat more systematically, in terms of the framework of six items outlined at the outset of section II. The aim here is as much to expand and refine our framework as to amplify our understanding of this case.

1. PERSONS IN STRESSFUL SITUATIONS. It should be noted that the stressful situation for all members of the Coyle family, including Mr. Coyle, arises from Mr. Coyle's deviant sexual behavior, his offense, and is compounded by his separation from his family and by his imprisonment. Background content available to the writer from interviews with Mrs. Morin, the caseworker, extends beyond what appears in the necessarily summarized case record. Such content indicates that Mr. Coyle had for some years been a moderate drinker and that the alleged offense was reported to have occurred while he was drinking. The girl in question was known to some of the social agencies in Putnam County. From these data, it is clear that Mr. Coyle was himself under certain pressures, though his behavior as a father and a worker was reportedly not adversely affected by his drinking. On the contrary, Mr. Coyle was considered to be a very fatherly person with his family. When Mrs. Morin describes Mrs. Coyle as "a sweet, passive, apologetic woman, with the aura of a little girl," one infers that Mr. Coyle's fatherliness probably fitted in well with some of Mrs. Coyle's personal needs. The crisis in the Coyle family arose when Mr. Coyle deviated widely from the expectations set for him in his role as husband and father—in this case, transgressing into a field of behavior tabooed for anyone in our society. Had the person who molested the girl been himself a minor, or had Mr. Coyle had sexual relations with an adult woman, the legal and total social situation would have been somewhat different.

What becomes clear, then, is that one important element in the definition of a stressful situation is the positions and relationships of the persons involved in the situation. In section III of this chapter, this element is discussed under the concept of *social role.* In this situation, Mr. Coyle's social role as father, husband, and worker are major factors in the stressful situation in this family. The sudden changes in role-relationships in the Coyle family, brought about by Mr. Coyle's offense, are one of the bases for defining this as a potentially stressful situation. Clearly, a realignment of role-relationships and a reallocation of role-functions were made necessary by Mr. Coyle's removal from his home.

Faced with the need for such changes in the Coyle family's daily living, each of the members of the family, including Mr. Coyle, adapted to the changes in a variety of ways. Mr. Coyle, in assuming the role of prisoner, apparently performed this role well, for we find him placed in an honor camp, at Long Pines, shortly after his imprisonment. At home, each of the children and Mrs. Coyle adapted in somewhat different ways —Mrs. Coyle initially by withdrawing from all roles but that of mother, Katie by being ostensibly a trusting daughter to her absent father, Patrick by somewhat uncertainly withdrawing from accustomed roles and seeking new supportive relationships, and Stephen by showing at least a front of aggressively facing up to peers with the facts.

Finally, let us come to what motivates, intrapersonally, the modes of adaptation used by each of the Coyle family members. To start with, Mr. Coyle was apparently under pressures, of which we have no knowledge, prior to his offense. We may consider his moderate drinking a mode of adaptation to such pressures. The statement that such drinking was moderate suggests that Mr. Coyle exercised some inner controls over his desires to drink. Drinking, in turn, is known to weaken such inner controls, and reportedly under the influence of drinking he succumbed to a desire that, so far as we know, he had previously channeled into socially acceptable outlets. With his conviction and imprisonment, we find him becoming a "good prisoner"—good enough to be placed rather early in an honor camp. Here again is evidence that Mr. Coyle's inner controls are normally quite effective. On the whole, he appears to make an appropriate adaptation to the demands and stresses of both his outer and inner world. The job of mediating responses to inner desires and conflicts and outer demands and pressures is carried on by the ego. We have thus some basis for saying, with the reservation that our data on Mr. Coyle are quite limited, that except for the situation of his offense, the reported facts indicate that Mr. Coyle has at least a relatively adequate ego. Indications are that he functions effectively most of the time. This is an important assessment for the caseworker in helping Mrs. Coyle to plan for the future of her family.

We have some evidence of Mrs. Coyle's ego functioning in her immediate and subsequent adaptation to the Coyle family's stressful situation. For the first year she felt overpowered and tried to deal with the situation by living a socially circumscribed life. (See item 10 in Observations and Inferences column for comments on psychological factors in depression.) We have learned, too, that her characteristic mode of adaptation as an adult woman has the "aura of a little girl" and that in her apparently "sweet, passive, apologetic" way, she was probably quite dependent upon her fatherly husband. In normal times, this kind of adaptation to the role of wife, given a husband with Mr. Coyle's fatherly attributes, may make for a relatively happy home life, although many women are now rejecting such dependent, little-girl roles in favor of more assertive roles within the household. The sudden changes in role-relationships and functions brought on by Mr. Coyle's offense seem to have called for more personal flexibility and ego strength than Mrs. Coyle had at her disposal. In retreating from the community, Mrs. Coyle used a mode of adaptation that is "regressive"—that is, a return to an earlier way of life when the ego is overwhelmed and accustomed modes of adaptation do not seem applicable. Her ego strength may be assessed from the fact of her self-recovery after a year. This fact has important predictive values for the caseworker who is formulating casework goals and plans with Mrs. Coyle.

The three central concepts of ego, social role, and mode of adaptation (to be expanded upon in section III of this chapter) seem to be tools that are helpful to us in analyzing a stressful situation like the Coyle family's. These concepts are keys to the analysis of major elements in stressful situations in which social caseworkers' clients are involved. Around these concepts, clients' feelings and attitudes, their perceptions of their stressful situations, and their goals for resolving their personal-social imbalances may be understood.

Note, finally, that in the Coyle family's stressful situation, both personally and socially unsatisfactory adaptations to problems that were beyond the conscious control of all the persons enmeshed in them appeared as personal-social imbalances.

2. SOCIETAL PURPOSES OF SOCIAL AGENCIES. Society has chartered and supported family welfare programs for situations in which children are being deprived of the necessary economic supports of the family. The death, illness, or departure of a parent may deprive children of a family income; for its restitution, the remaining parent may have to go out to work and leave the children unattended or ill attended. To keep the remaining family unit intact and the children supported not only economically, on a minimum subsistence budget, but psychologically and socially, federal legislation and state welfare codes have stipulated the conditions under which persons are eligible to apply for such assistance.

From such sources, caseworkers employed by county departments of public welfare, like Mrs. Morin, derive their societal framework for casework practice with a family like the Coyles. To implement our society's charges to the agency, the casework method may be used more or less extensively with clients. Note that Mrs. Morin has to evaluate (and account to her supervisor for) the appropriateness of investing limited casework time in this case. The path between society's charges to its social agencies and the specific techniques a caseworker uses with a specific client is a long one, but the steps between broad social goals and professional techniques employed to achieve those goals in a specific case are traceable.

The codes that govern the execution of a program are extensive and ideally cover all the types of conditions for which societal sanctions and limits are needed. The interpretation of these codes is sometimes a difficult one, and the values and biases of the agency's employees may influence the application of these sanctions in a given case. The employees know or can readily discover what the applicable regulations are. The employees thus clearly serve as both agents of society and servants of its public. One example—from the Coyle case—of how a caseworker's value judgments may affect the use of code stipulations will illustrate this point.

Remember that Mrs. Morin's first question concerning the Coyle family, prior to the initial interview with Mrs. Coyle, was whether the Coyle children had ever visited their father at the prison honor camp. Mrs. Morin says she raised this question because there was no evidence in the case record turned over to her that the children had ever done so. At the end of the first interview, Mrs. Coyle brought up her difficulties in budgeting for bus trips to the prison camp. Now the codes make provision for additional funds under certain special circumstances. What became apparent to Mrs. Morin, however, was that the prior worker, using her own value judgments about a sexual offender, considered the children's trips to see their father to be ill advised. Implicit in the prior caseworker's goals in the Coyle case was the maintenance of distance between the children and Mr. Coyle. Either the appropriate regulations for making such trips financially possible for the children were not communicated to Mrs. Coyle, or else Mrs. Coyle, sensing the caseworker's attitude, made no reference to her desires for her children to visit their father. A value-free assessment of role-relationships, adaptations, and ego strengths in the Coyle family's situation, plus a clear understanding of the social goals and intent of the regulations, would have made clear to the former caseworker that both the Coyle family and society could best be served by helping to make the children's visits to their father possible.

The interrelationships of society's purposes for its social agencies and the implementation of these prescriptions by the caseworker in relationship with the client deserve far more detailed analysis than can be given here. Clearly, however, what goes on between Mrs. Coyle and Mrs. Morin is affected by the agency's statutory bases, the agency's policies, and the agency's consequent definition of Mrs. Morin's role as caseworker.

3. THE CLIENT-CASEWORKER RELATIONSHIP. We have said that the client-caseworker relationship is the crucial medium in the casework method, its goal being the restoration of personal-social balances. Mrs. Morin aimed to develop with Mrs. Coyle a relationship that would help to fortify Mrs. Coyle's own ego strength in her family's stressful situation.

At the same time, the professional relationship offered an accepting and nonjudgmental medium for a discussion of Mrs. Coyle's relevant weaknesses. The nature of the developing relationship—its depth or intensity and the content discussed in this professional situation—was affected by the caseworker's assessment of stressful role problems and modes of adaptation in the Coyle family, the relative ego strengths of the family members, and the policy prescriptions by Mrs. Morin's agency on what problems were appropriate for service.

In her assessment, Mrs. Morin saw Mrs. Coyle as one who had been quite dependent upon her husband, who was now absent from the home. Mrs. Morin's role as caseworker—for the client-caseworker relationship is a role-relationship too—might have been defined as one that offered limited substitute role supports in the absence of Mr. Coyle. At the same time, it was clear that if this family was to become an economically self-sufficient, emotionally satisfying, and socially productive unit again, better able to face stressful situations, some modification in the little-girl–father relationship between Mrs. Coyle and her husband seemed desirable. Part of Mrs. Coyle's approach to her husband, Mrs. Morin learned, was that during her visits to him and in her correspondence with him at Long Pines prison camp, she never once let him know what a difficult time she was having at home. A little girl, seeking the approval of her father, may not feel comfortable telling him about her difficulties and pressures. By contrast, two adults, in a comfortable relationship with one another, can freely admit to one another their weaknesses as well as their strengths.

Mrs. Morin, having fostered a supportive, comfortable relationship with Mrs. Coyle, in which Mrs. Coyle could still be accepted despite her confession of weaknesses and in which her strengths were approved of, questioned Mrs. Coyle about her "covering up" by writing smooth and easy letters. Mrs. Morin could ask what Mrs. Coyle thought her husband might think of this, what he might feel, whether he might not sense a break in their communication with one another and an absence of shared feelings. In raising such questions, Mrs. Morin used the client-caseworker relationship to help Mrs. Coyle perceive how her mode of adaptation might be hindering achievement of her own goals in her marital relationship. To this extent, clarification and modification of relationships in the client's family life were being effected—and demonstrated—in the client-caseworker relationship.

It should be noted that Mrs. Morin did not approach this central problem directly or immediately in her contact with Mrs. Coyle but rather began by looking with Mrs. Coyle at her children's modes of adapting to their father's offense. Raising questions about the children's thoughts and reactions, Mrs. Morin entered the field of familial relationships with less stress than there would have been had the focus at once been upon Mrs. Coyle as a wife.

Recognizing that Mr. Coyle's behavior was an offense against social mores that the family shared, and that the family must, consequently, have been disturbed about it, Mrs. Morin wondered whether the children still did not think and feel somewhat differently about the situation in view of their own differing developmental needs. Katie, as a preadolescent girl, was likely to want to continue to see her father as unjustly accused. Being apparently closely identified with her mother, Katie could easily share her mother's defense against the reported situation, certain that her father had done nothing but drink a bit too much. In discussing with Mrs. Coyle how she might understand and handle Stephen's defenses, a front of battling bravado, Mrs. Morin pointed out how important the rules of the game might still be to one his age, but how someone could break some of the rules and still basically be "a wonderful guy." If Mrs. Coyle were clear in her own thinking about the situation, she could profitably, at the appropriate time, talk with Stephen as though he had some still unanswered questions about it all. Mrs. Coyle's recognition of her husband's drinking but her denial of the sexual offense, and her continued love and acceptance of Mr. Coyle, if communicated to Stephen, might help Stephen in his own specific feelings about his father's situation and in his general attitudes toward authority figures. Persons in authority, too, could in their way transgress; Stephen might realize this, adopt more of a "live-and-let-live" approach, and find little need then for his almost defiant defensiveness. Patrick, being older, was somewhat more removed from his father; the possibility of his regaining his balance through relationships with substitutes like his uncle was supported as appropriate action.

In short, in focusing on Mrs. Coyle's possible behavior as a mother in her relationships with her children around Mr. Coyle's offense, Mrs. Morin was first able to demonstrate the principle of adequate communication and ventilation of hidden feelings. Going from discussion of these relations to discussion of Mrs. Coyle's relationship with her husband was then a gradual step. Most important, in the very course of the client-caseworker relationship, Mrs. Coyle was experiencing the kind of open, accepting, and relatively defenseless relationship that was the content of casework processes, the problem being Mrs. Coyle's concealing and thus nonaccepting and defensive relationship with her husband. In her relationship with Mrs. Morin, Mrs. Coyle could be nonconcealing and relatively undefensive and still be accepted and even approved. If this kind of relationship was so satisfying when tested with a caseworker, might it not be so with Mr. Coyle also?

4. BASIC CONCEPTS FOR UNDERSTANDING HUMAN BEHAVIOR. In the discussion of the stressful situation in the Coyle family, references have been made to the concepts of ego, mode of adaptation, and social role. These concepts are discussed in some detail in section III of this chapter; their relationships to one another may be briefly indicated here.

The term *ego* symbolizes those creative forces in every person that, developing most rapidly in the early years of life, serve to mediate between the person's inner drives and conflicts and the demands of the outer world. An important function of the ego is the perception of both inner and outer stimuli. The stronger the forces of the ego, or the freer they are from attacks of anxiety, the more accurately or less distortedly the person perceives himself and the world around him, and the more appropriate and effective his behavior is likely to be.

Many of the cues a person perceives in social situations—in the family, at work, at play—call for appropriate responses from him in his position in the social situation. The well acculturated person in a relatively stabilized culture is likely to have learned the range of expected behaviors and other attributes for most of the positions in which he finds himself daily. For him, many of these behaviors have become accustomed or habitual, whether he is in the position of parent or child, worker or citizen in the community. The range of expected behaviors and attributes for each such position is called a *social role*. Each culture, according to its beliefs and values, prescribes its own definitions of the social roles of mother and father, male and female adolescent, physician or healer, and other universally found positions.

To the demands of these roles, persons make their own *adaptation*, with each person acting uniquely and creatively and yet each, in the same culturally defined role, acting somewhat similarly. Marked deviations in adaptation occur under conditions that may be intrapersonally stressful —conditions that induce troublesome or unusually inventive adaptations. Stressful situations are associated with the failure of or deviation from accustomed modes of adaptation, under intrapersonal or situational pressures.

Thus, schematically, the concepts of ego, social role, and mode of adaptation (and stressful situation) may be related to one another.

5. PRINCIPLES OF CASEWORK PRACTICE. In the Coyle family case record, there is evidence of the caseworker's use of many of the general principles of casework practice. The caseworker is at all times warmly accepting of Mrs. Coyle, respecting her as a person whose current problems in life at no time call for the allocation of blame or the crooked finger pointing at personal fault. The general principle of *acceptance* has philosophical roots in both democracy and Christianity, but it remains a guiding principle for the caseworker because many years of professional

experience have demonstrated that clients are helped to become self-dependent and self-respecting persons again only when, in their search for help, they are truly accepted and respected by their caseworkers.

The general principle of *communication* is illustrated by the ways in which Mrs. Morin fosters Mrs. Coyle's description of her situation and goals and the ways, in turn, in which Mrs. Morin demonstrates her own capacities for understanding and helping and clarifies her own role as caseworker. Through this give and take, an initial client-caseworker relationship develops and grows as a mutual and shared experience. The principles of acceptance and communication are not only based on professional experience of a trial-and-error sort; current theories in the social and psychological sciences offer generalized propositions on human development and behavior—the essentially reflexive or interactive nature of inner and outer determinants—that help to explain why the principles of practice mentioned above seem to work effectively.

Beyond this, the caseworker follows the principle of *individualization*, seeking to understand the unique constellation of factors in each client's stressful situation. Mrs. Morin, even in her relatively short contact with Mrs. Coyle, comes to know her as a person who is in many ways like other clients she has worked with, but who is, *in toto*, unlike any other client. If Mrs. Coyle is to be helped, she must be individualized and so understood by her caseworker.

These are but three general principles of casework practice—the principles of acceptance, communication, and individualization. Their essence is difficult to convey to a reader, without their seeming to be obvious and even platitudinous. In the complexities of practice, however, and in the illuminating experience of supervision of one's practice, one may discover how the subtle and unconscious rejection of such principles seems responsible for failures in practice. Six general principles are discussed in some detail in the first part of section IV of this chapter.

In addition to these general guides to practice with all clients, there is a group of differential principles. These latter principles relate differing casework goals and differing means of activities of casework to differing assessment formulations of clients in stressful situations. Differential principles prescribe that with clients in a given situation, these are appropriate casework goals and appropriate means to these goals. For example, under what specific conditions is the major goal environmental modification, or changes in role-functions in the client's situation? Under what specific conditions is a primarily supportive and nonquestioning approach called for? When does the caseworker use clarification of the meaning of behavior as a means of effecting changes in a client's stressful situation? Differential principles may be accurately applied only after a careful study and assessment of the client in his stressful situation—after his ego functioning, his characteristic and current modes of adaptation, and the social role components in his situation have been carefully assessed. A discussion of differential principles of casework practice appears in the latter part of section IV of this chapter. What differential principles Mrs. Morin used in her relationship with Mrs. Coyle should then be more apparent.

6. THE CASEWORKER AS THE BASIC HELPING AGENT. Mrs. Morin's capacity to apply her knowledge of human behavior under stress and her skill in establishing a relationship with Mrs. Coyle are apparent in the record and the discussion of it. Whatever is enduringly remedial about Mrs. Coyle's contact with the Putnam County public agency grows out of her relationship with a person like Mrs. Morin. Mrs. Morin (as well as her predecessors and successors) is, for Mrs. Coyle, the person who understands the family's stressful situation and the person who, aware of the regulations concerning services in the social agency, can help to connect the Coyle family with available resources in the agency. In addition, Mrs. Morin knows of other resources in the community, should the Coyle family need these. Mrs. Morin, for example, knew the correctional agency personnel and their functions; though she did not include this in the summarized case record, she told the writer that she reinforced Mrs. Coyle's expressed desire to keep in touch with the Adult Authority representatives who would be responsible for setting some limits to Mr. Coyle's indeterminate sentence. Upon Mr. Coyle's return, the use of a private family service agency might be indicated if problems arose for the Coyles during the readjustment period. At such time, of course, the Coyle family would no longer be eligible for social assistance.

In addition to being informed about and sensitive to the feelings and behavior of persons in stressful situations and cognizant of resources within the county agency and in other community facilities that might be useful to the Coyle family, Mrs. Morin was skilled in applying the principles of casework practice. She could define her role and relationship with Mrs. Coyle so that she could help her make the kind of modifications that not only would improve her adaptation to her situation but that might endure beyond the current situation as learned ego functioning. Such changes are not likely to occur in people without an appropriate supportive relationship. The reasons for this should become apparent in the discussion of the concept of ego in section III.

III. BASIC CONCEPTS RELEVANT TO CASEWORK PRACTICE

In order to provide tangible services and other kinds of casework appropriate to clients in their stressful situations, caseworkers engage, at varying levels of intensity, in the study and assessment of each case. This requires an analysis of the unique social, psychological, and biological determinants of the client's current stressful situation. Obtaining data on these determinants, the caseworker develops hypotheses for understanding the client in his situation.

The line of inquiry may focus almost completely on the present situation and its immediate antecedents. On the other hand, it may seek to include historical data on related past life experiences. How intensively a client and his situation are studied depends on many factors. Two that are basic are the *nature of the services offered by the agency,* as determined by its societal charter, which prescribes its goals, and the *agency's conceptual frame of reference for understanding and helping clients.*

Although the principle of individualization requires that each client be assessed and worked with on the basis of the unique components in his situation, it must be remembered that caseworkers do not begin each case *de novo.* Rather, they use generalizations and norms about human behavior derived from theories in the psychological and social sciences, generalizations enriched and refined by the knowledge gathered in decades of caseworkers' experiences in trying to help clients. These enriched and refined generalizations and norms are the frame of reference for caseworkers when they study and help to modify the modes of adaptation and the situational adjustments of their clients.

There are variations in the conceptual bases used by practicing caseworkers, but every caseworker uses a set of assumptions about human behavior to determine, among other things, in what ways a client in his situation deviates from the models in the caseworker's empirically fortified core of basic knowledge. On various dimensions, the client in his stressful situation can be understood and classified, or seen in tentative assessment categories. Some categorization is essential if the caseworker is to formulate and pursue an appropriate casework plan in a given case. Caseworkers' repertory of interventive activities is not limitless. Selection must be made from this repertory in each client-caseworker relationship, according to the caseworker's assessment formulations or classifications. Under certain conditions, certain caseworker actions are appropriate; under other conditions, other kinds of interventions are called for.

Conceptual tools for an understanding and typology of clients in stressful situations are found in the social, psychological, and biological sciences. Let us start our discussion of relevant social concepts by utilizing the situation in the Coyle family.

A. The Concept of a Social Role in Casework Practice Theory

All of us recognize the emotional and social deprivations suffered by Mrs. Coyle and her children in response to the offense and absence of Mr.

Coyle. Seen as a primary group, the Coyle family, like other families, consists of a network of intimate reciprocal role-relationships. Three sets of role-relationships overlap: those between husband and wife, among father and mother and child and child, and between wage earner and economic dependent. With the apprehension and imprisonment of Mr. Coyle, the social roles of husband, father, and wage earner ceased to be performed in the Coyle family as they formerly were. The absence of Mr. Coyle required a reorganization of social role-relationships and a reallocation of social role-functions in this family. The complexity of such realignments called upon the biological, psychological, and social adaptive and adjustive resources of the individual family members and of their community. This transition is schematized in Figures 1 and 2.

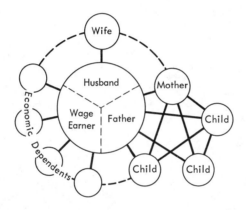

Figure 1. Role-relationships in the Coyle family, prior to Mr. Coyle's absence.

In Figure 1, wife, mother, child, and economic dependent are multiply interrelated with Mr. Coyle in his three roles of husband, father, and wage earner. Mrs. Coyle is simultaneously a wife, mother, and economic dependent (as the lines connecting these three roles indicate); she interacts with Mr. Coyle in each of these three roles. Each of the children interacts with the father as both a child and an economic dependent. Expectations for the behavior of oneself and others are built, as functions, into each of these roles in the course of living and interacting within this family. Many of these behaviors become accustomed and habitual ways of behaving. The mother and the children are able to do certain things, carrying out certain familial functions, by counting on the father to execute certain related functions. Seen in these social terms, the affective accompaniments of all communication among persons occupying related social roles in any primary group are not to be forgotten. These feelings are of major significance to the persons involved. However,

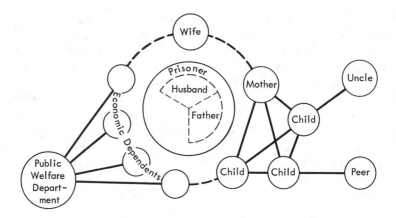

Figure 2.   Role-relationships in the Coyle family, following Mr. Coyle's absence.

initial emphasis is placed on the social interactions and social functions in these role-relationships, because without them, many of the shared basic biological and social needs of the family members may go unmet.

With the imprisonment of Mr. Coyle, many of Mrs. Coyle's habitual ways of performing her complementary roles of wife, mother, and economic dependent became inappropriate to the new situation. Mrs. Coyle must now behave in face-to-face interactions in the husband-wife relationship with Mr. Coyle, meeting him at Long Pines prison camp, more in the role of a public visitor to an institutionalized and restricted person. The privacy and intimacy of the husband-wife relationship are gone. Impulses to act in her accustomed wifely ways with her husband are likely to be screened, restrained, and modified, if expressed at all. Mr. Coyle's new role of prisoner is dominant in all situations and affects all other persons in their fulfillment of reciprocal roles with him.

At home, Mrs. Coyle's former modes of relating as a mother to her children no longer have the supports or accustomed interactions of father to complement her behavior. Some of the functions of the father must now be accomplished by Mrs. Coyle; other functions by the older son, Pat; others by the other children; and still others by persons and resources in the family's community, not previously involved in the Coyle family role structure in this way. Pat's uncle becomes for Pat a temporary substitute father. Stephen's peers may be invested with and called upon to give some of the responses Stephen formerly exchanged with his father. Katie may be thinking of an idealized father image as a replacement for her real father, no longer at home. The new role structure and allocation of role-functions brings into the family life, in Mr. Coyle's perception of it, an imagined lover as a replacement for himself in his relationship with his wife. In addition, as a replacement for Mr. Coyle in the role of wage earner, the Putnam County public agency enters the Coyle family's life, and, more personally, a social caseworker also becomes involved. Considering the reorganization of social roles in the Coyle family, what should the client-caseworker relationship—another role-relationship—be in this situation? How should the role of caseworker be defined and fulfilled to be maximally helpful to the Coyle family?

To decide on answers to these questions, the caseworker seeks a picture of the family in its stressful situation. Thus far, in this section, the Coyle family's situation has been described only in terms of social role changes or transitions. The discussion has assumed that *a situation is potentially stressful when a reorganization of role-relationships and a reallocation of social role-functions must be made in an on-going primary group. Accustomed and habitual modes of daily adaptation must, under such circumstances, be modified.* Old ways of doing things no longer seem applicable. *A situation is perceived as stressful,* however, not only whenever accustomed and habitual modes of adaptation do not apply, but *when the person's repertory of knowledge and skills does not readily yield new ways of adapting that seem personally satisfying, effective, or socially acceptable;* lacking appropriate social supports, *the person feels overwhelemed and, in extreme cases, powerless.* The link, then, between role-disturbance and personal disturbance is the concept of mode of adaptation, to which the next subsection of this chapter is devoted. We must first fill in this sketch of the concept of social role in terms of its relevance to casework practice by turning from the Coyle family and examining the concept more broadly.

The concept of social role serves as a link between the concepts of the individual person and the concepts of society and culture. Primary groups mediate, by interpreting and to some extent individualizing for each member, the beliefs and values of the culture and the expectations of the society for persons in a given position. Thus variant cultural expectations for such roles as mother, father, and preschool or school-age son or daughter are communicated. If, as Linton has said, social role is "the sum total of the culture patterns associated with a particular status," including "the attitudes, values, and behavior ascribed by the society to any and all persons occupying this status,"[3] it is in the primary group that

[3]Ralph Linton, *The Cultural Background of Personality* (New York: Appleton-Century-Crofts, 1945), p. 77. This concept of social role follows "one sociological tradition," as Robert Merton says. Merton proposes instead the idea that "each social status involves not a single associated role, but an array of roles," and so Merton develops a theory of role sets. This is not the place, however, to try to synthesize in summary fashion a large and divergent literature in concepts of social role. But, for one different perspective, see Robert K. Merton, *Social Theory and Social Structure*, 1968 enlarged ed. (New York: Free Press, 1968), pp. 41–45.

a range of acceptable role-performances is interpreted, narrowed down, and sometimes modified, the better to fit the needs and capacities of the persons involved. Whether a social role is performed in a satisfying, effective, and acceptable manner depends always upon the capacities, needs, and values of both the person occupying a given role and the persons in roles reciprocal to his. In short, the person learns through his primary groups what the expectations for a given social role in the group or the larger society are and then, in the network of role relationships that this primary group provides, normally prepares for and tries to fulfill the role-expectations. This latter process may be called role-adaptation, in which the person utilizes his resources to perform a role.

Because of personal needs, values, or capacities not immediately appropriate to the performance of the role as prescribed, the person may make an unsatisfying, ineffective, or unacceptable adaptation to a role. In some cases, he may attempt to adjust or modify the group's definition of the role, and in some group situations this may be an effective mode of obtaining a balance between personal attributes and social requirements. In some cases, role-adjustment may be unacceptable to the group, and the person may then attempt to perform the role as it is defined, but only with great personal effort and strain.

The concept of social role helps us to understand both the purposes of social services that use casework and the practice of casework within these services. The uses of casework have a long history in such social services as child welfare, corrections, family service, medical and psychiatric or mental health services, public assistance, and school social work. In addition, casework is used in crisis centers and other newer kinds of agencies set up specifically to help street people, or drug users, or persons affected by changes in the roles of women. In many of these services, community work and group work as well as casework are used.

Social Role in Public Assistance

Programs in public assistance have traditionally addressed themselves to persons lacking any alternative economic resources. The clients being served in public assistance programs are very often involved in stressful situations that may be understood on a social level, initially, in terms of the concept of social role.

Who are the clients who are eligible to use these agencies? In the categorical public assistance programs, clients have been the dependent child, the indigent aged, and the economically needy blind and disabled. Each of the persons in these groups occupies a marginal or deviant role in our society. Marginality and deviation, in and of themselves, make for potentially stressful situations for the persons occupying these positions. Our society is not structured through its formal facilities to support persons in these positions; our culture does not prepare its members with a repertory of modes of adaptation appropriate to these marginal and deviant roles. The child in our society normally develops through a sequence of social roles complementary to the changing roles of mother and father. He is able to perform these roles, within a range of satisfying, effective, and acceptable modes of adaptation, because he has the necessary parental supports. The "neglected" child—who is not provided with the minimal parental care possible when economic and other social, physical health, or psychological family conditions are inadequate— needs the support of supplementary or substitute parental role resources in the community. When parental roles are adequately fulfilled in relation to the child, he is not "dependent" on such supplementary resources.

Similarly, the needy aged person may become a client when, besides lacking private economic resources, the person suffers disruption in role relationships in his primary groups—familial, work, and peer or friendship groups. Other resources for financial help may not be available or acceptable. The social role of the aged in our society, defined by the expectations of our dominant culture, frequently includes segregation from normal affective and productive relationships, along with the loss of primary group associations and the complementary roles of mate, co-worker, and lifelong friend. The child of the aged person is now adult, no longer in need of the aged person's accustomed and habitual parenting. Industry and other economic institutions assume that the aged person cannot continue to produce effectively and displace him from his accustomed and habitual work roles. With increasing biological degenerative processes of the aging body and with the frequent death of elderly companions, the aged person is further delimited in his role-relationships. Seen in role terms, the aged in our society who are poor and/or sick are increasingly expected and forced to live in social isolation, focused on their memories of the past and their own developing somatic disabilities, encouraged to engage in hobbies and other pastimes they have never been previously prepared for. Social agencies providing only financial assistance to the needy aged fulfill but a very limited function when the total social situation of many old people is considered and the needs for services are explored.

Categorical assistance programs, such as aid to the aged or the blind, have been opposed on many counts. One reason is that the blame or onus for economic need seems to be placed primarily on the individual who fits the criteria for the aid category. Role concepts help us understand that there are many patterns of personal-social interaction in situations of economic deprivation. Role concepts help us understand also how our society alienates and extrudes to marginal roles persons who become in any way incapacitated. Failure to provide paying jobs is one way a society may cut off its less able members.

More generally, an unemployed worker may be unable to remain in the role of gainful worker either because of changes in the economy and its definition of a work role or because of changes in the worker's capacities for adapting to expectations for the job. Changes in the requirements for a work role may vary from the dissolution of the position to changes in the definition of role-relationships within a work group, brought on by changes in the personnel or technology of the job situation. Changes in personal capacities to adapt to a relatively unchanging work role may be rooted in somatic and/or value changes in the client. In any situation, the caseworker seeks to discover the sources of stress and to relate to the client in ways that may be corrective of any personal-social imbalance still existing after financial assistance has taken care of basic needs.

Social Role in Family Service

The family agency focuses with clients on difficulties in husband-wife and parent-child role-relationships. Role-restructuring and reallocation of role-functions occur in families not only, as in the Coyle family, with the loss of a key person—whether through death, desertion, institutionalization for illness or crime, or military service. These situations occur in families also with the addition of such roles as new baby, adoptive or foster child, stepchild, stepparent, grandparent, other kin, boarder, or visitor. In the course of attempts to integrate new social roles into an already structured, functioning, and ongoing primary group, realignments and reallocations become necessary. New complementary role-relationships must be developed, affecting all existing relationships within the group. The addition of persons in any of these roles in some ways inevitably alters the definition of the basic familial role-relationship of husband and wife. Whether such additions lead to stressful situations, either for those in the existing family unit or for the newcomer or for both, depends largely upon the adaptive capacities of all the persons involved. Clearly, however, the social roles of all—expectations for their behavior and other attributes—are redefined as much by the addition as by the loss of a role in the family's network of relationships. The meaning of the changes, how suddenly they occur, and how they are perceived by the client in a stressful situation can be illuminated by the family agency caseworker's generalized understanding of social roles and relationships among them in the family.

The concept of social role is a helpful tool, also, for partial understanding of the wife or mother or husband or father who comes to the
family service agency seeking casework help when the stressful situation
arises from changes in a person, with the structuring of role-relationships
and allocation of role-functions remaining rigid. Here, the stressful situation has as its source an imbalance between the other group members'
definition of a familial role and the person's changed needs, values, or
capacities for fulfilling the role defined in this way. The caseworker in the
family service agency has then to study and evaluate the situation and
determine what kinds of client-caseworker relationships are likely to help
modify the imbalances in the client's stressful situation. What changes
can the introduction of a caseworker into this network of interpersonal
and intrapersonal imbalances effect? And what should the role of a caseworker be in this situation?

Social Role in Child Welfare

This formulation goes beyond the client-caseworker relationship in family service agencies. Child welfare agencies have as a goal the resolution
of problems inherent in the roles of the foster child and the adoptive child
and in the complementary roles of biological, foster, and adoptive parents. The service of finding homes for children requiring foster-home
placement calls actively into play the caseworker's model of maternal and
paternal roles—that is, the ranges of attitudes and behaviors that theory
in child development postulates as satisfying and effective for the productive growth and development of children in our society.

   More specifically, the caseworker studies the patterns of role-expec-
tation and social interaction in each prospective foster family. With an
awareness of the foster child that is derived from study and assessment
of the child's needs, capacities, and limitations, the caseworker has a good
idea of the behavior the child is likely to manifest in a foster home and
can, in considering a variety of foster homes, select the one in which
expectations for the social role of seven-year-old girl or nine-year-old boy
are not too far removed from the role the child is likely to be able to fulfill.
Using the concept of social role in home finding, the caseworker asks:
what child attributes will fit and flourish in this prospective foster family's
network of role-relationships? What attributes exceed this family's role-
expectations and tolerances for child behavior? Through use of the casework method, what likelihood is there that the parental role-expectations
for a ten-year-old boy in this family might be adjusted? Using the concept
of social role in child placement, the caseworker asks what role demands
might not exceed this child's capacities for role-adaptation. What likeli-

hood is there that, living in this family, this child's growth and development will occur in desired directions?

It is, of course, a primary concern of the child welfare field to keep a child in his own home, with his own parent(s), wherever possible. Through early intervention, as in the situation in the Rodgers family described in section I of this chapter, a single parent may be given enough support to permit him or her to keep the child at home. Community resources, such as a day care center, may be drawn upon to supplement Dee Rodgers' child care capacities and to provide other kinds of support—for example, meetings with other parents—for a person in the difficult role of a single parent with very young children. The special strains and stresses of the role of single parent are of concern to social workers in both the child welfare and family service fields.

Social Role in School Social Work

The school caseworker, working with the pupil in trouble in a school setting, goes through a similar course of study and assessment, usually knowing through a referral statement from a classroom teacher or principal what social expectations the child is failing to meet. Such statements implicitly communicate how the social role of pupil is defined in the given situation and in what way the child is deviating from these standards. Here the caseworker has ready access to both objective and subjective data. Casework in such situations may involve direct work not only with the child but also with his parents. The child's performance of roles in extrafamilial settings is related theoretically to current experience and probably to past experience in the central role relationships between parents and children. The goal of school social work is to reinforce the child's potential strengths and capacities for satisfying, effective, and acceptable performance in the role of pupil. To achieve this goal in an institutional setting like the school, the caseworker works directly with the teacher and also with other school personnel, in an effort to help them understand some of what underlies the child's behavior, and to adjust their expectations for the role of pupil, so that a given child's capacities for role-adaptation to these standards may be understood and perhaps seen as falling within a somewhat broadened definition of acceptable behaviors for the role of pupil. Much of the work of a school social worker may consist of this kind of interpretation to school personnel. Through such interpretations and other consultation, school personnel's tolerances for children's behavior may be broadened generally.

Once understood and accepted by teachers, the atypical capacities of children referred for guidance may be somewhat modified in the classroom. Such changes have been seen to occur following a caseworker's interpretations to a teacher, which help the teacher to broaden his definition of the role of pupil and to understand situations in which individual children deviate from this model. In such a situation, with a greater consonance between social role-expectations or role-acceptances and the actual performance in this role of an individual child, the better balanced pupil-teacher relationship itself helps the child to develop, over a period of time, more appropriate performance in the role of pupil. Effective communication depends to a large extent upon consensus between interacting persons upon the expectations and attributes of their interrelated roles.

Social Role in Corrections

Casework treatment in institutional settings relies as heavily upon efforts toward role-adaptation in the client as upon role-adjustment in the primary groups, of which both the client and the persons (in related roles) who referred him are members. In the correctional field, the probation officer interprets the delinquent's behavior to the judge and to police officers. The delinquent's mode of adaptation to the combination of internal and external forces that directed him into the role of delinquent requires the same kinds of study and assessment as pursued with casework's other clients. As in other deviant or marginal roles in our society, stressful situations not only catapult the person into these roles but also induce further stress once the person has occupied the role. The client-caseworker relationship in the correctional field begins with the same questions for the caseworker as in all other fields: how can this relationship be of help to the client in his relationship with society, and what should the appropriate role of the caseworker include if it is to be effective with this client? In work with institutionalized delinquents and criminals, the caseworker has ready access to those who define the social role of "inmate" and who observe the client's daily role-performance. In such institutional settings, the caseworker is part of the world to which he is trying to help the client adapt more satisfactorily.

Social Role of Serviceman and Traveler

The work of the Red Cross with the kin of military servicemen and women focuses on a specific set of role relationships in our society, often reflecting the stressful effects of the separation of members in a family unit and a breakdown in communication among them. Travelers' Aid was another nationwide casework agency set up to help persons who, in the role of traveler, deprived of accustomed supports of their home community, have difficulties in the course of their separation from home. Note that stresses in the roles of serviceman's kin or traveler have to do with situations in which both former role relationships are disrupted and new adaptations are called for that may not immediately be possible. The parent who becomes ill at home has others in reciprocal roles and community medical resources to turn to. The parent who becomes ill while traveling, or while the son or daughter upon whom the parent is dependent is doing military service in another part of the world, may use the substitute relationships and the resources known to a caseworker in such situations.

Social Role in Medical Social Work

Persons making a transition into the role of patient, because of physical or psychological illness, may find this role adaptation a difficult one. The clinic and the hospital are institutions that reflect the culture of the physician. Like all institutions, they may be analyzed in terms of goals, functions, and traditions, resultant hierarchies of positions with their expected functions, and a consequent network of social role-relationships, in which the patient has his place. In a hospital, the medical director, staff physicians, residents, internes, the subhierarchy of nurses, the chief medical social worker, social work supervisors and other social workers, the occupational and physiotherapists, nutritionists, administrative and clerical personnel handling admissions, supplies, accounting, and other essential functions, the pharmacists, the ward attendants, and the custodial workers all have their expectations for the role of patient and in a variety of direct and indirect ways are related to and interact with the patient.

There are standards for the good patient, some of which are made explicit in the complex of rules and regulations governing behavior in medical facilities and communicated to persons (and their next of kin) when the former are initiated into the role of patient. On the whole, for reasons that (according to present theory) explain how people get well, the patient is likely to find himself in a role-relationship with others that is characteristically a dominance-submission or authority-dependence structure. The physician prescribes; auxiliary medical personnel, the nurses and the multiple therapists (physio-, occupational, etc.), all help the patient to comply with "what the doctor has ordered." The role of patient clearly calls upon a person's capacity to accept dependent and submissive relationships with others who have knowledge about getting well. Accepting this kind of relationship, without conflict about being in such a role during at least the initial phases of illness, a person is more likely to get well. But a person who has difficulty, for reasons of personal needs, values, or capacity or because of outside social pressures, in accepting such a position may be considered a "bad patient" and may suffer not only the physical effects of "not following the doctor's orders" but also the social pressures of performing a deviant role according to the sanctions of the surrounding medical culture. In such stressful situations, the social worker may be of assistance in helping the person to adapt himself more satisfyingly, effectively, and acceptably to the role of patient. Also, through interpretation to medical personnel, the social worker may alter expectations for a given patient. Since attitudes toward dependency are likely to have had their genesis in the early parent-child relationship of the patient, the knowledge and skills of the social worker in this kind of case may have to be of the highest order.

In addition, of course, in entering the role of hospitalized patient, the person is obliged to surrender temporarily many of his functions and obligations in his accustomed and habitual roles. Absence from the primary groups of the family, work, and the community may or may not come easily to the new patient. In either event, the family itself may suffer from the patient's absence, and the difficulties of kin may have direct or indirect ill effects upon the patient and his getting better. In cases of terminal illness, the attitudes and behavior of both the patient and those in complementary role-relationships must be considered. In all of these potentially stressful situations, the caseworker has a role to play. Precisely what it will be depends upon the needs and capacities as well as the deprivations of all persons in any such network of relationships. The caseworker may have the key to community resources needed to substitute for the patient's functions in the family. The caseworker may be able through a relationship with family members to offer other services aimed at helping all concerned adapt more effectively to a stressful situation involving illness.

Social Role in Mental Health Centers

"Mental health center" is a term that covers a wide variety of facilities. Included among them are a unit in a store-front community health service in an urban neighborhood, an adjunct of a psychiatric ward in a general hospital, an out-patient clinic in a complex of buildings comprising a large state mental hospital, and a crisis center with its suicide prevention switchboard. All of these facilities are likely to be staffed by teams that include social workers as well as psychologists, psychiatrists, nurses, and others. Their professional roles may blur in practice to the extent that an observer is unable to tell the differing educational backgrounds of participating staff members. The presence of social workers on such teams is likely to insure that the social components of mental health problems are addressed.

What is sometimes labeled "mental illness" seems to arise under diverse conditions, too complex to be discussed fully here. In brief, the stressful situations of emotionally troubled persons may be partially understood in role terms. Some such persons may have lost their ties with their society in ways that interfere with their performing key social roles within that society. Other persons may have become so oversocialized and habituated to their roles that they seem to have lost touch with their own individuality and spontaneity. In the latter situation, the persons have, in a sense, become their roles, performed mechanically and without uniqueness or creativity. In the former situation, the persons have become role-less.

Social workers in mental health centers help clients re-articulate with some segment of society—or with themselves—so that their lives may become more meaningful. The first bridge, in many cases, is the establishment of a viable client-worker relationship, starting with a demonstration or verbal clarification of expectations in the reciprocal roles of client and worker. Following this connection, casework intervention may aim to make the client's world more accessible to him through the social worker's direct dealings with important people in the client's milieu. At the same time, a caseworker may help a client reconsider his feelings and perspectives regarding the roles that have potential value for the client. Thus, in part, the personal-social imbalances of stressful situations may be ameliorated.

The concept of social role is a basic tool for the caseworker. Generally, social casework addresses itself to helping people who find themselves in marginal or deviant positions in society as well as in situations in which roles and their relationships have been misconstrued. Sometimes ambiguities about roles arise because of perceptual distortion. Sometimes ambiguities arise because of rapid situational or larger social changes. Roles and their relationships may have been suddenly restructured and role functions may have been hastily reallocated. Such changes make accustomed modes of adaptation inappropriate. Stressful situations have been seen to arise with the loss or addition of persons in primary group roles, with the modification of role-expectations in a dominant role in the person's life, or with the necessity of one's making a transition into a role, the demands of which are inconsonant with the person's needs, values, and capacities. This imbalance between intrapersonal biological and psychological strengths and the changing demands of social roles that the person is expected to fulfill is the core of the adaptative and adjustive difficulties with which caseworkers try to help their clients. The further usefulness of the concept of social role for the principles of casework practice is implicit in the statement that the client-caseworker relationship itself involves reciprocal roles, the caseworker's professional role varying in a given case according to the client's total situation and the social agency's goals.

Throughout the preceding discussion of the concept of social role, the term "modes of adaptation to stress" has been used. It is time now to consider the meaning of this term and its patternable forms, in their relations to casework practice.

B. The Concept of Mode of Adaptation in Casework Practice Theory

We have looked thus far primarily at the more objective phenomena in clients' stressful situations—changes in the structuring of social roles and realignments of role functions. We have noted that stressful situations are experienced subjectively as (1) the inapplicability or inappropriateness of habitual modes of adaptation for meeting changed role demands in a situation, or as (2) imbalances in a person's fulfillment of relatively unchanged roles, when relevant personal needs, values, and capacities are changing. We shall now turn to an exploration of the more subjective aspects of clients' modes of adaptation to stressful situations.

Study should reveal what the client's dominant modes of adaptation have been and should lead to the formulation of plans for appropriate casework intervention in an attempt to modify the imbalances between the person and his social world. The client's dominant and variant modes of adaptation are directly related to the goals of intervention as well as to the formulation of the role of the caseworker in this process. The ways in which clients adapt to stressful situations determine whether the subjective experience of stress is relieved or compounded.

Adaptations to stressful situations can be made on at least three different levels. Faced with a threatening situation, a client will first try to use his habitual modes of adaptation. When these have clearly failed to resolve the feelings of distress, he will "regress" to modes of adaptation used earlier in his life—fighting, pairing, or flight (discussed more fully below). Finally, if these approaches fail, in extreme situations, the client may become apathetic, totally resigned, mentally disoriented, and/ or immobile or hyperactive. It is essential that he achieve some endurable balance between his perception of the stressful situation and his mode of adapting to it.

If the client feels, more or less consciously, that by doing thus and so the situation becomes more tolerable, and by not doing something else, the situation will not become more painful, he is likely to cling to doing thus and so and meet with resistance any efforts to modify his mode of adaptation, even though to the outside observer his current approach seems in no way to be bettering his situation. His feeling is that he has reached a state of equilibrium, and he will reject any outsider's efforts to modify this precarious balance. He may therefore seem very protective of his mode of adaptation, utilizing it constantly and clinging to it, becoming quite emotionally attached to it. Efforts to effect any change in such a mode of adaptation obviously require a strong, supportive relationship from a helping person.

Now let us look at the Coyle family. Apparently nothing in Mrs. Coyle's background had prepared her to handle, through accustomed modes of adaptation, a situation in which she as wife and mother was expected to take over, in the face of feelings of shame or guilt, where her husband, suddenly imprisoned, left off. On the contrary, while the record provides us with no material on Mrs. Coyle's prior life, we have some cues suggesting that Mrs. Coyle was very closely attached to Mr. Coyle and probably quite dependent upon his fatherliness and his multiple functions in their household. We know that she gave birth to her first child when she was sixteen, suggesting that she had had no extensive experience in self-support or preparation for any work role. In the economic sphere, too, she was probably quite dependent upon her husband. Faced then with his departure, she says she literally shut herself up in her house. This was her initial mode of adaptation, one of social *flight*. From such behavior, one may infer her feelings of inadequacy to cope with the situation in any more active way. What might others have done?

In a similar social situation, but with a background and a repertory of adaptations somewhat different from Mrs. Coyle's, another wife and mother might have resorted to *pairing*—that is, entering into a dependent and solace-seeking relationship with another person perceived as stronger and able to help one handle a stressful situation where one felt powerless. Mrs. X might have taken the children and gone home to her own parents, or gone on a visit to an older sister, or asked a close friend to come and live with her. Mrs. Y might have related herself in a dependent way to her oldest son as a substitute for her absent husband or immediately sought the help of professional counselors in the ministry or other professional fields. Mrs. Coyle, however, did not resort to pairing, but rather to flight from her friends, among whom an outsider might believe she could have found a comforting companion. Yet Mrs. Coyle states that she avoided all friends for about a year, during which time she collected her personal resources and apparently, at last, decided that her current response was no longer adaptive—that is, helpful to her in reducing her feelings of stress.

Another possible initial mode of adaptation might have been found in the assumption of a *fighting* approach to others. Initially, Mrs. Z might have persistently directed a barrage of attacks at persons in the police and judiciary systems who had "falsely" accused and convicted her husband. Drawing no satisfying response from this target for her anger and aggression, Mrs. Z might have maintained her fighting orientation but redirected her attacks against neighbors, former friends, and her own and other children. In the course of attacking others, Mrs. Z might have been completely unaware that she was counterattacking the members of a society who, she felt, had done her an injustice. She might have been responding to a feeling that she believed they harbored against her as the wife of a criminal and prisoner, fighting them before they openly attacked her. It is quite probable that Mrs. Coyle did have strong feelings of anger in her initial response to Mr. Coyle's incarceration, but note that she apparently expressed none of these openly until she responded by getting "mad" when he questioned her fidelity.

In short, Mrs. Coyle initially did not adapt to her stressful situation by pairing or fight, but rather by flight. She maintained this dominant mode of orientation for about a year, when self-recovery occurred and what seemed a more constructive approach to her total situation began. The record is too sparse on this change in mode of adaptation for us to hazard a guess as to what forces might have precipitated her change at that time. What is apparent, however, is that Mrs. Coyle had achieved a state of balance during this period, protecting herself from the perceived additional threat of contact with friends.

Each of the children in the Coyle family apparently resorted to a somewhat different mode of adaptation. Pat, the older son, seems to have used, as one of his modes of adaptation, pairing with an uncle whom he may have seen as a strong person. One senses, too, an element of flight in his adaptation, avoidance of others who formerly knew him, leaving his home community when he could during the summer vacation. By contrast, Stephen, the younger brother, met the situation with what the caseworker reported as a defiant bravado air, a kind of fight rather than flight or pairing. Whether there is an element of denial in his adaptation, an intrapersonal defense process, we have no way of knowing; his saying to himself that others would not dare to disapprove of him because of his father's behavior would not square with the probable facts. One can, however, live and act as though something were so and thus not let oneself perceive any behavior in others that might disprove one's feelings. The data on Katie's mode of adaptation suggest that she remained well identified with her mother and attached to her father, probably also engaging privately in denial of his criminal behavior, and maintaining so strong a relationship with him as a person, important to her, as to discount whatever he had done as in any way affecting their relationship. The modes of adaptation in this single family, then, appear to include flight, fight, and pairing.

Now when we talk of the use of fight, pairing, or flight as modes of adaptation when habitual modes of adaptation fail, we are not suggesting that these three possible approaches arise out of the blue for use in response to stressful situations. We may think of these three modes of adaptation as ways of relating to others that were learned by all of us in our early years of growing up and subsequently abandoned as limited, primitive, unsatisfying, ineffective, or unacceptable ways of relating. To understand their origins, we must briefly review the general course of the early development of human beings in our society. To understand the genetic origins of these modes of adaptation is to have a framework for interpreting the cues a client gives a caseworker about how far he has "regressed"—or gone back—in attempting to regain his equilibrium in a stressful situation. By "regression," we mean that persons have returned to much earlier modes of adaptation in stressful situations in which current modes of adaptation have failed. Under such conditions, we may all fall back on abandoned ways of doing things—or "regress" to former and once-satisfying ways.

There are many sources for a more intensive review of personal development than can be presented here. In brief, however, for present purposes, it is sufficient to say that the very earliest mode of adaptation of the child under the age of two is to pair with a parenting person, an omnipotent one, who nurtures and protects the neonate, the infant, and the young child. The biologically based needs for dependence upon another who feeds, holds, fondles, carries, and keeps one warm are clear. At about the age, however, when the child is begun to be expected to become a more social creature and to conform with some of society's expectations—to be completely weaned and toilet trained and not to be destructive of property, in accordance with the values of the child's culture—the child becomes in subtle or overt ways pressed into doing things he may not want to do. The parental "no" becomes a repeatedly interruptive force in the child's ongoing activities and pursuit of his impulses. Whether this "no" is expressed verbally, reinforced with physical restraints, or expressed nonverbally and nonphysically by silent parental tensions and disapprovals, the child in the course of socialization is experiencing a sense of external restraint.

To such frustration, on some level, the child inevitably responds with anger and more or less overt counteraggression or fight. Fight may become a dominant or only a passing mode of adaptation, depending upon a variety of factors in the total familial situation. Normally, however, fight as a dominant mode of adaptation is repressed in our society some time before the child enters school, by at least about age six. By this time another major development has generally occurred; the child has incorporated some of the values of parenting persons, who, he feels, love him, and he has learned to inhibit the inappropriate expression of fight responses. In situations of stress, under threat, fight responses reappear. In times of external threat, with the threatening target clearly visible, fight directed against the attacking agent may be clearly an appropriate and socially sanctioned response. Where, because of unfortunate experiences in the course of a child's development, a child comes to believe that the world around him is a hostile place and he is always anticipating attack from others, fight may remain a dominant but apparently inappropriate mode of response to others. For most persons in our society, however, the conscience—the incorporation of cultural values mediated through parenting persons, which is usually on the way to becoming fairly well developed in most children by about the age of six—inhibits the primitive fight response of early childhood.

The third mode of adaptation to stress, flight, has multiple origins and expresses itself in many subtly different forms. One source of this mode of adaptation may be the attempt to resolve intrapersonal conflicts between a too-strict conscience and impulses to behavior that the conscience forbids. Unable, for example, at any time to express angry and aggressive impulses because of a too-stern, inflexible, and overwhelming conscience, the person may flee from and avoid as large a segment of the threatening living situation as possible. Like Mrs. Coyle, one may shut oneself up in one's house. Evidence of flight as a mode of adaptation to stress may then suggest an overwhelming conscience, a response learned with the early organization of a too self-punitive conscience.

On the other hand, flight may have its origins in far earlier experiences, in failures of the very earliest pairing relationship, where the child's needs for dependency upon parenting persons were not adequately met and where development of the child's capacity for pairing was inhibited. As a result, pairing's converse, a rigid independence and avoidance of or flight from others, may be learned. In some of the extreme forms of psychopathology, in the psychoses, this form of flight is most obviously seen. This does not seem to be the kind of flight to which Mrs. Coyle resorted in her initial response to stress, which was a form of flight involving an overworking conscience. Since this is a mode of adaptation learned later in life than the second form of flight we have cited (failure of early pairing relationships), we may postulate that Mrs. Coyle's withdrawal involved a lesser degree of regression. Had we been Mrs. Coyle's caseworker during the first year after Mr. Coyle's imprisonment, this kind of hypothesis would have been an important element in our planning. Current practice theory proposes quite different approaches to certain psychotic and nonpsychotic modes of adaptation. (See section IV of this chapter.)

In presenting this outline of the origins of modes of adaptation, we have had to be schematic and to oversimplify drastically some very complex developmental processes about which much is known and much still remains to be learned. We have not meant to imply that all pairing is regressive or that all developmental problems in regard to pairing are expressed only through repeated use of this early mode of adaptation. On the contrary, the person with an inability to form close and enduring relationships with others in the normal course of living or in stressful situations may be presenting, simply in upside-down form, evidence of such developmental difficulties in his earliest pairing relationships. In any case, role-maladaptations with one's parents or parent substitutes or other parent role maladjustments may be the determinants of such inability.

Nor did we mean to imply that fight could be expressed only in the most direct and open physical or verbal aggression. Clearly passive resistance can communicate as much hostility or fight as active attacks on others. Continually having to demonstrate or exercise superordinating power over others, manipulating them in various ways to achieve one's own ends, or in other ways exploiting people has a fight adaptation at its roots. But as a generally inclusive classification of initial modes of adaptation in situations of stress, the trichotomy of fight, flight, and pairing— of movement against, away from, or overdependently toward others— seems to stand the empirical tests of casework's experience with clients.

We cannot here give adequate discussion to cultural variations in norms for the modes of adaptation of pairing, fight, or flight. We must note, however, that as role-expectations for the same position vary from one cultural group to another, so do child-rearing practices and tolerances for the expression of dependent, aggressive, and avoidant behavior at various phases in the life cycle. Comparative studies of cultures suggest differences in the independence and aggression training of children, based in different cultural beliefs and values and related to differences in adult attitudes and ways of behaving in certain other culturally defined situations. There is some evidence from studies of psychopathology and culture that, although all known societies have their stressful situations, what is perceived as stressful may vary from culture to culture, as do the modes of adaptation that persons in different cultural groups tend to use in these stressful situations. We will not discuss here the more psychotic modes of adaptation—from freezing to manic-type behavior (see section IV); however, Clyde Kluckhohn nicely illustrates cultural variation in extreme forms of adaptive responses to stress as follows:

Malayans "run amok"; certain Indians of Canada take to cannibalistic aggression; peoples of southeast Asia fancy themselves possessed by weretigers; tribes of Siberia are prey to "arctic hysteria"; a Sumatran people goes in for "pig madness." Differentiated groups within a culture show varying rates of incidence. In the United States today schizophrenia is more common among the lower classes; manic-depressive psychosis is an upper-class ailment. The American middle classes suffer from psychosomatic disturbances such as ulcers related to conformance and repressed aggression. Certain kinds of psychological invalidism are characteristic of American social climbers. Feeding problems are more frequent among the children of Jewish families in the United States. The explanation of these facts cannot be solely biological, for American women once outnumbered men as ulcer patients. In some societies more men than women become insane; in others the reverse. In certain cultures stammering is predominantly a female affliction, in others male. Japanese living in Hawaii are much more prone to manic-depressive disorders than Japanese living in Japan. High blood pressure troubles American Negroes but is rare among African Negroes.[4]

Having reviewed the concept of social role and the concept of modes of adaptation as these concepts apply to persons in stressful situations, we are almost ready to put to use a typology for the classification of clients in stressful situations by discussing a few differential principles of casework practice in terms of this typology. We can now talk of the client whose social role is that of an unemployed worker and whose dominant mode of adaptation is a rather appropriate kind of aggression or fight; the unmarried mother whose dominant mode of adaptation is a markedly regressive kind of flight; or the foster child, aged twelve, whose dominant mode of adaptation is a very infantile, clinging, dependent kind of pairing. But we have omitted from our discussion thus far the concept of *ego*. In this concept, and related ideas, we have the tools for considering a third important dimension in the assessment of clients in their stressful situations. Let us now turn to the concept of ego.

C. The Concept of Ego in Casework Practice Theory

The concept of *ego* designates those intrapersonal forces that constantly strive to balance the person's diverse and sometimes conflicting needs and values with one another and with the demands of the outside world. (We have previously discussed such outer demands principally in terms of the concept of social role.) To the ego are ascribed the functions of

[4]Clyde Kluckhohn, *Mirror for Man: The Relation of Anthropology to Modern Man* (New York: Whittlesey House, 1949), pp. 201–2. Reprinted by permission from *Mirror for Man* by Clyde Kluckhohn, published by McGraw-Hill Book Co. Copyright 1949, McGraw-Hill Book Co.

perceiving, knowing, and problem solving, with all the creative and innovative possibilities in these processes. The ego's functioning is primarily rational.

When we are under great stress, however, and especially when we are feeling anxious, we may perceive the world around us or our self-image in distorted ways. Knowledge applicable to a problem at hand may completely escape us. We may feel unable to solve the problems we are involved in. Unaware of any inner conflicts, we may feel only a disabling discomfort or anxiety. We may feel overwhelmed by seemingly normal social pressures. At such times, other persons may question the effectiveness of our ego functioning, but they may ignore the evidence of psychological self-protectiveness in such situations (discussed under "defenses," below), sensing only our discomfort and the social inadequacy or apparent inappropriateness of our behavior.

Under such circumstances, clues about a person's past life should reveal whether current ego functioning is characteristic or atypical for this person. With historical evidence of repeated perceptual distortion, poor use of knowledge, and inability to solve life's normal problems—for example, unsatisfactory performance in the usual social roles of the family and at work or school—we may postulate that the person lacks the appropriate ego strengths. By comparison, a history of prior satisfying, effective, and acceptable adaptations to life's normal demands suggests adequate or strong ego functioning. We may thus consider a person to have a strong ego, or certain ego strengths, despite current difficulties in an exceedingly stressful situation.

With the threat of failure of ego functioning in a stressful situation, irrational or unconscious *defenses* may arise to protect the ego. For example, a person's intolerable angry feelings may be disguised by "projection" of such feelings upon others; that is, the person may distortedly perceive others around him as angry, and he may behave as though they were. A person may unconsciously "rationalize," or explain away, without being aware of this process, some unacceptable needs or feelings of his own. All such defenses—denial, displacement, reaction formation—are irrational forces, beyond the knowledge or control of the primarily conscious and rational ego. Thus, defenses serve psychologically to protect the ego against its becoming aware of feelings and drives or external realities that are unacceptable to it. Defenses are therefore not to be seen as negative forces. Rather, they often support a normally healthy ego under stress, and at some stages in child and adolescent development, the dominance of certain defenses may be quite apparent, normal, and facilitative of healthy development.

Nevertheless, for casework purposes, we must usually distinguish between rationally directed modes of adaption and irrationally or unconsciously directed intrapersonal and interpersonal defensive behavior. In some cases, intrapersonal defenses may serve to maintain, on a precarious and often only temporary level, one's intrapersonal balances. Interpersonal defenses, such as the protective modes of adaptation of fight, flight, and pairing, are similarly unstable techniques for achieving any lasting personal-social equilibrium. Generally, the extent to which an adult in normal living situations has repeatedly to resort to the use of such defenses is inversely related to the strength of his ego functioning. Since a client's ego strengths always—and his defenses, sometimes—are considered allies of the caseworker in helping a client to make a more effective and satisfying adaptation to a stressful situation, the assessment of ego strengths and defenses in the caseworker's study of a client is a major element of this procedure.

The caseworker is therefore always interested in how the client perceives his current situation, utilizes knowledge gained in past experiences, and tries to solve the client's problems. Evidences of perceptual distortion lead to inquiry about how the client has in his past life perceived similar situations. From such inquiry may emerge repeated themes in the client's perception of certain situations in the world around him. For example, persons in authority may always be seen as malevolent— whether they be the client's current employer, past bosses, teachers at school, the leader of a preadolescent gang, or a parent. Persons of equal status may always be seen as competitors, angling to displace one from one's current position—co-workers, a friend of the family, childhood peers, one's brother or sister. A client's feelings that his spouse rejects him in the current stressful situation may be found to be a repeated perception in the client's relevant life history; the caseworker may note that the client acts as though he anticipates rejection from the caseworker too. Such repetitiveness in perception of life's normally varied experiences suggests distorted perception and deviant ego functioning. It suggests an unsurmounted obstacle in one stage or another of the client's earlier development.

The caseworker is interested too in the client's capacities for problem solving and may discover, as with Mrs. Coyle, that after an initial period of withdrawal, the client manages to reorganize ego resources and to attack the problem more directly and effectively. Such evidences, from current and past living, suggest to the caseworker ego strength (or strength in ego functioning), which the caseworker may help the client to utilize again at the present time. In short, study and assessment of ego functioning enable the caseworker to ascertain what the client has to work with in his efforts to regain a more stable personal-social balance.

Beyond this assessment of ego capacities and defenses relevant to the problem at hand, the caseworker seeks to determine the client's *motivations* to modify his current situation, and to discover in what ways the client wants the problem situation to be resolved. The concept of motivation is a complex one, and it cannot be explored here in much detail. From our discussion of the ego, however, as comprising the primarily rational and conscious capacities of the client and from our description of the irrational defenses as processes arising to protect the ego from knowledge of threatening feelings and drives, it should be apparent that there are motives and other pressures operating outside of a person's awareness. Although the defenses keep the ego from knowing about such unconscious feelings and drives, these forces remain active and in no way become ineffective. Thus conscious and unconscious desires may be in conflict. Other motivational conflicts are seen in ambivalence, when we feel both positive and negative at the same time about any given object or goal. Merely a conscious desire to behave in a certain way, or not to behave in a certain way, may have insufficient force to change a current mode of adaptation that is rooted in irrational motives or feelings.

Thus Mrs. Coyle, during the year in which she withdrew from the community, could have gotten no help from friendly and rational counsel to "get out more, see people, and you'll feel better." One cannot approach irrationally motivated, defensive behavior with rational advice and expect any change. Knowing this, the caseworker attempted to help Mrs. Coyle with those aspects of the problem situation that Mrs. Coyle was clearly motivated to tackle—that is, to do the best she could in her relationships with her children and her husband and to assist in her husband's release from prison. To have advised or pressed Mrs. Coyle to find employment when she was motivated primarily to be a good wife and mother and when she seemed to perceive her working as oppositional to her success as a wife and mother would only have driven her into a job situation in which she would have failed, as she had done once before when forced to work. Such an experience of failure would have only further reduced her chances of effectively utilizing her ego capacities at work at a later time when the obstructing feelings and drives were clarified and she would be thus more single-mindedly motivated to become self-supporting. Incidentally, advice or pressure to find work, when Mrs. Coyle was not so motivated, would also have made the client-caseworker relationship an ineffective one for helping Mrs. Coyle in any other phase of adaptation to her problem situation.

It should be clear, then, that we are sometimes multiply conflictingly motivated in regard to a problem situation. As long, moreover, as our anxiety endures and the conflicts that lie at its base remain unclarified, our motivations are likely to be confused. What we may think consciously that we want to do and what we may actually be able to do remain irreconcilable. When we say that the caseworker is concerned about the client's ego capacities, clearly more than this must be known about the client's intrapersonal functioning. We must see to what extent motivations and ego capacities are consonant and to what extent intrapersonal conflict is manifest through evidences of anxiety and other defenses in the client. We must explore not only ego capacities but the extent to which the client is free and unconflictingly motivated to use them to resolve his stressful situation and to modify his mode of adaptation. And in focusing on ego functioning, we must not forget the world of social realities—opportunities, job demands, and obstacles—with which the client's ego may be in contact.

In summary fashion, then, we have touched on the concept of ego and have alluded to a few other concepts that help to explain the functioning of the ego. We have discussed the crude dichotomy of strong ego functioning and weak ego functioning. We have suggested that the latter condition may be merely a situational response to overwhelming stimuli from the client's inner or outer world, or it may be a characteristic, almost lifelong condition, indicating some deficiency in the development of the person's ego. We have proposed that the ego is subject to conflict with other forces in the client's intrapersonal world and that especially under such circumstances motivations may be multiple and confused. In planning to work with clients, caseworkers therefore attempt to assess not only the client's relevant ego strengths and weaknesses but also his motivations for handling his current situation.

For the classifications and typology that we will use in section IV of this chapter in our discussion of differential principles, we now have a framework of three basic, related concepts: social role, mode of adaptation, and ego functioning. Knowledge of concepts of this type helps the caseworker to understand clients in their stressful situations. Let us put aside further discussion of these basic concepts until we have completed our discussion of the general principles of casework practice in the first part of section IV, which follows.

IV. PRINCIPLES OF CASEWORK PRACTICE

We have just completed our discussion of basic concepts relevant to the caseworker's understanding of clients in stressful situations. We turn now to a second area of knowledge for the caseworker: principles of casework practice.

We discuss first (subsection A) some principles of practice that are considered *general principles.* They are applicable under all conditions of casework practice, beginning from the first moment of meeting a client, before the caseworker may know much about him. In subsection B we go into *differential principles,* which are clearly related to assessments and subsequent classifications. Differential principles are applicable, differentially, in light of the different conditions judged to be relevant in different cases. Differential principles may be applied only after the caseworker has sufficient knowledge of a client in his situation—that is, has derived enough understanding of the client through the procedures of study and assessment—to decide whether to apply one or another of these differential principles.

There are thus principles to guide the caseworker in practice, not only when the client in his situation is as least partially understood but also in the initial inquiring phase of the casework process. We start now with a discussion of these latter general principles.

A. General Principles of Casework Practice

THE PRINCIPLE OF ACCEPTANCE. It must be remembered that when the client and the caseworker first meet, the client usually approaches the interview weakened by the damaging effects of involvement in a stressful situation. The caseworker approaches this same interview strengthened by professional education and experience and by the supports of the definition of the role of social caseworker provided by a social agency, in keeping with its societally prescribed goals. A relationship between two persons thus begins with the two persons in quite unequal positions of security and power. All that these two persons are likely to share is a concern about the client in his problem situation.

The caseworker carries to the initial meeting certain assumptions about society and about individual human beings, their characteristic modes of adapting to stressful situations, and their ego functioning. These assumptions provide the caseworker with a basis in knowledge for respecting the client as a person, under any circumstances; this respectful approach to clients is essentially an expression of a compound of attitudes that are based in scientific assumptions about human behavior. For such assumptions (as those cited in section III of this chapter) may lead the caseworker not only to an understanding of the meaning and causes of the client's behavior but also to a mode of meeting and interacting with the client—without blame. Truly to understand the determinants of a client's behavior in a stressful situation and the possibilities of modifying any elements in the constellation of determinants in such a situation, or the direction of their movement, requires a positive interest on the part of the caseworker in the person involved—a concern and a professionally disciplined curiosity about the person, the problem, and its solution.

In casework settings, therefore, the caseworker approaches the client with a genuinely warm interest, with concern about the situation, and with curiosity about its determinants and their modifiability. The case-worker meets the client, accepting him as a person who is in trouble. Acceptance is the opposite of blame. Midway between acceptance and blame is a kind of neutrality. The caseworker is neither blaming nor being neutral about the person or his problem. The caseworker wants to understand and manifests a positive and undivided interest in what the client does and says about himself and others in his situation. The caseworker, in short, accepts the client where he is—as a person involved in a stressful situation, thus far only partially resolved or totally unresolved.

In this early interaction of the client-caseworker relationship, the client approaches the caseworker with certain expectations regarding the caseworker and, consequently, with certain attitudes or predispositions to behavior with the caseworker. These expectations and attitudes may be related to the way in which the client was initially referred to the agency—whether, for example, abruptly and forcefully, by persons in authority, or gradually and as a result of his own decisions, because of his own feelings of discomfort. Beyond the situational factors surrounding his referral, there is likely to be a whole repertory of stereotypes that the client has learned in his cultural group and developed out of his own interpretations of past experience with persons in positions of authority or power and knowledge—with doctors, teachers, or police officers, and previously with his own parents. The client may, consequently, approach the caseworker, whom he more or less consciously classifies in a similar position, with attitudes of submissiveness or dependence, hostile suspiciousness, or overt or covert anger, or of social distance, withdrawal, and self-concealment.

As these attitudes become manifest, the caseworker observes them and accepts them as cues that help in the understanding of the client. The caseworker does not, as perhaps in a nonprofessional relationship, sit in judgment of the person and his behavior as acceptable or nonacceptable. Nor is such client behavior likely to be perceived by the experienced caseworker as personally evoked in response to the caseworker's own behavior or attitudes. The caseworker sees the casework role as a symbolic one, representative to the client of many reciprocal roles in his past and current experience. The client's reactions are learned ones out of past and recent situations. The caseworker is not being, personally, submitted to, attacked, or withdrawn from. The caseworker can, therefore, accept the client and seek to understand the relevant forces behind his behavior.

The caseworker's accepting response helps the client to lower his social defenses; submission, attack, and withdrawal are modes of adaptation when omnipotent or threatening power is perceived or assumed to exist in another. The caseworker's acceptance of the client may in time communicate to the client that his defenses are inappropriate; since they serve no purpose in this situation, they may be dropped. The ultimate effect of the caseworker's accepting approach to the client should be a response from the client of counteracceptance. When the client-caseworker relationship is, at least tentatively, characterized by mutual acceptance, what has been called "rapport" may be considered to have occurred.

THE PRINCIPLE OF COMMUNICATION. In any interaction between two persons, for true communication to occur between them, the meanings of the terms and other symbols they use and act upon must be shared meanings. The persons may agree or disagree about the issues they discuss, but if they are truly communicating, each must understand what the other means by what he says and does. Each must understand, in short, the role of the other.

It is assumed that in his initial communication, the client explains the difficulties in his current situation. He explains these conditions not always as clearly as he perceives them, but rather as fully as he believes the caseworker's presence allows him to recount them. The caseworker is, after all, a stranger. Normally, one exercises restraints in telling a stranger about one's personal problems; one may not give evidence of weakness, insecurity, and inadequacy in one's life or one's self to another person, until one is sure how the other person will use such information. There are some persons, it is true, who are so bereft of trusting and accepting intimate relationships in their familial, work, and leisure-time associations that the transient person on a bus or train, a bartender, or a strange-city acquaintance, in the role of stranger, may become the recipient of the person's private concerns. But normally the stranger must identify himself as an available, receptive, and nonblaming listener before the troubled person begins to unburden himself. If the listener's being a stranger also adds to the security of the person under stress, we must admit that the professional role of the caseworker may have some of the attributes of this role too. The caseworker, however, communicates much more than this in the definition of the caseworker's role.

For as the client begins to define his own position in the stressful situation in which he finds himself, the caseworker regularly communicates by deed and statement the attributes and potentials for this client in the reciprocal role of caseworker. In a variety of ways, the caseworker makes clear in what ways the client can be served by the agency and what the agency expects of the client in view of his situation and personal capacities. In defining explicitly what is involved in the client's use of the agency, the caseworker is in part defining what the nature of the client-caseworker relationship may be and what activities and attitudes the client may expect from the caseworker.

The principle of communication in casework practice calls for clarification and, where necessary, reclarification of the conditions under which two people engage in a professional client-caseworker relationship. By demonstration and by explicit statements the caseworker makes clear the role of caseworker. In turn, the caseworker calls for clarification of the client's role in his stressful situation and, at times, in their interactions. The extent to which correcting the client's misassumptions and misperceptions of the interview situation aids in his perception of the larger stressful situation in which he is involved varies from case to case. But an assumption underlying the principle of communication in casework practice is that the caseworker's contributions to interview role-clarification may help in this direction.

THE PRINCIPLE OF INDIVIDUALIZATION. Section III of this chapter, on social role, modes of adaptation, and the ego, outlines generalized knowledge about human behavior. The usefulness of any such framework of concepts and assumptions begins to be tested, however, when we try to apply the principle of individualization. Through the use of some such conceptual guide to understanding behavior, the caseworker comes to understand not only in what ways *this* client in his stressful situation is like other clients, but also in what special ways he differs from the others and how he may be helped. For the principle of individualization stipulates that the caseworker try to relate to and help each client as an individual—as a person in a situation involving a unique combination of biological, psychological, and social forces.

In the procedures of study and assessment, the caseworker wonders about the following kinds of questions: In *this* client's situation, what are the social role problems? What are the client's dominant and alternate modes of adaptation? What are his ego strengths (and weaknesses)? What are his needs, if any, to resolve his problem situation? Although clients in their problem-situations may sufficiently resemble one another to be grouped or classified together, so that the general lines of casework followed trace a similar pattern, the principle of individualization reminds the caseworker of refinements and uniqueness in the specific situation that any general classification conceals.

This is where the sensitivity of the caseworker is especially needed —why casework, increasingly based on scientific knowledge, will always remain an art. In her many years of casework experience, Mrs. Morin had dealt with other clients in stressful situations in many ways similar to Mrs. Coyle and her situation; there had never, however, been and never could be a second client situation precisely like the Coyle family's, in all of its elements. There would thus never be a client-caseworker helping relationship exactly duplicating that one. By contrast with the mass dispensation of some social services—whether on the emergency "breadlines" of the Depression of the 1930s or in the operation of our current social insurance programs—the casework method requires sufficient individualization of the client in his situation to provide effectively the tangible services and other interventions required, according to the caseworker's knowledge of the specific problems and possibilities for resolving them in *this* client's situation. To do this, individualized study and assessment are necessary, followed by appropriately individualized casework.

THE PRINCIPLE OF PARTICIPATION. If a client is to be helped to extricate himself from a stressful situation and to regain a personal-social balance that is satisfying and enduring, he must be involved as an active participant in the corrective activities of the casework process. This, in essence, is the principle of participation.

If, in attempting to help a client, an inexperienced caseworker tries to "take over" the solution of a problem, reactions from the client will vary, depending upon his own dominant modes of adaptation. In all cases, however, the caseworker will be communicating his feeling that the client is unable to help himself; whatever feelings of inadequacy may afflict the client under stress will be reinforced. Yet a primary instrumental goal in all cases is to build upon and utilize the client's ego strengths and to reinforce whatever feelings of adequacy he has. Therefore, within the client-caseworker relationship, the client's active participation is to be expected and encouraged. His problem is his own; its resolution is to be shared by the joint participation of client and caseworker.

In the early days of social work practice, the significance of this principle was not realized. The social worker was a giving and doing-for person, well intentioned but as ignorant as all other persons at that time of how human beings behave under stress. In the course of "taking over" for the client, the social worker placed him in a necessarily subordinate position. Clients' responses to such subordination varied, of course, from a passive acceptance and growing dependence upon the omnipotent source of charity to a resentment and distrust of the social worker's charitable efforts. More important, however, were the possible effects upon the client as a potentially self-dependent person—upon his feelings and attitudes concerning his own capacities and competence. In taking over certain functions of the wage earner, the social worker was inducing a restructuring of roles in a family and a reallocation of role-functions, was feeding into certain defensive modes of client behavior, and was failing to utilize the client's own ego strengths and motivations in his own problem resolution.

In current practice, the principle of participation guides the caseworker to elicit from the client his own definition of the situation, his own analysis of his current and possible alternate modes of adaptation, and his active use of all of his own resources to achieve the goals both he and society consider satisfying, effective, and acceptable. In this context, the important corollary *principle of client self-determination* must be mentioned; in the course of the client's participation, the responsibility for decision making in regard to many elements in the stressful situation is almost always his, once the caseworker has helped him clarify what the alternative courses of action and their consequences may be.

THE PRINCIPLE OF CONFIDENTIALITY. If the client is to participate fully in the resolution of his problem situation, accepting the caseworker as a trustworthy and competent person, communicating with a minimum of social defenses a picture of his current role, and helping to individualize his situation, he often must be assured both directly and indirectly of the social agency's policy regarding the confidential nature of interview content. What the client tells the caseworker is never discussed outside the confines of the professional relationships that are aimed at helping the client. In practice, this means that the content of case records is never discussed in public or social circles—on a bus or a train or at a party. It also means, for example, that what a wife tells a caseworker is never subsequently communicated to her husband by the caseworker without the express permission of the client. Moreover, letters requesting information about the client from other professional or social agency sources are never prepared without the permission of the client. In entering into a client-caseworker relationship, the client is generally expected to remain protected, within the limits of the law, from harm to himself deriving from what he divulges to a caseworker. This, in essence, is the principle of confidentiality.

In effect, there have arisen some still unresolved legal questions about this principle. Should a client confess to criminal action in the course of casework treatment, what is the caseworker's responsibility to the client and to society? If the caseworker is an agent of society, so designated by society's chartering and support of the social agency, what does the caseworker do under such circumstances? How is the principle of confidentiality interpreted if an agent of the judiciary makes an inquiry about a client?

What is clear is that the social and psychological problems of clients may be discussed with caseworkers without fear that such facts will be handled irresponsibly. If a client asks whether discussion about a transgression will be kept confidential, the caseworker may, on occasion, have to reply that no such guarantee can be given about the situation and that the client will have to decide for himself whether or not to discuss the matter. But such situations are rare, and in general the principle of confidentiality is a rigorous guide to the caseworker in his subsequent use of interview content.

THE PRINCIPLE OF CASEWORKER SELF-AWARENESS. The caseworker, like the client, is a human being with complex personal motivations. The caseworker has learned and lives by many of the beliefs and values of the dominant culture. Every caseworker, in professional relationships with a great variety of clients presenting a multiplicity of problems and giving evidence of their many different cultural backgrounds, finds personal impulses or attitudes entering the client-caseworker relationship. The principle of self-awareness requires that the caseworker be sufficiently conscious of responses to a client to separate what goes on in the professional relationship that is professionally motivated—that is, aimed at helping the client—from what is personally motivated—that is, aimed at fulfilling the caseworker's own personal drives. Biases or prejudices that operate in the caseworker's personal life, negative attitudes toward members of a sociopsychological or ethnic group, obviously have no place in a casework relationship. The caseworker whose own father was alcoholic or whose own mother was neglectful is likely to have special feelings about a client whose problem situation involves alcoholism or parental neglect. Overidentification with a client who is a child in such a situation or a negative approach to a client who is alcoholic or neglectful of her children prevents the caseworker from following the primary casework principle of acceptance.

The principle of self-awareness calls upon the caseworker to examine all personal feelings in this relationship—both positive and negative —that are responses to this client as a person in a stressful situation. To this end, the procedure of casework supervision is an extremely helpful one, especially in the early years of practice, for some of the caseworker's personal responses may not be clearly perceived as personal without the searching eye of a professional outsider or supervisor.

In the course of time, caseworkers (like other self-critical professional persons) may come to understand and control in one way or another their personal blindspots and limitations that interfere with their practice. In a broader sense, however, the principle of self-awareness calls upon caseworkers to make use of themselves in their relationships with clients in ways that enhance the clients' ego development and not primarily their own. In effect, and especially in the early years of practice, the principle requires caseworkers consciously to keep a double focus in interviews, upon the client and upon themselves interacting with the client. If caseworkers in their initial years of practice seem somewhat self-conscious in interviews, this is an attribute of early practice that wears off as the professional helping use of oneself becomes habitual behavior. Then, the professional person may be said to have learned the role of caseworker. At this time, self-awareness does not cease; it becomes merely a familiar aspect of practice, particularly when something seems to have gone wrong in a professional relationship with a client.

The principle of *self-awareness* is the sixth and final general guide to casework practice with all clients to be discussed in this chapter. Together with the principles of *acceptance, communication, individualization, participation,* and *confidentiality,* the principle of self-awareness helps caseworkers to foster client-caseworker relationships that are productive of at least partial resolutions in clients' stressful situations. But what principles guide caseworkers in their differential approaches to clients? We discuss these formulations as differential principles in the next subsection.

B. Differential Principles of Casework Practice

Differential principles propose that, under certain conditions, certain casework goals and techniques are appropriate. Under other conditions, other goals and techniques are appropriate. To understand what the conditions are for each client in his stressful situation, the caseworker engages in the procedures of study and assessment with each client. Then goals for casework and means for their achievement may be decided upon, with due regard for relevant agency policy.

Such decisions always, of course, remain tentative. Acting upon them is a way of testing the hypotheses of assessment formulations. The complexity of human adaptations and the processes of social adjustment in stressful situations call for continuing refinements and modifications in judgment as casework progresses. Goals and techniques appropriate today for Client A may be different not only from those appropriate for Client B but also from those appropriate for Client A at a later interview. By then, changes in the client's relations to his social situation may call for modifications in the casework plan. Determining factors in the case may be more precisely understood.

Differential principles, then, provide a guide to the initial selection of casework plans with a client, upon the formulation of an initial assessment, as well as a guide to later decisions about changing casework plans in the light of changes in the client's total situation and reassessments of it.

In proposing the differential principles for practice that appear in this section, we recognize the breadth of their current formulation and the fact that they are by no means simple rules of thumb. They are, nevertheless, extremely helpful guides to the art of casework practice in that they connect, however generally, plans and techniques for intervention with assessment formulations. In the years ahead, these principles will be much further refined and expanded. What we learn in the future about ego functioning, modes of adaptation to stress, and the social role component in stressful situations should lead to the reformulation of differential principles, related much more precisely to our increasing knowledge of techniques in casework interviews.

ENVIRONMENTAL MODIFICATION AND EGO SUPPORT.[5] In most agencies where casework services are offered, clients may come for help with problems that lie almost completely in their social worlds. These are problems primarily of changes in social role relationships, with no basic ego malfunctioning of the persons involved. For example, the wife whose husband is besieged with a long-term disabling illness may be a person with marked ego strength, quite capable of making an effective and satisfying adaptation to the situation. With the caseworker, she clearly expresses her need for some help in regard to her responsibilities as a mother, perhaps through the use of a day care center for her child. She seeks help also in regard to finding employment. Her capacities and motivations for fulfilling a variety of possible work roles are apparent. The family will need some short-term financial assistance until she finds such work. The client's feeling about her husband in his current plight and about the changes in her own life and family are well within the range of "normal" reactions to an unexpected and distressing situation of this sort. She is upset, but admiring of her husband's determination to get well and back to work as soon as possible. She reports that he does not feel threatened by her move to work outside of the home.

The caseworker is sensitive and responsive to the client's feelings about the situation. The caseworker is understanding and supportive and especially encouraging about the plans that the client and her husband have made. The caseworker sets as a goal helping the client with the location and use of appropriate community resources, in an effort to lessen the stresses in the current family situation. Reallocation of some maternal role functions and assistance in regard to the role of wage earner are clearly called for. These are elements in the goal of environmental modification.

---

[5]For the basic formulations from which the differential principles were originally developed, the writer is indebted to Florence Hollis, "The Techniques of Casework," in *Principles and Techniques in Social Casework: Selected Articles, 1940–1950,* ed. Cora Kasius (New York: Family Service Association of America, 1950), pp. 412–20. Although in the years since their initial proposal, Hollis and others have elaborated on and refined these formulations, and some alternative prescriptive statements and minitheories have appeared in the literature, we still lack any empirical evidence to question the validity of the fundamental ideas outlined in the following pages.

Because people, in addition to their feelings about themselves and others involved in a problem situation, often have mixed feelings about seeking help from others, the caseworker is certain to be accepting and respectful of this woman as a client. In addition, the caseworker is especially supportive of the client's direct and realistic approach to the handling of the family's problem situation. The client-caseworker relationship is developed as an objectively accepting and warm one. The client's desires and planning are genuinely approved of. The client's clear perception of the situation and what needs to be done evokes a direct and positive response from the caseworker, who informs the client about and helps her to use the necessary community resources. These include public and private employment services, agency information about jobs, and sources for temporary financial help. The caseworker communicates clearly in what ways the agency itself can and cannot help financially in such a situation. The client is related to as a competent person who, helped with certain initial environmental or social-role difficulties, can manage from there on by herself. All of this approach, of course, assumes that the diagnostic formulations concerning the client's situation, her essentially positive adaptation, and the kinds of strong ego functioning that such adaptation indicates are valid.

In a stressful situation involving a client who presents evidence of inadequacies in current role functions, whose current mode of adaption to this loss seems appropriate (not markedly regressive), and who demonstrates the possession of a clear perception of the problems and what may be needed for their solution—which is evidence of effective ego functioning—the goals and techniques of environmental modification and ego support are applicable.

The objectives of ego support and environmental modification are appropriate in a second type of client situation. For example, a client presents a history of difficulties in keeping a job. He seems to react with partially concealed hostility to each of his employers or supervisors and finds some excuse to quit each job after a short period of time. The mode of adaptation to what he feels are the excessive demands in his work roles is as follows: he withdraws in response to his feelings of hostility and unexpressed aggression toward those to whom he is responsible at work. Exploration of his ego functioning in other situations reveals that he has recently and for many years engaged in markedly distorted perceptions of persons in authority, regularly imputing to persons in such positions attitudes of distrust and malevolence. He explains that he has no close friends to turn to; since he took to the road at age fifteen he has repeatedly resolved his problems by withdrawal. A brief stay in the Navy was terminated by a discharge because he "got sick." He is at first vague about what was wrong, then tells about the strange ideas he had about his body and its allegedly deficient ways of working. He is no longer troubled by such thoughts.

The evidence indicates long-term use of the defense of projection, the client periodically feeling quite distrustful of others and fearful of harming them; however, he never injured another, always "moving on" instead. In regard to ego capacities, the client has often felt inadequate to the tasks he faces at work and is not, on any deep level, motivated to "settle down" and keep a job, though he says he would like to. With the caseworker, he is superficially friendly but somewhat reserved, saying that he does need financial assistance and does want help in finding a job.

The psychiatric consultant in this agency sees this man as a border-line, ambulatory psychotic, at the present time well enough not to need medical care. It seems clear that this client has adapted to his intraper-sonal stress by becoming a wanderer. In this marginal social role he is subject to a minimum of social pressures.

In regard to job placement, the client talks of having enjoyed work-ing as a short-order cook; he likes to cook, but he does not like the rush at mealtimes and "being told what to do." He has thought of seeking employment as a night watchman. The caseworker notes that this selec-tion of work role suggests that the client has a nice appreciation of his own limitations; few jobs would place less strenuous social or interper-sonal demands upon him.

With clients who behave in this fashion, as well as with the essen-tially "normal" person in an acutely stressful social situation, approaches aimed at ego support and environmental modification are appropriate. In the latter type of case, the caseworker works more directly with the client toward the client's effective use of existing community resources. With a person who has difficulties in adapting in most social situations, the caseworker may have to be more directly active in structuring for the client social-role and other environmental situations that he can with some success fulfill. This may involve interpretations of the client's rele-vant capacities and limitations to persons with whom the client lives or works, so that their role-expectations for him may be more in line with what he is likely to need and be able to do. Casework techniques are not now known that may effect appreciable changes in the ego functioning of persons whose adaptations for many years and in most social roles have been markedly regressive. For such persons, casework efforts are directed toward environmental modifications and specifically social role-adjust-ments within which such clients may function with an optimum of satisfac-tion and effectiveness. In their efforts to make successful adaptations to these roles, such clients can be helped by the ego-supportive casework techniques of encouragement and an unquestioning clarification of daily realities when these are distortedly perceived by the clients.

At all times, the client-caseworker relationship is kept on a simple and objectively accepting but uninvolved level, without fostering in the client a deep emotional attachment or overt responsiveness of feelings—especially negative feelings—to the caseworker. More intensive or deeper professional relationships are necessary in casework situations where changes in ego functioning or in basic modes of adaptation are the goals. Especially with borderline psychotic clients, it is important for the caseworker to remember that clients' intrapersonal balances may be quite precarious—that the psychotic adaptation is a mode of defending against overwhelming motivations and feelings and against more intimate relationships than the psychotic person feels able to handle. Any serious mental aberration is a defense, a compromise, a way of reaching a kind of personal-social balance. With such clients, the caseworker tries to support and encourage the use of such ego strengths as the client manifestly has, without becoming involved at any deep level in the client's feelings.

We may now broaden our statement of our first differential principle of casework practice:

In a stressful situation involving a client who presents evidence of inadequacies in current role-functions, and whose mode of adaptation seems either (a) appropriate (not markedly regressive) or else, at the other extreme, (b) markedly inappropriate and regressive, and who demonstrates the possession of either (a) a clear perception of the problems and what may be needed for their solution—evidence of effective ego functioning—or (b) markedly inaccurate or distorted perception of the problems—evidence of grossly ineffective ego functioning—the goals and techniques of environmental modification and ego support are applicable.

CLARIFICATION OF THE EFFECTS AND MEANING OF BEHAVIOR. For some clients, like Mrs. Coyle (see section II of this chapter), study reveals the use of certain regressive modes of adaptation—not marked regressions—from which some self-recovery may have been made. These clients demonstrate a basic kind of ego strength. Moreover, the client's fulfillment of major social roles—in the family and/or at work—seems at least moderately effective and satisfying. Some relatively slight distortions in the perception of self or others are apparent, however, and, in acting upon these perceptions, the client fails to resolve the stressful situation as enduringly as he might. Should the distortions remain, the client may soon find himself again faced with similar problems. For example, if Mrs. Coyle had gone on seeing herself as a little girl, unable to express appropriate anger to a husband on whom she was totally dependent, future situations in this family might well have reactivated her flight (from the community) mode of adaptation, rather than stimulating her to face up to her own and other people's negative feelings.

With an assessment of relatively strong ego functioning, of some but not marked regressive modes of adaptation, and of a rather satisfying and effective performance in key social roles, the caseworker may engage with clients in the goals and techniques of clarifying the effects and meaning of the client's behavior.

What does this differential principle mean in practice, in terms of what the caseworker does and the kind of client-caseworker relationship needed to foster such treatment? It should be recalled that Mrs. Morin helped Mrs. Coyle to understand her children's different reactions to their father's offense and imprisonment. In explaining their behavior, Mrs. Morin went into what the behavior meant for each child at his level of development. She also touched on the effects of their behavior and the possible advantages of helping Stephen to modify his. Mrs. Morin then helped Mrs. Coyle to clarify her own feelings about the situation, actually dealing with her perceptions of her husband's and her own behavior. What is the theory underlying such clarification?

When, in a stressful situation, perception becomes distorted, this process is unconsciously used by the client as a defense against what the client vaguely expects to be painful stimuli. What the client shuts out or distorts are potentially threatening or painful facts. Mrs. Coyle saw her husband as innocent of the crime for which he was convicted. To have seen him as guilty would have been painful for her. She saw him as a strong father figure who could not tolerate any expression of anger from her; to have seen him in any other way would not have permitted her to feel comfortable in her self-perception as a little girl who needed fartherly protection. People behave "as if" distorted perceptions were truths. Mrs. Coyle did not dare express her anger to Mr. Coyle. As a result, however, in trying to conceal her anger and other related negative feelings, she behaved as though all things were going very well at home. The effects of this behavior were that she communicated to Mr. Coyle not only what she believed to be a lack of anger and her full devotion to him but also, indirectly, her holding back of something. Communication between them was incomplete. Mr. Coyle became suspicious and hypothesized that she had a lover. The effects of Mrs. Coyle's behavior were contrary to what she intended them to be, even though she expended great effort in controlling her show of feelings.

Understanding the meaning of Mrs. Coyle's behavior, as well as the untoward effects of it, Mrs. Morin was able to help Mrs. Coyle achieve her own ends through the process of clarification. She said, in effect, "When you do thus and so, though *this* may be your desire, what actually happens is *that.*" Moreover, in supporting Mrs. Coyle through her testing out of the previously unused or forbidden behavior (expression of anger with her husband), Mrs. Morin helped Mrs. Coyle to see that there was no extrapersonal need to fear and inhibit this kind of behavior. When expressed, its effects were not the painful ones Mrs. Coyle had anticipated.

Having seen how one's behavior and perception of self and others are interrelated—this is the *meaning* of the behavior—we may postulate that this kind of dramatic change in accustomed behavior may affect subsequent perception and correct distorted perceptions. Mrs. Morin never dealt directly with Mrs. Coyle's perception of herself as a submissive little girl. Instead, she focused on the *effects* of behavior deriving from this perception. Mrs. Coyle's report that she felt, in essence, more grown up after her crucial visit with Mr. Coyle suggests that her changed behavior did affect her perception of herself. That such changes may be relatively enduring has been demonstrated in other similar cases.

The client-caseworker relationship, where clarification of the effects and meaning of behavior is indicated, is a somewhat more intensive one than in cases where environmental modification and ego support are the treatment goals. Where clarification is the goal that guides casework intervention, the client has obviously reached a kind of partial balance, using modes of adaptation that to the outsider may seem ineffective or unsatisfying but that to the client seem terribly important and self-protective. One may, therefore, because of this self-protective balance in the client situation, expect any unskilled questioning of a client about the effects or meaning of his behavior to be met with various forms of resistance. The unskilled questioner may be ignored or withdrawn from; he may be attacked. Examining and clarifying the effects or meaning of a client's behavior call, therefore, for a strong, positive client-caseworker relationship in which the caseworker has demonstrated a warm interest in the client and a capacity to understand him in his stressful situation. Such understanding shows a complete respect for the client's own motivations and goals.

Within a mutually trusting relationship, the client can admit to the caseworker some of the dissatisfactions in his current situation and can express his desires to modify current ways of doing things. With such cues, the skilled caseworker can begin to study with the client how what he does affects others and how they respond to him, how his actions result in undesired effects. With support from the caseworker, the client may act experimentally on his newly clarified perceptions. In this process, the caseworker works primarily with the client's present ego strengths and current conscious thoughts, not delving back into the client's past to experiences that may lie at the roots of his current behavior. The focus of content is current situations that are stressful; the goal is to clarify the effects of current behavior based on "as if" perceptions.

Because the client-caseworker relationship is a necessary support for the client who seeks to understand and change some of his habitual ways, the caseworker tries to keep the dominant feelings between them positive. Evidences of resistance from the client indicate probable negative feelings toward the caseworker and provide a cue that the pace of casework may be too fast or the area of discussion an upsetting one to the client's current balances. In the use of clarification, coupled with a sound, emotionally positive client-caseworker relationship, clients' resistances are not themselves examined or clarified, lest a negative relationship with the caseworker develop. The client's use within the interview situation of more effective behaviors in his dealings with the caseworker may, after their relationship is well developed, be used to help the client clarify his understanding of how his actions affect others.

It should be clear, finally, that clarification of the effects and meaning of behavior always requires some elements of ego support and often includes environmental modifications too. Ego support is addressed, however, to helping the person maintain himself at his present balance, where changes in the level of ego functioning are either unnecessary or beyond the help of available skill or current knowledge. Ego support is used in conjunction with clarification in regard to those components of present ego functioning that seem effective and satisfying and then, later in the process, when desired changes have been tested by the client. For example, Mrs. Morin was very supportive of Mrs. Coyle in regard to her newly tested expression of anger with her husband. If clarification of and change in the "little girl" aspect of Mrs. Coyle's behavior were desired, Mrs. Morin should, obviously, not have been supportive of Mrs. Coyle's inhibition of angry feelings. On the other hand, with the borderline psychotic client discussed above, a caseworker would clearly want to be supportive of the client's reported efforts to control angry impulses to act upon his grossly distorted perception of a new employer.

Clarification of the effects and meaning of behavior is appropriate with clients considered to be mildly neurotic or moderately distorted in their perception of self and others, when, on the whole, key roles in their lives seem to be filled with moderate effectiveness and satisfaction, their modes of adaptation to stress are not markedly or enduringly regressive, and their level of ego functioning is a relatively high one.

V. THE PLACE OF CASEWORK
IN LARGER CONTEXTS

We shall conclude this chapter with some observations on how social casework relates to other modes of social work practice and to other social processes. To understand the "whys" and "hows" of social work with individuals and families, we must not only consider the moral and cognitive purposes for casework intervention and some principles of practice but also see these "whys" and "hows" in their larger social contexts.

Early in this chapter, there appeared a summary record of "child neglect" in the Rodgers family and the initial steps taken by a caseworker to change the situation. The goal in this case was to bring a quite removed Mrs. Rodgers and her two very young children into their neighborhood's activities, which was done through the formal resources of the Canby Street Day Care Center for 2½-year-old Joe, the children's health care unit, and the informal relationships of other mothers in the community. An assumption of the social worker was that as Mrs. Rodgers found acceptance and satisfaction in her experiences with local persons, she would become less expectant of rejection in her approaches to others. It seemed to have been at least partially this attitude that had kept Mrs. Rodgers and her two children so isolated prior to the social worker's visit. From information in the fuller record on the Rodgers family, we gather that Dee Rodgers, ever since her removal from the Indian village in which she had spent her first ten years, had tried to adapt to her alien environment by withdrawal. This pattern of avoidance was the core of the child neglect complaint that brought the caseworker to her apartment on Duncan Street.

In the behavioral science literature, a family like the Rodgers family might be referred to as anomic or alienated. In essence, this would mean that the family felt—and were, in fact—cut off from communication of a meaningful sort with others in the world around them. They might feel powerless to do or be otherwise, much as most persons in stressful situations feel, and abandoned, as well. They might feel that what matters to other people does not matter to them and that, in fact, there is very little in life that they value. In ultimate terms, a sense of hopelessness might override all other sensations.

The centrality of alienation as a human problem in our times is counterbalanced, in a limited sense, by the centrality of social integration as a prime goal of the social welfare field. The great British social policy specialist, Richard Titmuss, some years ago cited social integration as the unifying aim of the social services, and more recently Norman Polansky wrote, "During the next decades, the most pressing task confronting American social work will be the defeat of personal and social isolation," a problem extending to "all segments of society, affluent and poor."[6]

A problem of these dimensions calls for a multifaceted attack. While social work is not the only professsion to be aware of and responsive to this social malady, it is heartening for caseworkers to recognize that our

[6]See Richard Titmuss, *Commitment to Welfare* (London: Allen and Unwin, 1968), p. 22; and Norman A. Polansky, "Beyond Despair," *Shaping the New Social Work,* ed. Alfred J. Kahn (New York: Columbia University Press, 1973), p. 66.

profession includes group workers and community organizers, as well as other kinds of social workers. There are large-scale aspects of this problem that call for social changes extending far beyond what can be effected through social work with individuals and families. Neighborhood workers in community organization or community development are helping to provide the kinds of organizations and local resources that are needed by, and ideally will attract, persons who have become remote like Mrs. Rodgers. At higher levels of government, social policy specialists on children, the aged, the poor, the ill and handicapped, ethnic minority groups, and other segments of the population who are at high risk in regard to alienation are working to provide the policy underpinnings for better societal opportunities and supports of many kinds. As the social worker worked directly with Mrs. Rodgers and her children to help them use the resources of their neighborhood, that worker should have gotten some sense of support from the awareness that other social workers, teamed up with colleagues in other professions, were probably instrumental in having those resources like the Canby Street Day Care Center established. For this to happen, social workers of varied special skills and with somewhat different concentrations of knowledge and understanding had quite different but interrelated jobs to do at all levels of government and in the community.

Thus the social worker who specializes in work with individuals and families never works, as a professional, alone. But similarly, neither does the social worker whose primary concerns are social policy development, the delivery of social services, the improvement of social integration at the neighborhood level, or the completion of tasks coupled with the optimal development of persons through small-group programs work alone. For some individuals, in almost any kind of society, the capacity to use what that society has to offer and to make contributions to the common welfare may be blocked or warped, and for such persons some kind of one-to-one relationship may be essential. What social workers do at all levels of intervention is part of a total professional effort aimed at social integration.

Awareness of the interdependence of the different specializations in skill and knowledge among social workers has led, in recent years, to proposals about unitary or generic principles of practice within the profession. Common values, of course, guide the profession. And it is, moreover, stimulating to try to distill out the shared features of social work practice represented, for example, by the three central chapters of this book. Experience in the field in recent years has suggested, moreover, that there are times and situations when it would be advantageous if the same person could provide services at many levels—with individuals on a one-to-one basis, in small groups, and in the community. For example, in less densely populated rural areas, a social worker who is skilled in many aspects of practice might be much more flexible than one who is skilled only at one kind of practice. The problem is that social work practice at any level involves a sizable body of knowledge, as well as skill. One must have a keen and applicable understanding of the kinds of situations one is addressing as a social worker. Clearly, the more one has to know about a wide range of matters, the less one can know well or in any depth about any one matter. Similarly, there is a limit to the number of skills one can master with real proficiency.

With the expansion of knowledge in the human sciences basic to social work practice, the period of preparation for practice has been extending. As basic understandings grow, so does the development of new social work modalities for resolving newly defined or interpreted human problems. Since both knowledge and skills must be taught in social work, what was for many decades an education of about two post-baccalaureate years has now ramified into educational programs at many levels of postsecondary schooling, all proposing to prepare social workers with varying levels of expertise.

Our only purpose in bringing the matter of changing educational programs into this chapter has been to indicate the limits we have felt obliged to impose on what could be adequately presented here. An entire volume on social work with families would inevitably, today, focus in large measure on work with families as units. The development over the past few decades of social systems views of families has made the rationale for treating families as systems impelling. As difficulties in family life have come to be interpreted through the concepts of social systems theories, so workers of many disciplines in the family treatment field have developed techniques for addressing these problems through the simultaneous involvement of the members of a family. Yet in this chapter, in neither the Rodgers nor the Coyle family case did the social worker have direct professional dealings with anyone other than the woman of the family.

I make this matter explicit for a few reasons. First of all, it should be clear that every problem concerning a member of a family does not necessarily require the social worker to interact with all members of the family. In fact, in a family like Mrs. Rodgers's, the presence of her two preschool children was important for the social worker's assessment of the seriousness of the neglect complaint, and some interaction between the children and the visiting social worker was inevitable and essential; but focusing on Dee Rodgers and helping her to reduce her remoteness from the community clearly seemed the proper goal for the children's sake as well as Mrs. Rodgers's. Much interaction between these young children and the social worker might well have been a threatening situation to add to Mrs. Rodgers's discomforts. In the Coyle family, while at some stage later than our record carries us there might have been good reasons for the social worker's considering with Mrs. Coyle the possibilities of the total family's meeting with the worker, Mrs. Morin's views of the family were clearly in social systems terms. At least the perspectives on social role changes in the family, with Mr. Coyle's imprisonment, were in part a systems approach to understanding the family situation. The changing knowledge bases for practice may be most influential in helping social workers to understand human problems in new ways. These new ways of understanding inevitably affect what social workers do in their interaction with clients, but to see and understand families in holistic ways does not mean that social workers must always deal directly with families as total systems.

The issue of educational level is relevant because there are more or less advanced kinds of intervention social workers may engage in; in addition, preliminary to the treatment of families as groups—a complex process, as any reader of a recent issue of *Family Process* can see—is the kind of work done with, first, Mrs. Rodgers, and second, Mrs. Coyle. In a chapter aimed at presenting some of the fundamentals of social work with individuals and families, we have traveled a good distance in presenting discussions of some basic concepts for understanding the person under stressful conditions and the relationship of these concepts to general and differential principles of casework practice. Having gone this first lap together, we are all free now to continue in a variety of possible directions.

SELECTED BIBLIOGRAPHY

Social Work with Individuals and Families

BARTLETT, HARRIETT M. *The Common Base of Social Work Practice.* New York: National Association of Social Workers, 1970.

BRIAR, SCOTT. "Family Services and Casework," pp. 108–129 in *Research in the Social Services: A Five-Year Review*, ed. Henry S. Maas. New York: National Association of Social Workers, 1971.

DE SCHWEINITZ, ELIZABETH, and DE SCHWEINITZ, KARL. *Interviewing in Social Security: As Practiced in the Administration of Retirement, Survivors, Disability and Health Insurance.* Washington, D.C.: Social Security Administration, U.S. Department of Health, Education and Welfare, 1971.

DE SCHWEINITZ, KARL. *The Art of Helping People Out of Trouble.* Boston: Houghton Mifflin, 1924.

FRIEDLANDER, WALTER, and APTE, ROBERT Z. *Introduction to Social Welfare.* 4th ed. Englewood Cliffs, N.J.: Prentice-Hall, 1974.

GARRETT, ANNETTE MARIE. *Interviewing, Its Principles and Methods.* 2nd ed. New York: Family Welfare Association of America, 1972.

KADUSHIN, ALFRED. *The Social Work Interview.* New York: Columbia University Press, 1972.

MAAS, HENRY S., and ENGLER, RICHARD E. *Children in Need of Parents.* New York: Columbia University Press, 1959.

PERLMAN, HELEN HARRIS, ed. *Helping: Charlotte Towle on Social Work and Social Casework.* Chicago: University of Chicago Press, 1969.

POLANSKY, NORMAN A. *Ego Psychology and Communication: Theory for the Interview.* New York: Atherton Press, 1971.

POLANSKY, NORMAN A., BORGMAN, ROBERT D., and DE SAIX, CHRISTINE. *Roots of Futility.* San Francisco: Jossey-Bass, 1972.

REID, WILLIAM J., and SHYNE, ANN W. *Brief and Extended Casework.* New York: Columbia University Press, 1969.

ROBERTS, ROBERT W., and NEE, ROBERT H., eds. *Theories of Social Casework.* Chicago: University of Chicago Press, 1970.

Knowledge Basic to Social Work Practice with Individuals and Families

The baker's dozen of books listed below is intended merely to be illustrative of the kinds of source books that social workers draw upon for an understanding of persons and families. Some books use sociological perspectives, others are psychological or biological in their origins and focuses. Some books consider large-scale social change as it affects persons (Campbell, Dubos, Wheelis). Some books focus on personal/social changes in the course of normal development over the life cycle (Caldwell, Carson, Maas). Some books address the strains of being in relatively powerless positions—by being black (Billingsley), or ill (Davis), or poor (Finney), or handicapped (Goffman), or old (Townsend), or in a variety of stressful situations (Levine and Scotch).

BILLINGSLEY, ANDREW. *Black Families in White America.* Englewood Cliffs, N.J.: Prentice-Hall, 1968.

CALDWELL, BETTYE M., and RICCIUTI, HENRY N., eds. *Review of Child Development Research: Child Development and Social Policy.* Chicago: University of Chicago Press. 1973.

CAMPBELL, ANGUS, and CONVERSE, PHILIP E., eds. *The Human Meaning of Social Change.* New York: Russell Sage Foundation, 1972.

CARSON, ROBERT C. *Interaction Concepts of Personality.* Chicago: Aldine, 1969.

DAVIS, FRED. *Illness, Interaction and the Self.* Belmont, Calif.: Wadsworth, 1972.

DUBOS, RENE. *So Human an Animal.* New York: Charles Scribner, 1968.

FINNEY, JOSEPH C., ed. *Culture Change, Mental Health and Poverty.* Lexington: University of Kentucky Press, 1969.

GOFFMAN, ERVING. *Stigma: Notes on the Management of Spoiled Identity.* Englewood Cliffs, N.J.: Prentice-Hall, 1963.

LEVINE, SOL, and SCOTCH, NORMAN A., eds. *Social Stress.* Chicago: Aldine, 1970.

MAAS, HENRY S., and KUYPERS, JOSEPH A. *From Thirty to Seventy: A Forty-Year Longitudinal Study of Adult Life Styles and Personality.* San Francisco: Jossey-Bass, 1974.

TOWNSEND, PETER. *Family Life of Old People: An Inquiry in East London.* London: Routledge and Kegan Paul, 1957.

WARWICK, DONALD P., and KELMAN, HERBERT C. "Ethical Issues in Social Intervention." In *Processes and Phenomena of Social Change,* ed. Gerald Zaltman, pp. 377–417. New York: Wiley & Sons, 1973.

WHEELIS, ALLEN. *The Quest for Identity.* New York: W. W. Norton, 1958.

CHAPTER THREE

THE METHOD
OF
SOCIAL GROUP WORK

Gisela Konopka and Walter Friedlander

For social work is international in scope and interracial. Its methodology is useful in solving the human problems of the happy and adequate, as well as the handicapped and unhappy.[1]

I. GOALS AND PURPOSE OF SOCIAL GROUP WORK

The capacity to effect shifts in values is immeasurably strengthened through group participation and cohesion. Values represent our orientation to society and our attitude toward human welfare. In the last analysis adjustment is the name for the process of living up to a set of values.[2]

---

[1]Miriam Van Waters, "Philosophical Trends in Modern Social Work," in *Proceedings of the National Conference of Social Work* (1930), p. 3.

[2]Saul Ginsburg, "Values and the Psychiatrist," *American Journal of Orthopsychiatry* 20, no. 3 (July 1950): 478; and Anthony N. Maluccio and Wilma D. Marlow, "The Case for the Contract," *Social Work* 19, no.1 (January 1974): 28-36, explains the value of participation of the group members in decisions about group activities.

Our discussion of social group work will emphasize an approach to human problems—systematized and based on as much scientific understanding as we have. We know, however, that in actual practice, every worker enters with all *his* or *her* qualities, hopes, fears, and creativity, and whatever we know or say about "people in general" never completely explains the specific person or group we are trying to help.

Our knowledge is derived from many different disciplines, from sociology, psychology, psychiatry, physical and biological sciences, economy, and history. Besides supplying general knowledge, these disciplines force us to approach problems with clear purpose and with a determination to look for facts.

The *professional* endeavor of the social group worker is to use this knowledge in relation to a *specific* situation or a person and to accept the helping role, adding to the scientific understanding the warmth of the person-to-person approach and the deep respect for uniqueness of the individual and the group effort. It is this helping attitude that differentiates the professional practitioner from the pure scientist. It demands a constant alertness to feelings as well as thoughts, and it does not allow for high manipulative action for outside purposes. Because of the immense power of the group process, the social group worker must be especially sensitive to the forces playing in the group, but sensitive also to ethical demands and to any urges of his own that might drive him to misuse the power of his central position.[3]

With this frame of mind, we enter the discussion of one of the basic methods in social work, *social group work.*

Definitions are agreements born out of experience, discussion, and compromise. They seldom are completely self-evident, and they are dynamic—they change in time. The great French historian Mark Bloch, in speaking of history, said,

> Assuredly since its first appearance on the lips of men, more than two millenniums ago, its content has changed a great deal. Such is the fate of all truly living terms in a language. If the sciences were obliged to find a new name each time they made an advance—what a multitude of christenings! And what a waste of time for the academic realm![4]

With this caution, we present our present-day definition of social group work, keeping in mind that social group work, as all social work, is concerned with interaction behavior:

[3]Paul Glasser, Rosemary Sarri, and Robert D. Vintner, *Individual Change through Small Groups* (New York: Free Press, 1974).

[4]Mark Bloch, *The Historian's Craft* (New York: Alfred A. Knopf, 1953), p. 21; see also: Hans Falk, "Social Group Work and Planned Change," in *Social Work Practice,* ed. Alfred J. Kahn (New York: Columbia University Press, 1964), pp. 209–30.

The group worker enables various types of groups to function in such a way that both group interaction and program activity contribute to the growth of the individual and the achievement of desirable social goals.[5]

A *method* is a "special form of procedure in any branch of mental capacity" (*Concise Oxford Dictionary*). Certainly procedure does not stand by itself. It only makes sense when it leads somewhere and when it relates to a problem to be solved.

It will be the task of this chapter to fill the definiton of social group work method with life and meaning.

Values Underlying the Professional Use of the Group Work Method

Our *general goals* in social work have their roots in religious and humanistic values. We base our work on the respect for *every* human being and recognize his rights to fullest development of his capacities while he respects and contributes to the rights of others according to his capacity. Few people will disagree with this principle. The problem is its application and practice. It leads us into the general problems of a democracy —namely, how to combine individualism and the concern for a whole community; it raises the question of how to help people in their own terms rather than our own and yet represent values necessary in an interdependent society. The social worker can never escape these problems. Science can tell a social worker "what is" but not necessarily "what should be," and yet we expect the social worker not to be dogmatic and not to judge individuals according to his own values alone.[6]

Therefore, the first assignment of the group worker is to learn to understand himself as much as he is able. A young social worker, for instance, was very disgusted with the "superficiality" and materialistic values that her group of teenagers presented. They were interested only in money-making projects for their own club. There is no question that one would want to help such a group to see the needs of others, yet had this worker really understood herself and the values that these children presented? Had she realized that she had come from an environment that had provided early for many of the pleasures that these youngsters had to seek by common endeavor? Had she realized that her capacity to consider others had grown out of many satisfactions she had received

---

[5]The 1949 Statement of the Executive Board of the American Association of Groups Workers, in *Social Work Yearbook* (1954), p. 480; see also: Peter J. Burke, "Participation and Leadership in Small Groups," *American Sociological Review* 39 (December 1974): 832–43.

[6]Lewis A. Coser, "The Functions of Small-Group Research," *Social Problems* 3 (July 1955): 1–6.

before she was able to give to others? And was she really thinking in terms of the others, or was she thinking mainly of herself by being "disgusted" with them? It is in such small incidents that we learn something of what we call the "professional attitude."[7]

Professional discipline is hard to learn and demands a great deal of insight into oneself. It is not the requirement of a cold impersonal attitude and it is not a rejection of basic values. It is an increased sensitivity towards other people and a constant effort to project oneself into their situations while not losing one's own identity. In social group work—because of the intensified interaction of several people with each other and because of the unique position of the group worker as agency representative and as helper—there can be a great temptation to by-pass this professional self-discipline. We then either have the "leader" who might be authoritarian or paternalistic or enthusiastic but who does not allow the true development of the group members, or we might have the standoffish, cold, purely observant, and perhaps dull group worker who thinks "not getting involved" is the badge of a profession.

Human Needs Served by Social Group Work

The goals of any group are determined by a basic value system of respect for every person and his needs. Sometimes social work was concerned only with the economic needs of human beings, sometimes only with psychological ones. Yet to anyone in practice even in the early days of social work, it was clear that economic needs could not be separated from many others: the need to be loved, to feel security, to be an important person in one's own right, and to have enjoyment.

In the art gallery in Hamburg, Germany, hangs a painting by the famous fifteenth-century painter Lucas Cranach. It is a gay picture. It presents a young woman who is surrounded by many little children, some of them being held by her, others scampering happily through the grass and biting into some fresh apples. The painter named this scene *Caritas (Charity)*. The painting shows a deep understanding that giving does not consist only in food but also in a happy, warm, and relaxed relationship. To respect the human being the helper must not feel "removed" from humans but must know that he is only helpful if he himself feels "part of the human race" and understands the many varied human needs. In social case work, this was expressed by the Charity Organization Movement in its demand, "not alms but a friend."

---

[7]The distinction between "social group work" and "work with groups" is discussed in Robert W. Klenk and Robert M. Ryan, *The Practice of Social Work* (Belmont, Calif.: Wadsworth, 1970), pp. 168–71.

Social group work, rising mainly around the turn of the nineteenth century when there was an emphasis on social reform movements and when labor was awakening, accepted early the fact that people needed more than economic assistance. It also understood from the beginning of its history that people needed to participate in the solution of their problems and that they resented "handouts." We must not forget that labor's fight was from the beginning not only for increased wages but also for the eight-hour day, which was a recognition of the individual's need to be more than just a workhorse. It was also at this time of history that social workers were fighting child labor, again because of their recognition of the right of individuals to grow up as healthy, well-rounded, educated human beings and not only to be used by others.

With the understanding of human needs beyond bare necessities grew the understanding of the child. It is not an accident that the emphasis on understanding of children occurred at the same time as the fight developed for generally improved living and working conditions in the industrial society, at the same time as women's rights were demanded, and when there was a general yearning to put into practice the individual and humanitarian ideas of the French and American revolutions. We find at the same time the beginning of youth movements, the foundation of the Campfire Girls and Scouts, the concern with providing of playgrounds, and the publication of Jane Addams's beautiful book, *The Spirit of Youth and the City Streets.*[8]

We find a number of books describing institutions that were first identified with social group work as the youth-serving agencies: the settlement houses, the YW and YMCAs, and the Jewish centers. We will not go into this here, but the social group work method can only be understood when we see its background not in terms of agency affiliation but in terms of what needs the agencies served. A professional worker coming from the Charity Organization Societies could do a great deal to help a person talk out and work out his problems or to help tangibly with financial and other services. But in addition to this the client needed to establish himself in his own group and this, too, required skill. We cannot cut up people to match the kinds of services we can supply. Small-group techniques may be useful in short-term teaching in social work studies.

Early social services were usually quite generic ones. They were focused (mainly) around the social problems faced by the settlement houses out of which many of our social services have grown—for instance, the Children's Bureau, public health nursing, recreational ser-

---

[8]Jane Addams, *The Spirit of Youth and the City Streets* (New York: Macmillan Co., 1909); and Klenk and Ryan, *Practice of Social Work*, p. 163.

vices, nursery schools and kindergartens, help to delinquent gangs. In social group work particularly, we have focused strongly on those needs that can be fulfilled mostly through group association. Let us look at those.[9]

Large industrial centers are filled with lonely people who cannot find friendships by themselves. A group worker once visiting in a neighborhood to invite some older people to a newly established club program heard a woman say in tears, "I should go down on my knees to thank God for your visit. I have prayed every night that God should take me out of this miserable lonely life and now there are people who care and there are friends." Three months later it would have been hard to recognize this desperate woman when she was presiding at a club meeting; the club was preparing for a short camping trip and was working out ways to take everybody along, even those who did not move easily.

A capable young woman, married and secure in a college community, remembered her excessive shyness and loneliness when she was an adolescent, and she wrote:

> I had been told by my parents that I was not ugly and that I could make friends, but for some reason I did not dare to join in what others were doing. When there were parties I painfully tried to serve only refreshments and stayed away from the others as far as possible. In one of the church groups I joined the group worker did not persuade me to enter activities, but simply sat down beside me and talked about some of the things that I was interested in. He then called on somebody else who "happens to have the same interests" and for the first time I learned that I could talk with others. In his sensitive way he had understood that I could not join activities immediately, but needed confidence in being able to relate to one person at a time. In this group I gained confidence in myself but I also learned how to help others.

Loneliness is perhaps the most heartbreaking state in which a human being can be. This does not mean that we have to be with others all the time. One can be alone and not be lonely. If a person has gained confidence in himself and feels accepted he can stand being alone, but he needs this reassurance first.

A little twelve-year-old boy, condemned to death because of an incurable disease and incapable of walking around, was able to stand much of this situation because of the great love of his parents and his strong scientific interests. Microscope, slides, and scientific books were close to his bed, and yet he said wistfully, "I wish I could find some boys

[9]Lois G. Swack, "The Unique Aspects of Short-Term Teaching," *Journal of Social Work Education* 10, no. 1 (Winter 1974): 90–95; and Sheldon D. Rose, "Group Training of Parents as Behavior Modifiers," *Social Work* 19, no. 2 (March 1974): 156–62. Small-group techniques may be useful in short-term teaching in social-work studies.

of my age who would be interested and with whom I could talk. Most of the kids who come, come only to see my things. They are only interested in them, not in me." Here again, the group of the same age meant a great deal, though love and understanding of parents helped.

Being *important,* being valuable to others, feeling one's own worth is another basic need of all human beings. And this can only be found in interrelation with others. The young child receives a feeling of worth, or should receive it, in his family (and this is the reason why work with the family is of such utmost importance), but the older we become, the more this must be supplemented and underlined in our relationships with contemporaries. Even the five-year-old new to school can let mother or father leave if he (or she) is sure that he is liked by the others in the kindergarten and that he is able to stand up among them.

Feeling of self-worth comes with achievement in individual endeavor, in acquired skills, and in interrelationships. Some of you might have seen the excellent film "The Quiet One," which is the history of a boy who had received little love in his early life and because of delinquent behavior came to a training school where he was helped by the psychiatrist, the caseworker, and the group counselor. If you have seen the film you will remember the calm and self-confidence that comes to the boy when he is capable of molding a clay bowl. This is individual achievement. You might remember his rage and disappointment and self-doubt when he thinks that the counselor does not love him because he also loves other boys. Here the question of relationship with another human being has arisen. In group work, we are dealing continually with those very realistic feelings of rivalry, self-doubt, and fear, but at the same time we have the gratification of seeing the change brought about by a child's mastering direct skills, by the group worker's acceptance, and by the group's acceptance. This does not apply to children only. In an experiment in California with obese adults, it was found that self-confidence and the capacity to diet were greatly enhanced by group treatment—partially by the kind of discussions that were conducted in the group but mainly by the help that came from seeing others "in the same boat" making the same kind of effort. This insight has found wide acceptance in self help groups.

We know that people who are not accepted cannot give love and that people who do not feel respected cannot respect others. Marie Jahoda and Dr. Nathan Ackerman made a study of people in psychoanalysis who expressed strong anti-Semitic feelings.[10] They found that these patients had very low self-esteem and suffered from loneliness and frus-

---

[10]Nathan Ackerman and Marie Jahoda, *Anti-Semitism and Emotional Disorder* (New York: Harper, 1950); and George E. Simpson and J. M. Yinger, *Racial and Cultural Minorities: An Analysis of Prejudice and Discrimination* (New York: Harper, 1958).

tration. "They reject themselves and annoy others."[11] Because they hated themselves, they had to "project" this and hate others. We find similar mechanisms in other hatreds, as against Blacks, Indians, or other races or nationalities. Low self-esteem is never the only cause, but it is an important factor. We also see it over and over in work with delinquents: their unconcern with the feelings of other people is very closely related to their feeling that nobody cares about them. We see this expressed clearly in an excerpt from discussion among young male offenders:

> Harry brought up the intense hostility that he has felt towards his father and at the same time the death wishes that he had. He brought out the fact that when he took off from X he felt that the lack of family concern was such, and, particularly, that his father's hostility was such, that he just didn't care what happened to him. He stated that at that time he would not even have cared if he had killed Mr. A. . . .[12]

We cannot "make" parents love their children. But casework services will help reveal why the family relations have been disrupted so badly and perhaps help the parent to gain more understanding of the child. Group work services will be effective in helping the young person establish new and satisfying relationships with others outside the family. We recognize the family as the most important factor in the development of the young person, but we must realize that strength comes also from other associations and that the associations must be especially gratifying if the family relationships have broken down. The group in the training school or reformatory might give the first feeling of "understanding," and the beginning of insight into one's own responsibility and feelings might come in those group discussions. Beyond this, the group worker's role will be to help the young person to find other satisfying human relationships after leaving the school or the prison. The young person needs not just "occupation" but a slow building up of self-confidence and confidence in others—and this comes only through experience. For far too long we have left this experience to accident. Consciously planned group work services are an important part of rehabilitation work with delinquents. (Certainly none of this works if the total living situation is degrading—as many unfortunately are.)

We do not consider only the youngster who has encountered severe problems. *Growing up* is not an easy process. We cannot protect the growing person from all the pitfalls, but we can enrich him or her and try to supply the nourishment that the growing human being needs so

[11]Ibid., p. 55.
[12]Gisela Konopka, *Group Work in the Institution* (New York: Association Press, 1954), p. 262.

that he or she becomes strong and develops the capacities we consider part of maturity.

It is our jobs as adults, as people with more contacts or information, as representatives of agencies which have a social purpose, to provide a bountiful table from which members may take intellectual or emotional nourishment.[13]

It is certainly not only through social group work that young people are helped with the growing-up process. They receive help through many institutions of our society—for instance, the family, the school, and the church. Social group work enters into the life of the youngster who goes through a normal development in those informal settings where he tries his wings in relation to his friends and in relation to a community. The group worker's grave responsibility is to give the opportunities for growing up—to provide this bountiful table of which Margaret Berry speaks —and also to allow for trying out capacities and making mistakes.

GROUP WORK AND RELIGIOUS PREJUDICE AMONG SMALL CHILDREN[14]

We usually think of the preschool child as least affected by racial or cultural tensions. Yet the four and five year olds learn early the attitudes of their environment. Example: A small preschool group consisted of: Bert, a Jewish child, age 4; George, a black child, 4; Chris, 3 ½, and Jim, 4, two white boys of Irish-English parentage. Greatest anxiety in this group was seen in Bert, who was referred because of extreme aggressiveness with other children. He was removed from nursery school because he could not adjust to regulations. Bert was the youngest of three siblings with strict parents who had little understanding of and patience for the needs of a young child. They lived in one of the most dilapidated districts of the city with little playgound space. In the neighborhood lived mostly people of Jewish and Italian background and blacks. In the home were also the grandparents, orthodox Jews. It is clear that many other factors, besides his cultural background were involved to produce disturbances

[13]Margaret Berry, "First Steps in Social Action," in *Roundtable,* National Federation of Settlements (June-July 1951), p. 1; Daniel Thursz, "The Arsenal of Social Action Strategies: Options for Social Workers," *Social Work* 16, no. 1 (January 1971): 27–34; and Arthur J. Frankel and Paul H. Glasser, "Behavioral Approaches to Group Work," *Social Work* 19, no. 2 (March 1974): 163–75.

[14]This case, published in Gisela Konopka, *Social Group Work—A Helping Process,* 2nd ed. (Englewood Cliffs, N.J.: Prentice-Hall, 1972), pp. 105–6, was presented by Prof. Gisela Konopka at the Annual Meeting of the American Orthopsychiatric Association in Chicago, 1947, and is included here with the permission of Prentice-Hall.

in Bert. In play intervals Bert showed much anxiety toward adults and a great need to release active energies. In the group he showed reluctance at first in playing with George, the black child. Apparently helped by George's outgoing and warm-hearted behavior Bert soon teamed up with him. His conflict about being Jewish came into the open around Christmas time. The children listened intently to the *Night Before Christmas* when Bert suddenly pointed to Santa Claus saying: "Bad Santa Claus, I don't like him," and slammed the book shut.

Two weeks later, without any provocation, Bert suddenly shouted profanities, among them, "Dirty Jew, dirty Jew." Each time he said this, he looked provokingly at the group worker. Through the caseworker's contact with the mother, we knew that Bert had only recently received a severe beating because he had said "dirty Jew" at home. It was clear that the child was struggling with his own status in being Jewish.

It was planned to use the Christmas party the following week to show him that being Jewish was as good as belonging to any other religion. Bert was delighted with the Christmas tree. His mother had said that he felt deprived in not having one at home. He and his sister had rigged an umbrella with cotton and twigs pretending this to be a Christmas tree and had hidden it so the grandparents would not see it. At the clinic, Bert touched the twigs and the ornaments of the tree, exclaiming over them. When the children sang, the worker asked Bert whether his family did not light candles at home, too, and whether he did not want to sing his song for all of them. Bert hesitated, but when the worker herself started the Chanukkah Song, a very surprised and happy look came over Bert's face. He sang while the other three boys admired the different language. Encouraged by the admiration of his little friends and the first recognition of his being Jewish by children who were not, he asked whether he might hold a candle. With the Christmas tree in the background, ice cream cone in one hand, and the candle in the other, Bert proudly said the Hebrew benediction. The importance of the event became clear when an excited and happy boy ran downstairs at the end of the party and told his mother," I lit the Christmas tree and I lit a candle and I sang a Chanukkah song and she [pointing to the group worker] knows it, too." Through this experience, Bert got a feeling of acceptance from the adult and from the other children, who admired and enjoyed his performance. He was able to accept himself as a Jew among non-Jews.

One of the specific tasks of the group worker is to be aware of each individual in the group and understand *differing* needs. Consider Joan, a twelve-year-old who has a tendency to always comply with what the adult says or what other children suggest. She is not happy with this passive role. Joan needs strengthening of her capacity to be independent. Mary in the same group cannot accept any decision that does not completely follow her own desires. She needs to keep her valuable capacity to have independent ideas, and yet she needs help to be able to accept those of others. The dependence-independence struggle in growing up and probably all through life is a basic and difficult one. We want to help people to come to some balance and some inner satisfaction in regard to this. This is one of the needs with which the group worker works constantly. The group worker needs to give each member of the group the opportunity to observe the group norms and to participate in group interactions.[15]

Acceptance, a a feeling of worth, the need to be independent, and being capable of *accepting dependence* and of *being part of the whole* are some of the needs we have discussed in talking about social group work.

Human Capacities Strengthened by Social Group Work

In addition, there are some basic *capacities* that we think can be strengthened considerably through group endeavor. These are human capacities that do not completely grow by themselves but need strengthening and trying out. One is the capacity to *overcome frustration in a healthy and constructive way.*

There is no life without frustration. From the moment when the infant fails to get *immediate* gratification in learning to relate to societal demands—for instance, when drinking from a cup or eating with utensils or sharing toys and people—to the harsh demands of sickness or of loss of loved ones, life continually offers frustrations. We have put values on how we deal with frustrations. Mental hygiene concepts are clearly value oriented. For some reason, we are embarrassed to use the words "good" or "bad." The avoidance probably arose out of the genuine wish to get away from harshly judgmental attitudes. Yet the words we use as substitutes, for instance, being "mature" or "well adjusted," really contain also our value judgments of the way a person deals with life's problems. Since we are all human, we know we will never achieve the complete ideal. Sometimes there has been a tendency in teachers or social workers to expect the ideal. Yet we must know that all we can do is help the human being with his inner strength; we cannot expect a person to never show any weakness.[16]

There has sometimes cropped up a theory of introducing frustra-

---

[15]Alfred Kadushin, *The Social Work Interview* (New York: Columbia University Press, 1972), p. 19; and A. Barcal et al., "A Comparison of Three Group Approaches to Underachieving Children," *American Journal of Orthopsychiatry* 43, no. 1 (1973): 143–41.

[16]Derek Jehu et al. *Behaviour Modification in Social Work* (New York: John Wiley, 1972).

tion into group situations so as to make the youngsters learn. We know, however, that the natural frustrations that occur are sufficiently manifold. Margaret Mead has described one primitive society where mothers and relatives tease four and five year olds by showering love on a younger child and pushing the older one away so that the older child will learn to overcome his resentment of not being the only one given affection. Many initiation rites in primitive societies inflict a great deal of pain to teach the youngster to be able to accept pain. We consider this unnecessary. Being part of a family group or a group of contemporaries includes the need of sharing, and one can learn without additional infliction of pain. The simple fact that a beloved group worker has only two hands and, therefore, cannot walk hand in hand with ten children at once is something that children experience with some pain and that he learns to overcome. The adolescent with sexual drives and with a great desire for independence continually experiences the inability to completely follow his wishes—this in itself is frustration. In group work, we are helping with this process by allowing for expression of negative feelings; at the same time, we help individuals to think through and work through the fact that frustrations are unavoidable. The group worker who tried to eliminate all frustrations would not be helpful, nor would the one who worked too harshly with youngsters.

We may help not only by encouraging acceptance of frustration that cannot be changed but also by helping people to see that there are some frustrations that need not persist, that should be eliminated by a constructive working toward change in the environment. In one of our cities, for instance, the curfew was set unreasonably early for teenagers, and some of the youngsters dealt with it by simply breaking the law. They complained about the curfew to the group worker, and they indicated their intention of defying it. In this discussion, the group worker helped them to see that their complaint was probably reasonable but that action should relate to a lawful change of this order. The group worked on a project of collecting evidence for the unreasonableness of the set hour and together with some of the interested parents presented the evidence to the city council. This is an example of learning how to deal with frustration in a constructive way by citizen action and by working together.

Since human beings are interdependent, the capacity to cooperate needs strengthening. We can make, and we have made, the great mistake of equating cooperation with uniformity. In recent years, warnings have been sounded against this tendency, and they were justified. Riesman, in his book *The Lonely Crowd,* has made a strong case against our exaggerated ideas of having to do everything in a group and of stamping people into a given pattern.[17] He is afraid that we do not allow for enough individuality. This danger is great. The social group worker's very specific task is to enhance the capacity of the individual to be different, to be himself, and yet to be able to cooperate.

What we mean here by "cooperation" is the willingness to involve oneself in work with others and to strengthen the group's goal even if one does not agree. One of the "democratic disciplines" (as Edward C. Lindeman named them) is to accept the fact that in a democracy, one sometimes is in the minority. This does not allow one to simply move out or to sabotage the decision of the majority. It does mean responsible cooperation while continuing to work for one's ideas. The English form of parliament has developed this to a very high degree. But cooperation is something that does not come by itself to the human being. It has to be learned.

Groups usually start making decisions by having one group member decide for all, or by a wild shouting match—with those shouting loudest winning, or by a primitive form of majority vote. Group members learn only slowly the important possibility of discussion of issues, weighing of facts, accepting divergent opinion without hating those who express opposing views, and, finally, deciding on a course of action in which everybody participates without resentment. Again, though we are talking about an ideal that is hardly ever completely fulfilled, we are nevertheless striving towards it.

In talking about the capacity to cooperate we have already talked about the capacity *to make decisions*. Decisions certainly are not made only in a group. They are also made inside of the individual. We all know people who cannot make decisions. They either follow the crowd or one other person, or they can never make up their mind. Although perennial hesitation is often very painful to the individual, perennial following of others is more harmful to our society as a whole. Again we see how social workers are working both to help the individual and for the good of society. Our skill will lie in strengthening the individual who seems to be incapable of making a decision by finding out what is blocking him. It is not a simple matter of "just making up one's mind." It is often related to much fear, to low self-esteem, to a wish to be loved, and to a fear of losing love if one takes sides. If this is the case, we must give the person, whether a child or an adult, the opportunity to *experience* that he does not

[17]I [Gisela Konopka] agree with his warning against conformity. However, I think Riesman twists evidence too much according to *his* thesis.

lose love if he takes a stand. There are similar dynamics in the cases of those who just follow or those who show a great deal of anarchism. Each time we will have to look for the causes while at the same time creating opportunities for genuine experience—not only "talking through."

The final need and capacity with which we often deal is the realistic need for *achievement.* A thirteen-year-old boy met the social group worker with whom he had worked individually and in a group when he had been five years old. The problem at the time had been that this child had been extremely shy and very unsure of himself. Did he remember the worker who had helped him? He remembered her only vaguely but felt great affection for her. (The human relationship, therefore, had had meaning.) He remembered nothing he had talked about and none of his violent play with puppets that had brought out a great deal of his sibling rivalry. But he remembered clearly that he had been able to cut out a wooden animal by using the jigsaw, and he still thought of it with great pleasure.

In no way do we want to say that the working out of feelings at that time was not important. Yet we also see how extremely important it was to this child to have had tangible evidence of achievement. It would not have been a pleasurable experience if the boy had been pushed into it. One of the skills of the group worker lay in helping the boy find proof of his abilities when the boy had considered himself such an incapable individual.[18]

In a group of young men and women who had severe seizures, the patients strongly favored the meetings in which they could talk freely about their problems. But they considered as a high point of their experience the meeting where for the first time they dared to dance with each other and where some healthy people had been present. Again, it was the realistic offering of an experience of achievement that added to the improvement of their mental health.

There are many other needs and capacities with which the social group worker deals. Group work is a dealing with life and, therefore, with the manifold aspects of life. Like all social work, it is concerned with the human being as a whole and as a part of his environment. We have stressed here those needs and capacities that group relations can especially help: the *need for companionship,* for *self-worth,* for *opportunity* and *capacity to be independent or dependent* in accordance with the reality situation; the *capacity to overcome frustration,* to *cooperate,* to *make decisions,* and to *achieve as an individual* through *group participation.*

---

[18]Special tact and patience is needed for group work with street gangs who are harmful to others and themselves. Irving Spergel, "Selecting Groups for Street Work Service," *Social Work* 10, no. 2 (April 1965): 47–55.

II. THEORY OF THE SOCIAL GROUP WORK METHOD

The great cosmic force in the womb of humanity is latent in the group as its creative energy; that it may appear the individual must do his duty every moment. We do not get the whole power of the group unless every individual is given full value, is giving full value.[19]

We have discussed the needs and capacities with which social group work is predominantly concerned, and we have defined the goals that group work helps people reach. Every human being needs such help in the normal course of life. Therefore, group workers work with the growing child, with groups of teenagers, with young adults who might want more knowledge of organized planning, with mature adult committees who want to contribute to the community, and with our senior citizens whose capacities we seem only recently to have discovered. In every instance, the goal of the group worker is to make the individuals and the group as a whole realize *their* potential to conduct their affairs by themselves.

Social group work does not serve only in the areas of prevention and of general human development. Sometimes problems become so great that the individual seeks for or is asked to look for specific help. Sometimes problems in the community—for instance, race relations—become so tense that specific service is sought. When social group work attacks those acute problems, it usually acts in cooperation with other professions and citizens because of the great amount of specialized knowledge that is needed. The social group worker becomes part of a team in child-guidance clinics, in mental hospitals, in camps for handicapped children, in institutions for disturbed or delinquent children, or in agencies especially concerned with community problems, such as the Urban League or housing authorities.

The social group work process is goal related; some of its applications differ. However, *the elements of process are always the same*. In our discussion of group work practice, we will draw examples from different settings.

Application of the Scientific Method to Social Group Work

The scientific method used in most professions—for instance, in medicine or law—can always be described by its functional steps: fact finding,

[19]Mary Parker Follett, *The New State*, 4th ed. (New York: Longmans, Green & Co., 1934), p. 342; Walter A. Lurie, "Intergroup Relations," *Encyclopedia of Social Work (1971)*. pp. 668–76; and Paul H. Glasser, *Treatment of Families in Conflict* (New York: Group for the Advancement of Psychiatry, 1970).

diagnosis, and treatment or fact finding-assessment-action. Those steps often do not follow one another but occur at the same time. Let us see this in practice:

> We are in the reception cottage of an institution for delinquent girls. One of the group worker's functions is to meet with the girls every second day for a two-hour discussion to help them understand the institution into which they move as well as to let them express their own fear, their apprehension, their hostility, and perhaps their hope. It is also one of the goals of her work to help them gain some confidence in an adult who is identified with the institution. This is a meeting in which four newcomers are present as well as three girls who arrived a few days previous to this meeting. The worker welcomes the four new girls and asks the three others whether they can bring the group up to date about what has been discussed. Jean quickly sees the opportunity to tell the girls that she thinks it "a crying shame that we are here anyway but at least Miss X (the group worker) and Miss Y (caseworker) are people with whom one can talk." According to Jean none of them has really done anything serious and she is sure it is the same with the new girls. Joyce, another of the girls who has been here previously, fumbles with her handkerchief and looks uncomfortable. The group worker asks whether Joyce wants to say something. Joyce shakes her head. One of the new girls blurts out, "Well, I'm not such an angel." Joyce nods, still very inhibited. . . .

Every aspect of this meeting must clearly register in the group worker's mind. At this point she is "gathering facts." She begins to learn not only about the history of the girls (she might be able to read this up in a record) but also about how they feel about their situation. She learns something about the interrelationship with which she will be faced. She must watch to find out whether Joyce's apparent reluctance is only related to her own insecurity or whether perhaps Jean is beginning to play a dominant or inhibiting role in the goup. When the group worker has found this answer, she will have to look deeper to understand even more. She will begin to learn what this dominance means to Jean, whether it gives her satisfaction or actually frightens her, and what it means to Joyce —whether her dependence grows out of fear or latent love.[20]

While the group worker observes and begins to understand (accomplishes fact finding and diagnosis), she cannot leave out the third step, "treatment." The group worker cannot only observe. Her encouraging Joyce to talk is already a step toward treatment; she is giving Joyce the feeling that somebody cares about her, and she is giving the rest of the group the assurance that she is aware of their discomfort or joy, even if they do not freely express themselves. Her not pushing Joyce into an answer after the first encouragement is part of treatment, because it

[20]Frankel and Glasser, "Behavioral Approaches to Group Work."

signals to Joyce that her reluctance is respected and that she is allowed to go at her own pace. It also sets the atmosphere for the session and lets the less inhibited member speak up more freely. We thus see that the three steps in the scientific process are not necessarily separated.

To use the scientific method, we need a theoretical framework. We have discussed the *philosophy* underlying social group work; this gives us "what should be." *Theory* includes our present understanding of individuals and of their relationships with others. Social group work, like all social work, is based on an eclectic theory of individuals and groups.

Theory of Individual Dynamics

The understanding of the individual is based on a modified psychoanalytic theory with the added understanding of cultural components and knowledge from social psychology and sociology.

One of the crucial concepts in understanding the individual is that of the *importance of early childhood experiences,* experiences that greatly influence the development of personality. This theory does not include a deterministic point of view; it allows for the capacity of the individual to grow and change in the course of his life. Childhood experiences have great impact on personality development, but we assume that later experiences also have importance.

A second vital concept is that man's actions are *influenced by unconscious motivation as well as by his capacity to act consciously and rationally.* This second concept has direct relation to the practice of social group work because the social group worker constantly deals with the development of the individual as well as with helping him or her to relate to others and to make a conscious effort to improve society. The capacity to deal consciously with difficult inner forces is a functioning of the ego, which develops its strength through constant interaction with others.

The *life stages* as we understand them now are best expressed by Erik Erikson in his book *Childhood and Society*.[21] The first year of a child's life serves to establish a *sense of trust,* which is developed through a relationship with a loving adult. The next stage is that of the *sense of autonomy. The child learns about the boundaries* of his self-determination as he begins to feel his own self. The third stage is developing a *sense of initiative;* the child continues to understand himself as a separate human being but experiences the interplay of his own desires with those of others. The fourth stage is the *sense of industry.* It is around the time of beginning

[21]Erik H. Erikson, *Childhood and Society* (New York: W. W. Norton, 1950), p. 159; and idem, "Identity and the Life Cycle," *Psychological Issues* 1 (1959): 1–171.

school when the child wants to engage in real tasks. Erikson describes adolescence as the period of the *sense of identity,* when the search for one's role in society begins. I think it is also the period of beginning commitment—to people or a cause. At the same time, the young person feels a *sense of intimacy,* which is the beginning of interest in the other sex and, in later adolescence, courtship and marriage. Adulthood is the period of *parental sense.* This does not mean exclusively biological parenthood but also productivity and creativity. Finally, the human being enters a period of integration, which develops what Erikson calls the *sense of integrity.* He sees in this the capacity of the well-integrated adult to accept himself as different from others and yet able to love and accept others. While the person defends the dignity of his own life style, he can accept the different styles of others.

In accepting this developmental theory of the human being, the social group worker tries to understand whether an individual with whom he works in the group has had a satisfactory development during those stages or whether he needs to relive some of them. The group worker also tries positively to work out experiences that will make such a development possible.

Related to this theory of development is the social group worker's assumption of the importance of *changing group associations* to the individual and of the importance of the individual's impact on such associations. The individual belongs during his life to three kinds of groups: (1) the *primary group* into which the individual is born, the family, (2) the freely chosen *friendship groups,* and (3) the *vital-interest groups.*

For the young child, the primary group plays the most important role. The family is most important in the development of the individual. Friendship groups develop later and change during different age periods. In early school age, they are diffused and change frequently. They are determined by such outside circumstances as living communities or school associations. The friendship group is most important in adolescence, when relationships to contemporaries are more important than relationships to adults. The adolescent group usually shows a very close bond; it is a small group with intense relationships. The individual's role in a contemporary group becomes almost all-important. It is at this time that values that had been accepted throughout childhood are frequently rejected. It is a crucial period in which adults need to be especially understanding and yet must avoid imposing on the adolescent.

In adulthood, friendship groups usually diminish in importance. Associations consist mostly of vital-interest groups—groups with specific purposes such as union groups, professional associations, and civic associations. Most adults start their own primary groups (founding of a new family), but this time in a reversed role. The person who was a child becomes a parent. This reversal of roles is not always achieved easily, and the increased use of group discussions on family life demonstrates the necessity of learning about this new position.

Social group workers will use in different ways this theoretical understanding of individuals, their development, and their relationship to others. The emphasis will depend on the group. In "growth-oriented" groups—as in most therapeutic groups, for instance—the worker will have to be aware of each individual's specific needs and will sometimes have to offer group experiences that resemble those of the primary group, the family.

In "task-oriented" groups, such as adult community groups, the worker will have to understand the needs of individuals but will focus more on the accomplishment of group goals. The worker's diagnostic understanding, therefore, relates not only to the individual and his relationships but also to the spoken—and sometimes unspoken—purpose of the group.[22]

Group Process

What concepts does the group worker need to make a diagnosis of the group? Again we want to stress that these concepts can never be completely separated from those related to the individual. If the individual is part of the group, his behavior is determined not only by his inner forces but also by the people around him. What group workers, therefore, must understand besides the individual dynamics are group dynamics or the concepts of the *group process.*[23]

We understand a *group* to be several people who are interacting with one another and who form an entity separate from other entities. It is important to remember this definition of the group, because we clearly distinguish it from people who are together just by accident. Several people standing at a bus stop and waiting for a bus do not form a group. They just happen to be together at the same time. The group worker works mainly with groups where there is interaction and where individu-

[22]The distinction between "growth-oriented" and "task-oriented" groups was made by Gertrude Wilson in her article, "Social Group Work—Trends and Developments," *Social Work* 1, no. 4 (October 1956): 66.

[23]"Group process" is that net of psychological interaction that goes on in every group. The "group *work* process" means that a conscious helping force, the group worker, has entered this interplay of relationships. Emanuel Tropp, "A Methodology of Group Counseling in Group Work Practice," *Child Welfare* 50, no. 4 (1971): 218–28; Eileen D. Gambrill, Edwin J. Thomas, and Robert D. Carter, "Procedure for Sociobehavioral Practice in Open Settings," *Social Work* 16, no. 1 (January 1971): 51–62; and J. S. Wodarski, R. A. Feldman, and N. Fax, "Social Learning Theory and Group Work Practice with Asocial Children," *Clinical Social Work Journal* 1, no. 2 (1973): 78–93.

alization is possible. The degree of interaction might vary sharply from one group to another, and it also differs from one individual to another.

To understand the individual in the group, we must understand his relationship to others. The pattern that makes up a group is a pattern of acceptance or rejection among different human beings. It is almost frightening to consider how much power each of us has over another human being. Our power is that of acceptance or rejection. Sometimes one individual is isolated from the rest of the group. He might be in it, but he is not really accepted. When the group worker sees this, it is his task to understand why the isolation has occurred and what it means. Has this person been isolated because of some behavior that has offended the rest of the group? Or has he been isolated because of something that lies outside of the group—for instance, the status of his family? Was he incapable of participating in something the group wanted to do because of his own incapacity or poor health or lack of money? Or has he offended the group by aggressive behavior? Is he perhaps a rival to the one most powerful member of the group who prevents everyone else from showing acceptance? By raising these questions, we see that a single aspect of the group process, the isolation of a member, forces us to search for both the *intra*personal and the *inter*personal reasons for the position of the group member.[24]

Sometimes an individual is in an even less favorable position than isolation. He is *rejected* by the group and exposed to open hostility. Again we must search for the reasons before we try to change. Is he the scapegoat on whom falls the group's hostility because the members feel guilty for certain behavior and use their weakest member to quiet their own conscience? Or is he a youngster who is so disturbed that he brings upon himself the hostility of the group? In an adult group is he the person who constantly interferes with the purpose of the group but makes no constructive suggestions in his own direction? According to the way these questions are answered, we will work with the inner problems of the individual concerned, with the attitudes of other members around him, or with social environment.

As part of the group process we observe *subgroups.* No group does all things together, and group members feel varying attractions for one another. Every group develops some subgroups. But to diagnose a group, we must find out whether these subgroups threaten the unity of the group: whether they are born out of hostile factions among group members or out of dogmatic adherence to certain opinions, or whether

[24]Cf. Lurie, "Intergroup Relations," p. 670; and Henry S. Maas, "Group Influences on Client-Worker Interaction," *Social Work* 9, no. 2 (April 1964): 70–79.

they actually are friendly formations that are a sign of some stronger cohesion between individuals.[25]

An important factor in group process is *group bond*. It represents the feeling of cohesion that makes for a group. If we would define *bond* exclusively as "the sense of belonging," we could measure a group's effectiveness by group bond. But group bond can also be destructive. Its strength might have been produced by threat or by serious dependence of the members on one another. Exemplifying group bond created by threat are some of the gang groups, which show strong group cohesion mainly produced by the iron hand of the gang leader. An example of a group bound by the dependency of one member on another was a group of women that had met since their childhood and that had prevented the members from going out and making new relationships by strong disapproval of anybody who tried to do so. Group bond, therefore, may be a powerful aspect of the group process in either a constructive or destructive sense.

We must understand *group hostility* and *group contagion*. A very gentle person may sometimes express an unaccustomed amount of hostility because of the fact that he is part of a hostile group atmosphere. Hostility might spring up against individuals who would not have been treated negatively if they had been met individually. We can observe this often in relation to minorities. Group contagion is a phenomenon we have observed but whose dynamics we do not yet completely understand. We do not know why in some instances contagion will work like a charm and why, for instance, a whole camp will be in an uproar because two or three children are upset. In another instance, these same children may have no influence on the others.

There is probably no student who does not know the power of group contagion when it comes to examinations. Even the calm and quiet, self-possessed student can be pulled into a pool of painful uneasiness by the anxiety of the group living through the common experience of examinations. And anyone who has had to stand up against persecution and cruel interrogation knows how much it meant that there were others who were going through the same ordeal. These are aspects of the phenomenon of group belonging and group contagion.

Closely related to them is *group support*. We are all aware of the fact that stealing is seldom done by one child alone. There is always a gang

[25]Ronald Feldman, "Group Integration, Intense Personal Dislike, and Social Group Work Intervention," *Social Work* 14, no. 3 (July 1969): 30–39; Carl Goldberg and Merle C. Goldberg, *The Human Circle: An Existential Approach to the New Group Therapies* (Chicago: Nelson Hall, 1973); and T. G. Walker, "The Decision-Making Superiority of Groups: A Research Note," *Small Group Behavior* 5 (January 1974): 121–28.

whose members give each other support and courage to carry through. This is delightfully presented in Saroyan's *Human Comedy*. The phenomenon of group support has been used effectively in groups formed for therapy purposes. One of the main reasons for group treatment of mentally or emotionally disturbed people has been the support that comes from others "who are in the same boat."

Group conflicts and how they are solved must be carefully observed. We know that there are different ways of conflict solving: withdrawal of one part of the group ("we give up," "we sulk," "we run away," "we start our own group"), subjugation (whoever has the greatest power makes the others do what he wants), majority rule (the largest vote determines action regardless of arguments), minority consent (majority rules but the minority does not feel defeated, agrees to action), compromise (the two conflicting subgroups meet "halfway"), and integration (the conflicting opinions are discussed, weighed, and reworked until the group comes to a decision satisfactory to everyone. Integration is the most mature solving of conflicts.[26] In observing how a group solves its conflicts, we can determine its stage of maturity. It is the group worker's responsibility to help a group move towards mature capacity.

It is important that we learn to treat the family not only as a social institution but also as a "group." Conflicts in the family group require special attention. The skill of the group worker may play an essential role in solving such conflicts.[27]

In recent years there has been growing interest in the understanding of small groups. Research has not yet produced many new discoveries. It has mainly served to point out questions or to confirm knowledge that had grown out of practice.[28]

Summary of Theoretical Framework of Social Group Work

In group work we combine our understanding of both individual and group dynamics. The formulating of this combined knowledge and its

[26]Albert Bandura, *Principles of Behavior Modification* (New York: Holt, Rinehart & Winston, 1969); G. Aplin and R. Gamber, "Group-Work Counselling: The Case for a Specialist Provision in Intermediate Treatment," *Social Work Today* (London) 3, no. 22 (1973): 5–9; and Ronald A. Feldman and John S. Wodarski, *Contemporary Approaches to Group Treatment* (San Francisco: Jossey-Bass, 1975).

[27]Suzanne K. Steinmetz and Murray A. Strauss, "The Family as Cradle of Violence," *Society* 10, no. 6 (October 1973): 50–56; and Gertrude Wilson and Gladys Ryland, "The Family as a Unit for Service," in *Social Work Practice* (New York: National Conference on Social Welfare, 1964), pp. 119–41.

[28]Gambrill, Thomas, and Carter, "Sociobehavioral Practice in Open Setting."

translation into basic principles of action is group work's specific contribution. The next step will have to be research into evaluation of the use of this combination. Diagnostic thinking in group work can never rely exclusively on an understanding of the group process or on an understanding of individual dynamics. It derives its knowledge from a combination of both.

With this theoretical orientation in mind, we can return to the three steps in the scientific method and see them in application.

Fact Finding

Fact finding in social group work is done by means of (1) observation and listening in the group, (2) occasional individual contacts with a group member or with members of his or her family, and (3) home visits and a sound knowledge of the economic and social influences of the neighborhood and work place from which the individual or his parents come.[29] Fact finding in social group work, therefore, relates to the understanding of the individual, to his role and his relationships in the group, to the kind of impact the group has on the individual, to the individual's impact on the group, to the whole group atmosphere, to the interpersonal relationships outside of the group, and to the social and economic environment. We realize that this is a big order. Yet without this knowledge, group work cannot be effective.

Let us observe the fact finding aspect of the social group work process:

> *Example 1:* This was the first meeting of a club of 12 fourteen- to fifteen-year-old boys of Mexican parentage in a settlement house of a northern state. The boys had come to the house saying that they wanted a place to meet and to play basketball. The group worker met them in a club room to discuss what the settlement had to offer and to get acquainted with the boys. They had stated their club goal: basketball. The additional facts the group worker saw in the first meeting were: a group of boys with little cohesion, some of them rather solemn and defiant, others boisterous and aggressive. There was sharp rivalry between two of them, one of whom was strongly supported by three other boys. When this subgroup decided on something, the others had little chance. There was much questioning of the worker, why he was there, whether he could provide them with the desired space, and whether he would "always be around." This was said with suspicion, not with hope. There was caginess about giving a father's occupation or outright disdain of the "old man's job."

[29]Theodore M. Newcomb, *The Acquaintance Process* (New York: Holt, Rinehart & Winston, 1961).

Facts stemming from the worker's knowledge of the neighborhood were: This was a minority group in a predominantly Italian and German neighborhood. The Mexican group was the most recent newcomer and had some language difficulty. The group also occupied the least desirable and lowest paid jobs. Almost all the men were unskilled laborers. Housing was poor. From other sources, including school and court and probation department, the worker knew that several of the boys had been in difficulties before the court and some were on probation. Schools in this neighborhood were crowded, and the teachers could not give too much individual attention to those children who had a language handicap.

From psychological knowledge, the group worker knew that these boys were adolescents struggling with dependence and independence feelings: they wanted to be "grown up," but they were afraid of it at the same time. They had great difficulty in establishing their own self-image because of the conflict between the values of their present environment and what their fathers represented to them. The group worker, as an adult, represented to them in the beginning a person of whom one had to be suspicious. The rivalry between the boys was an important fact to note. Additional facts would be needed to understand the reasons for it. The group worker also had to be aware of every individual being different; he had to be cautious not to stereotype the young men.

The process of *diagnosis* [assessment] of these facts will be discussed below. We will first give some additional examples:

Example 2: A teen-age group as part of a YWCA is starting in a suburban area of a large city. The girls are quite sophisticated, seem poised and capable of planning. Their first meeting is mainly used to plan a backpack trip. Although superficially the meeting seems to run very smoothly, the worker realizes a constant referral to the fact that this trip must be better than anything another group puts on. There is also (twice) referral to two girls who want to join but might "ruin" the whole endeavor because of their "nonconformist" behavior.

By being attentive to undercurrents, the worker is capable of looking for additional facts. She finds that sororities are still strong in this school setting and that there is much painful discrimination connected with them. She finds rigid moral codes among the teenagers with little acceptance of those who deviate even slightly. She knows there is much rivalry among the parents of the youngsters to "keep up with the Joneses" but also a genuine concern on their part to create a better life for their children. Parents in most of the families in the neighborhood have come from hard-working families and are now trying to offer their children every economic and social opportunity. This is a community in a state of upset and fluid values. Schools are not too overcrowded, and there is a high degree of intellectual stimulation. There are many young women who want more outlet for their energies as well as for a certain idealism that is not yet clearly focused. The work (mostly business) of the parents is not looked down upon by the girls, but there is resentment.

Example 3: Heavy gang fights have occurred in a neighborhood in a large urban area. The people involved are seventeen- to eighteen-year-old boys with the occasional help of "girl auxiliaries." At times it has been found that some of the adolescents have been using drugs. The group worker begins to work in the neighborhood, meeting the gangs at their hangouts.

The group worker must learn much about the people involved before he can be of help. He must begin to get to know them individually. He sees the power Jack has over the other boys and observes his demand for authority. He learns of Jack's ambition to be a pilot and his certainty that he can never reach this goal because he cannot find the money for training. He learns about the general feeling of hopelessness in this group and the bitterness that "everybody else gets the breaks. The only way is to help ourselves." This is done either by destroying others or by flight into a dream world helped by alcohol and drugs. The group worker sees the housing where six or seven people live in one room and where father and mother, brothers and sisters sleep together. He learns about the extreme importance of money because it represents power and plea-sure gratification. He begins to realize that the "legitimate job" is often the most important thing to those youngsters, but that they do not know any way of getting one. The worker gets to know the families, their broken hopes, their feelings of futility, and their quarrels, but also their strength.[30] He learns about the far-too-heavy load of the probation offi-cer. His fact finding with this group relates to the same factors as we have described in every other case, although the institutions with which he will deal predominantly might be different ones—employment agencies, vo-cational counselors, perhaps housing authorities or citizen committees concerned with housing.

Example 4: A group of young adults asked for a series of discussions on marriage counseling. The questions they posed in the beginning were highly sophisticated and mainly related to child rearing and the choice of a partner. Yet in the first planning meeting for the series, the group worker recognized uneasiness. Through a frank question raised by the worker herself—whether there were any specifics they wanted to discuss beyond the purely intellectual problems—a flood of feelings was released. Behind the sophisticated surface were many very baffling questions regarding facts of sex knowledge and hygiene as well as their relation to standards set by family, community, and church.

[30]Edward E. Sampson and Arlene C. Brandon, "Effects of Role and Opinion Devia-tion on Small Group Behavior," *Sociometry* 27 (1964): 261–81; and Kadushin, *Social Work Interview,* p. 19.

The facts the worker had to investigate were the situation of the group in relation to the subject, the specifics of church affiliation, and the individuals' stages of emotional and social development. If the group worker had not been sensitive to the "feeling tone" of the meeting, she would have missed the real needs of the members.

In children's institutions, in group homes, in mental hospitals, in child guidance clinics, or in discussion groups conducted in family service agencies, the group worker has an additional tool to help with fact finding. This is information coming from the social case worker or from other members of the team. From the beginning, in a child guidance clinic, for instance, every expert on the staff collects all the information he can to gain a better insight into the child's problem. The caseworker usually has interviews with the parents to get the developmental history of the child and to try to gain some insight into family relationships. The pediatrician makes a careful physical examination, and the psychologist gives the child several standardized tests that illuminate the child's intellectual functioning at the given time.[31] The psychiatrist, by means of interviews, will try to gain insight into the problems as the child sees them.

After one or two weeks of such investigation, the staff meets to bring together all this information, to learn from one another, and to work out the best method to help the child and the family. The group worker brings to this conference his observation of the child in relations with other children, the way the child approaches materials and activities, and the way the child relates to an adult whose affections he has to share. Sometimes observations contradict each other: a child may appear shy in individual interviews and be aggressive in a group situation. Such contradiction only proves how much we need all those observations. People act differently in different situations, and to understand people best, we must see them in as many situations as possible. To a child, an adult is somebody so different from the child's contemporaries that we should never base our conclusions only on observations in the interview relationship. The concepts of "role" and "role expectation" relate to this phenomenon. Human beings act differently according to expectations they assume others have of them.[32] Sometimes those are perceived in accordance with reality, yet often they are not.

---

[31]It is too widespread an error that tests always show the inborn capacity of an individual. Actually, they can only indicate a person's present functioning. Sometimes emotions can block existing intelligence and prevent a child from using it well. Also, social circumstances as well as the standardization of tests on different cultural groups make them increasingly questionable.

[32]Sampson and Brandon, "Effects of Role and Opinion Deviation," pp. 264–68; and A. K. Boer and J. E. Lantz, "Adolescent Group Therapy: Membership Selection," *Clinical Social Work Journal* 2, no. 3 (March 1974): 172–81.

Diagnosis and Treatment Plan
(Assessment and Action)

We have borrowed the word *diagnosis* mainly from medicine. It means ascertaining the symptoms of a sickness so as to be able to distinguish it clearly from other diseases. In presenting the kinds of facts the group worker collects, we have implied that the worker is looking not only at the surface of individual or group behavior but also behind this surface behavior to try to determine exactly what situation he is dealing with.

When we use the word *diagnosis* in medicine or psychiatry, we think of the use of a given term for a cluster of symptoms. The physician observes, for instance, that a child has a red rash, high fever, sore throat, and that he vomits. The doctor diagnoses the measles. We have not established such diagnostic entities in social work. We talk about social breakdown areas such as delinquency and broken families, yet those do not always present the same combination of symptoms. At present our diagnostic skill in social group work will not be expressed through a given nomenclature but will be expressed in the summation of the symptoms and the understanding of some underlying causation of the group process as well as individual behavior. Let us, therefore, return to the previously given examples and take our next step in relation to diagnosis and resulting treatment plan. We had left these situations at the point of establishment of facts.

EXAMPLE 1: Our fourteen-year-old boys of Mexican parentage in a settlement house have been seen as adolescents coming from a discriminated-against minority group with little identification with their fathers and with low capacity of trust towards the adult or towards each other. Through our psychological knowledge, we know that the age of development of trust lies early in childhood and that it grows out of an identification with a beloved parent. Many of the boys, therefore, will need to recapture this opportunity. A group worker whom they can trust and respect may help them to develop confidence in themselves and in others.

As adolescents they also need an outlet for their spirit of adventure and for their growing feeling of independence. Besides identification with an individual, they need identification with their own heritage and pride in their background.

As a group they present a loose structure with little opportunity for a sense of belonging and with a potential for dictatorship or gang anarchy. The summary of the group worker's diagnosis and of the implied treatment goal would, therefore, be:

1. Adolescent boys with normal adolescent drives
2. Deprivation of satisfaction in childhood and, therefore, need for identifica-

tion with a father figure or in some cases with an accepting and consistent mother
3. Need for a positive self-image related to the nationality background
4. Poor group cohesion with danger of extreme group development toward dictatorship or anarchy

EXAMPLE 2: The YWCA group in a suburban area: The facts showed adolescent girls with a strong drive for status and for success in competition. There was confusion about values. There were great capacities for cooperation and a wish to contribute to the "good of society." Translating those facts into diagnostic terms would probably mean:

> This is a group of adolescent girls who show a comparatively healthy development. Trust in adults has not been severely damaged, but the confusion of values is intensified by the confusion among parents and relatives in their neighborhood.

Work with these young people must relate directly to adolescent needs, as by providing ideals incorporated in an adult other than their parents, and must offer opportunity for free and independent discussion and questioning of values and opportunity for actual acting out of idealistic drives through projects that contribute to the community.

Such work must be done with the highest group work skill. It is not enough to introduce "worthwhile projects"—sewing for deprived children or collecting for hospitals. Here, instead, is a great opportunity to help the girls really understand their community in a wider sense, to learn to participate genuinely in a democratic society. They can learn how little it means to people to get "things handed down" to them. They can learn to form committees with young people from other neighborhoods, learning from them and sharing with them. In working on a variety of projects, the girls will begin to see the overall picture of a community, and they might learn to see and to understand the conflict in which their parents are caught. Such a group had a meeting with their parents in regard to some of the discriminatory practices that the young people resented bitterly. One of the girls said, "But our parents never have time to think through such things." One of the mothers answered bitingly, "How can they when you girls want a new pair of jeans every month?" In a common enterprise, the conflicting values came to light; mutual understanding grew from the discovery that it was not always only "one side's fault."

Needs of self-importance must be met through opportunities for heterosexual activities and successful social life. Outdoor activities and sports, planned and worked out by the girls with the help of the group worker, can mean a great deal to an insecure and competitive group of adolescents. High individualization will allow an outlet to those with great gifts and to those youngsters who feel left out.

EXAMPLE 3: The gang of seventeen- and eighteen-year-old boys was the one in which we saw the strong influence of poor housing, poor family relationships, and the feeling of having no importance in this world. The summarized diagnosis would resemble the one for the Mexican boys. Because of these boys' age and their greater need for adult responsibilities and privileges, we add:

1. Urgent need for provision of jobs or qualified training facilities
2. A long period of support by a person whom they trust
3. Constructive outlet for participation in change of environment is very important and might contribute not only to this change but to the self-confidence of the boys
4. In some cases, referral for medical help

EXAMPLE 4: The young adult group that asked for marriage counseling needed help in expressing problems and in coming to terms with their own and community standards. Diagnostic thinking in relation to this group:

1. Comparatively well-adjusted young adults with the normal fears and apprehensions of this age entering into the adult responsibility of marriage
2. Help needed with direct teaching of facts in a free atmosphere of group discussion allowing for expression of feelings and of doubts
3. Group needs help with awareness of the fact that these problems are common and nothing to hide
4. Group cohesion might become very strong as is often the case after such discussions. New diagnostic thinking will be needed at this point to determine whether continued group meetings will be helpful to this group

The latter remark presents a caution in all group work. Diagnosis never stops with its initial establishment. We must constantly watch it and either confirm or change it if facts change.

In recent years the need for intimacy has been well recognized. It has lead to group techniques as "encounter groups," "sensitivity groups," "marathons," etc.[33]

[33]Carl Rogers, "The Process of the Basic Encounter Groups," in *Challenges of Humanistic Psychology,* ed. James F. Bugental (New York: McGraw-Hill, 1967), pp. 261 and 268; Emanuel Tropp, "Social Group Work: The Developmental Approach," *Encyclopedia (1971),* pp. 1250–51. See also: W. H. Masters and V. E. Johnson, *Human Sexual Response* (Boston: Little, Brown, 1966); and Harold I. Kaplan and Benjamin J. Sadock, *Sensitivity through Encounter and Marathon* (New York: J. Aronson, 1972).

They have raised expectations of "instant love" (like "instant coffee") and have become a surrogate way of life for many. Group workers must be aware of new techniques but always evaluate them in the light of varying individual needs and basic respect for the integrity of each person.

Treatment (Action)

In talking about *treatment,* we are again using a medical term. We mean the actual application of the social group work method. The tools we have at our disposal are the group process (the interaction of the members with one another), the program media (activities, discussions), the worker's understanding of the members, his capacity for "empathy," his disciplined and conscious use of himself in relation to the members.

What is *discipline and conscious use of oneself?* In the beginning of this chapter, we talked about the professional attitude and the insight the worker must have into himself. Whenever we want to help other human beings, we must establish a relationship with them that is meaningful to them. The establishment of such a relationship is a specific skill of the social worker.

All of us have had experiences in our lives when another person became meaningful in a helpful sense. Often this occurred in a love or friendship relationship. The relationship gave us the feeling of being wanted, of being important to the other person, of feeling comfortable enough to be ourselves without pretense. It usually made us more capable of doing the things we had to do, and it gave us an inner happiness.

There is no professional relationship that can completely replace this kind of experience. Love and friendship in their deepest sense are such great gifts that they cannot be imitated. The professional relationship cannot reproduce them. It does, however, offer growth experience through acceptance and understanding. It gives the group member the feeling of being completely accepted as an important individual human being with all his weakness and with all his strength. It gives both the individual and the whole group the feeling that the worker shares with them their vital concerns and is not imposing his own wishes upon them.

This feeling and its genuineness can only be established if the worker learns to be extremely sensitive to the members' needs. This is the reason why in selecting students, schools of social work will look for the quality of compassion as well as for intellectual capacity and rational understanding. "It is the sensitivity of the socially vital layman raised to the Nth power which makes the difference between amateur and professional skill in working with social relationships."[34] This focus on the group members does not prevent the group worker from also considering the demands of society. But it does prevent the worker from fulfilling mainly his own needs. None of us can work without some satisfaction, and this certainly should not be denied to the social group worker. In fact, if the worker does not derive any satisfaction from his work, it will become stale and cold. We would hope that the flame that brought the worker into work with people will be kept alive and continue to warm all his contacts. We mean only that he must not use the group for his own purposes. If the worker is an enthusiastic stamp collector, he has every right to get some of the youngsters interested in this when he feels that they have a certain curiosity in this or similar areas. But he cannot make all his club members philatelists just because this is his interest. Perhaps the worker is a person who has a great need for acceptance and admiration. He still has no right to transform all his clubs into admiration societies for him. The latter is a great temptation in group work since the group worker is in a position where he can command a great deal of adoration and since his position can give him opportunities to make members dependent on him. This danger is especially great in working with deprived and unhappy groups because the social group worker is so largely the giver of tangible and intangible gratification. The worker needs much self-discipline to remember that the goal is always the independence and competence of the group members.

Conscious use of self also includes the capacity to set limits when necessary. To set limits in a constructive, not punishing, way is a great skill and demands much sensitive understanding of others and oneself. We have often swung from harsh authoritarian approaches to unlimited "permissiveness." Yet neither has been helpful to the individual. Our goal in all educational efforts is to help individuals to "internalize" limits. They themselves should be able to recognize the times and muster the power to curb their instinctive drives. It starts quite early in childhood when we help a child to learn the difficult art of "postponing" gratification, of waiting for food and not screaming, of being able to accept that there is a "tomorrow" for play, no more the same evening, that Dad gets tired out by a wild game but is willing to resume it another time. And we learn more and more difficult limitations: sharing the parents with a new baby, sharing toys, taking turns, listening to others. If we were never taught all

---

[34]Bertha Reynolds, *Learning and Teaching in the Practice of Social Work* (New York: Farrar & Rinehart, 1942), p. 51; see also: Eileen Blackey, *"The Process of Group Deliberation"* (New York: Council on Social Work Education, 1965); and Pallassana R. Balgopal, "Sensitivity Training: A Conceptual Model for Social Work Education," *Journal of Education for Social Work* 10 (Spring 1974): 5–11.

this—and it is usually and best taught in the gentle give and take of everyday living—we would become difficult and unhappy members of society.

The group process itself, the relationship between the members, is one of the greatest teachers, whether we consider children or adults. In adult discussion groups, we have often heard a member being chided by others when he tried to dominate the discussion, or we have seen a shy nonparticipant brought out of his passive role by kind and helpful coaxing of other members. Yet sometimes the group cannot, does not want to, or does not know how to act. It is then that the group worker must enter; the worker has received a cue to make use of the group work method in practice.

III. PRINCIPLES OF SOCIAL GROUP WORK IN PRACTICE

All of us have a need to belong and when the belonging is tied with significance and worthwhileness we are enabled to rise above our personal feelings and to lose and find ourselves in the joint enterprise.[35]

No two people will practice group work exactly alike. Social work does not want to produce puppets who follow strictly established patterns. The most helpful group worker is the one who can use basic principles in a creative and disciplined way. These principles are:

1. The function of the social group worker is a helping or enabling function. This means that the worker's goal is to help the members of the group and the group as a whole to move toward greater independence and capacity for self-help.
2. In determining his way of help, the group worker uses the scientific method —fact finding (observation), analysis, diagnosis—in relation to the individual, the group, and the social environment.
3. The group work method requires the worker to form purposeful relationships to group members and the group. This includes a conscious focusing on the purpose of the sponsoring agency and the needs of the group as expressed by the members and as implied in the member's behavior. It is differentiated from a casual unfocused relationship.
4. One of the main tools in achieving such a relationship is the conscious use of self. This includes self-knowledge and self-discipline in relationships without the loss of warmth and spontaneity.
5. Acceptance of people without accepting all their behavior. This includes a basic respect and love for people, a warmth relating to their strength as well

[35]Saul Bernstein, "There Are Groups and Groups," *The Group* 13, no. 1 (October 1950): 6; Herbert Barish, "Self-Help Groups," *Encyclopedia (1971)*, pp. 1163–69; and Harold Weissman, *Individual and Group Services* (New York: Association Press, 1969).

as to their weakness. It is not sentimentality, and it is enhanced by understanding of individual needs and societal demands.

6. Starting where the group is. The capacity to let groups develop from their own point of departure without immediately imposing outside demands.

7. The constructive use of limitations. Limitations must be used judiciously in relation to individual and group needs and agency function. The forms will vary greatly. The group worker will mainly use himself, program materials, interaction of the group, and awakening of insight in the group members.

8. Individualization. It is one of the specifics of the group work method that the individual is not lost in the whole but that he is helped to feel himself a unique person who can contribute to the whole.

9. Use of the interacting process. The capacity to help balance the group, to allow for conflict when necessary and to prevent it when harmful. The help given to the lonely member, not through individual attention by the group worker, but by relating him also to other members. Help given to the leading member by enhancing his gifts so he may become a democratic leader who increases the capacity of the group.[36]

10. The understanding and conscious use of nonverbal program as well as verbal materials (discussion).

To illustrate "group work in action," extensive excerpts of a single group's meetings are given below. The commentary will point to the conscious use of the group work method and will include significant observations. This record will be followed by brief notes on meetings of other groups to highlight application of the group work method to other settings.

The Group of Seizure Patients[37]

BACKGROUND AND SETTING. The outpatient department of a large hospital served many patients with epileptic seizures. The caseworker working in this department and the head of the neurology department realized that these patients had many problems in addition to their medical condition. Epilepsy is a disease still regarded with great suspicion by people who know little about it. It has the Biblical stigma of the "falling sickness." Epileptics are often treated like outcasts.

Actually, the disease can now be quite well controlled if the patient is under competent medical care. It should not prevent the person from leading a normal life. Yet superstition gathering around epilepsy has made life very hard for those who suffer from it. They have difficulty in

---

[36]Emanuel Tropp, *A Humanistic Foundation for Group Work Practice* (New York: Selected Academic Readings, 1969); and Kurt W. Back, *The Story of Sensitivity Training and the Encounter Movement* (New York: Russell Sage Foundation, 1972).

[37]All names are fictitious. This group met in the 1950s. The record is still presented because: (1) the problem of discrimination against epileptics is still acute; (2) the group work approach is well illustrated.

getting employment, they are regarded with suspicion and fear by their families, and they seldom have a normal social life.

In this hospital, both the neurologist and the caseworker realized that the seizure patient could not get enough help from the hard-pressed physicians. Because of the specifically social problems related to this sickness, they felt that group treatment would be helpful. The services of a social group worker were secured to start with a group of these patients.

Such a group had to be a *formed* group. The first question that arose for the group worker was how to choose a small group of patients who would be congenial and helpful to one another. There were about one hundred seizure patients attending the clinic; out of them a group of about eight or ten was to be selected. The patients' records gave comparatively little information on personality and background. Group workers frequently find themselves in such a situation, in which they can use only the most obvious criteria for selecting patients. In this case, patients were chosen according to their age, their expressed wish to get some additional help, and the doctor's impression that they needed such help. Out of the ten patients invited, seven became regular members of the group. They were:

JOE, nineteen years old, college student, comes from a large family, grand mal seizures.[38]

LUCY, twenty-two years old, housewife, married, one child and pregnant at the time of the meetings. Grand mal with nocturnal seizures. (Seizures occur only at night.)

MARGE, eighteen years old, college student, only child, petit mal.

FERN, nineteen years old, secretary, orphaned, large family, grand mal.

DON, twenty-six years old, clerk, lives separated from his parental family, grand mal.

ED, twenty-five years old, salesman, only child, grand mal.

RAY, nineteen years old, salesman, parents divorced, only child, grand mal.

Ted, Lucy's husband, twenty-two years old, laborer, no seizures, came as a guest to the group. The group met in a pleasantly furnished room in the hospital. To create an informal atmosphere, the worker had prepared coffee and cookies, the meeting being in the afternoon. The group worker (W designates group worker in the record) was early to greet everyone who came. Lucy was the first one to arrive, and the worker and she began to get acquainted.

---

[38] *Grand mal* are those seizures that are characterized by unconsciousness, the patient falling to the floor and in some instances writhing. Teeth are clenched, and there is some foam at the mouth. *Petit mal* are epileptic seizures characterized by a short fleeting moment of unconsciousness. Often the environment is not aware of the attack.

RECORD OF FIRST MEETING (EXCERPT):

It was at about this time that Joe entered. Joe kept his head down during the discussion, but mostly when he was speaking. There was discouragement and some cynicism in his voice. Both Lucy and *W* asked him about his studies, and he told us that he was taking history and art. He enjoyed history. He added with some disgust he was going to school longer than he needed to. Lucy spiritedly entered this discussion. She said that she would be interested in learning more about psychology and psychiatry. She said that she herself was very tense. She knew that this was not good for her. She would like to know more about what makes people tick.

Group worker observes gestures and movements as much as the spoken word. Here we see indication of Joe's embarrassment and discouragement.

Marge entered smilingly. She looked like a child, a bit apologetic. She expressed her delight at coffee and cookies being available. When *W* poured the coffee half of it spilled on the floor. There was delighted laughter among all three of them and a loosening up of the atmosphere.

At this time Fern, a nineteen-year-old girl, entered. Fern and Lucy discovered immediately that they lived in the same neighborhood. They talked about the distance from the hospital and about the poor streetcar service. This led into their talking about how long one has to wait at the clinic until one is seen by the doctor. Fern said with some anger that sometimes she waits from 10 o'clock in the morning until 4 o'clock in the afternoon. Fern asked the others how often they had to go for their medical appointments. Lucy and Fern said that they were going regularly. It was significant that the two students sounded most discouraged. They said they did not keep appointments regularly. Marge said that she had had no grand mal seizures for months, but after this interval she had four in a row, and she was very unhappy about this. Joe rather evasively said he had them quite often. Lucy reported hers occurring at periods she could not quite determine, yet it was often.

Members begin to relate to purpose of the group.

W began to give the reason for the meeting. She told them that though not everything was known about their sickness, it might be helpful to discuss some of the questions they had about it. It might be of some help if one loosened up, and maybe seizures would be a little less frequent. They would be the first group to try this. Lucy said that she thought this marvelous and that we should try to find out as much as we can. The more people are

Group worker states purpose of meeting. Sets tone by being frank about the limits of help that can be given.

able to talk freely with each other about it, the more we might learn about it. She also felt that she was so much under an inner strain that it would be very helpful for her to talk to others about it and get some indication of what to do. Her husband had first thought that she should not have a second baby because it might be too much of a strain for her. She hoped, though, that she could learn to relax and that this would improve her seizures. Anyhow, she wanted to try.

Fern: "If only people would not always think that we are just crazy, that we are something like mentally sick. You have no idea how my brothers treat me. You know, I did not grow up with my brothers, because my mother died very early, but when they see me, they just stare at me all the time, and they watch me, and I hate that. I have a very nice roommate at the place where I am, and we went along very well, but when I had my last seizure, she was present, and she was very good about it. But now she, too, is watching me all the time and always so cautious and says: 'Fern, sit down,' and 'Don't get excited.' I hate to be treated that way."

First expression of resentment. It comes early, because of the informal atmosphere and the realization that one has nothing to hide in this group.

Lucy: "Yes, this is true, and very often your own family doesn't understand. But it is amazing how well my husband accepts it, and how good he is about it and understands it. It certainly is terrible when it happens when your relatives are present. For instance, just for the first time when my brother-in-law came to visit us, I had a seizure. One hates to be seen like that by one's own family."

Marge: "You feel that way because people always take us so dramatically. I will never forget the first time I had an attack. I was seven or eight years old. I was in school, and when I woke up my teachers were standing around me and what frightened faces they had! One of my best friends shouted over the whole place: 'Marge had a fit, Marge had a fit.' This made me so embarrassed. People would not shout about somebody having headaches would they? I know that that is the reason I never again wanted to be in a group with others."

Joe: "People in general are quite kind to me. All my friends just make me comfortable and then they don't talk about it much afterwards."

Joe is the least comfortable of the group. He hides his feelings.

Fern brought up the question of what type of seizures they had, whether it was petit mal or grand mal. Joe asked about the difference; he had never heard those words. *W* asked whether anyone knew

This shows how Joe tries to forget about his condition. Group worker first involves other members in the difference. Fern was the only one who tried to explain. *W* gave the information in more detail. This opened up everybody, and they described their symptoms.

the answer; gives information, when needed.

W had the impression that they were filled with so many problems that they had to jump from one point to another. They went into the question of drug treatment. In describing the symptoms, they mentioned that the most horrible thing was the headache right after the attack. The drugs did not help but made them very drowsy, and they were yearning for a drug that would not do this. Fern and Marge were able to describe some combination of drugs that they were taking. They too complained of the drowsiness. *W* said that she would ask Dr. Mann, the chief neurologist, or another one of the physicians to talk to them, and this was greeted with great enthusiasm.

This whole discussion shows the need of the group members to talk about their sickness. It also gives the outsider a good insight into the feelings of seizure patients.

Fern then said with strong feeling that she would like to know whether this disease is hereditary. Her brother pressed her saying that she should not get involved with any fellow, because she should never marry and have children. At this point Lucy spoke with great conviction that this was all wrong, that there was not a hereditary factor in this, but that one should discuss it with the husband beforehand. She said, "You will live with this man day and night, and he will find out anyhow. It is better to tell him beforehand, and if you both have decided to go along with it, then you just make up your mind not to be so worried about it, and you can have children and raise them happily. I had my own child, and I know that it is a healthy child." Lucy continued talking about how she met her husband and said that as a youngster she did not dare to go out as other girls did. Marge interrupted her and said, smilingly, that Lucy should not think that others dare to go out. She never had gone out with any boy either, because she was much too afraid. Fern said that she felt very strongly about all this and wanted to know the answer in regard to heredity. *W* gave Lennox's explanation of the fact that having seizures is not hereditary but that there might be some disposition toward it in people. This was well understood by the group, and even Joe joined the discussion at this point, trying to explain it. Lucy added with conviction: "You simply cannot live always thinking about it. For many years I could not even look above my own nose. Yet I began to see that it is impossible to live that way, and I began

Realistic help given by one group member to others. This is especially helpful since it comes from a "fellow sufferer."

Open admission of "inadequacy," because others have lived through the same problem.

Worker gives information and support.

to think about people and somehow the sickness did not matter that much." Marge added that it was such a relief to see others who have the same problems. Joe was comparatively quiet during this discussion. *W* asked him whether he had friends. He said that he had quite a few.

Everybody in the group felt that they had to discuss further the problem of predisposition, but they were already interested in another aspect of the sickness. Fern said, for instance, "Why does everybody act so 'hush, hush' about our sickness? Why doesn't anybody talk about it?"

Lucy: "I think it is because nobody has enough knowledge about it, and they consider it something so horrible."

W explained how not so long ago cancer was also a "hush, hush" sickness. It had much to do with the distressing symptoms and the fact that little was known about it. Fern said with great conviction, "People should know, then, and we should help them to know, and we should know ourselves." Marge asked shyly whether there is a law against marriage of seizure patients in the state, and *W* said that there was not such a law. Joe said with resentment: "But there is a law about not being allowed to drive a car." Marge felt resentful about this too.

W had to interrupt and remind the group that they had to close. *W* asked some questions: (1) Did they feel they wanted to go on? There was general enthusiastic response. (2) Did they want more members and would it be all right to invite some older members, since the hospital was not serving many in their own age group? Fern said seriously, "I think it would be very good if we have as many as possible to talk things over with; and if we have some older people, these older people have gone through things that we might still have to go through, and we can learn from them." Joe underlined this, and Lucy added that age does not make much difference when people are adults. Marge said that the more people they had in the group, the more people would know what to do and how to understand themselves.

Joe began to collect his books. While they were getting up, Fern said that they should not be so formal to each other in this group and that they should call each other by first names. It was also Fern who added that it might be good if some other

Sometimes the worker must limit members. Her limitation is set by time. It is helpful not to run meetings with much emotional content for too long a period. This allows for stimulation of the members' own inner forces after the meeting.

Questions are raised to increase the group's participation and feeling of responsibility.

fellows were in the group because poor Joe must feel very isolated. Joe smiled for the first time.

Lucy suggested she would like to bring her husband because it would be good for him "to see others who are in the same boat as I am." With feeling for the others, she added, "Don't think that you are funny or crazy. He knows me, and he understands this." The others thought that this would be a good idea. *W* suggested they might wait a little longer on this, until they had talked among themselves a little more. Lucy agreed readily, and Fern said it would be better "when we know a lot and can tell them, and I sure wish that we could tell them."

Other plans they discussed in the last minute were to go out together and to visit Lucy when she had the baby.

Summary—First Meeting

In this first meeting, the worker established an atmosphere of informality so that free expression of thoughts and feelings was possible. The members of the group began to relate to each other primarily on grounds of a feeling of having common problems. The worker played an enabling role in relating members to each other. She was sometimes supportive and at times gave simple explanations. She observed carefully and used this meeting for "fact finding" as well as for giving some direct help.

Fact finding included observing the roles played by individual group members: Lucy, the pacifer, reliever of tension; Fern, the "trigger," the one who asked questions; Marge, the timid follower; Joe, the waiting observer. The worker learned that some of those roles hid strong feelings. Lucy was really fearful, in need of her husband's support; Joe was wearing a mask. A sense of belonging had been initiated, and the group members had been able to show unusual frankness in relation to their sickness.

Second Meeting—Summarized Account

Ed and Don came to the group for the first time. The free and open atmosphere prevailed. It is significant for the group process that the entrance of every new member changes the tenor of the group considerably. From the beginning, Ed established himself as a leader admired by the group. He was a young man with far greater calm than the rest of the members, at least on the surface. He was the only one who had satisfying social contacts in another social agency providing group work services, and he told the members about the way he handled his going out with young women.

Don's presence meant something very different to the group. He was the oldest member and a very tense person. His hostility and frustration were close to the surface. He expressed them by overwhelming everyone else with medical terms and showing off with his knowledge. He tried to dominate the group meeting by telling the members what they had to do. His presence was also helpful because it forced the group members to stand up for their own thoughts and to accept a more difficult member.

RECORD OF THIRD MEETING (EXCERPT):

Joe asked to discuss the question of car driving. Ed expressed a strong feeling about how much a car means to him that it is always needed, that he had driven a car since he was fourteen years old, and that it was a terrible feeling not to be able to drive now. He also thought that too much time is wasted on buses. He added, "Friends offer to drive me from work, but I don't like that."

Joe agreed and said that it was horrible that he was not allowed to drive. He underlined that a state law did not allow seizure patients to drive. *W* asked them whether they considered the law reasonable or thought it should be changed. Ed started telling about a beautiful new car he had had when he was told not to drive because of his seizures. He made up his mind to drive only until he could sell it. "I drove it and then I had a seizure. I smashed it to bits, and so I couldn't even sell it." Joe confessed that he too had driven a car and had backed into a door. They agreed that the law forbidding driving was reasonable. Ed added: "I rode with a friend of mine, one of my best friends; we both were not hurt, but we could have been."

Group worker had given support when societal limits were unjustified. She had also the responsibility to help members accept justified limitations. Her question opens up discussion to allow members to think this through together.

Lucy: "I really don't need it so badly, but it must be very hard on a man because I know that the man always wants to do the driving." *W* could see in Ed's face that he wanted to talk about this more, because his face worked and looked very pained. Finally he blurted out, "I tell you, I learned a lesson, I tell it here just among us. I had a girlfriend and she went with me in my car. But when she learned that I should not drive, she told me not to. And just a few days later I smashed up the car. Now she doesn't talk to me anymore. I have walked ten miles back and forth and I have begged her to listen to me, but she just slammed the door and did not want to hear what I had to say."

There was a storm of strong sympathy for Ed. Lucy said, "She is not worth caring about so much, if she doesn't listen to you." Ed said in a low voice, "But it is my fault. How can she trust me with other things if she cannot trust me with not driving when it is forbidden?" *W* said to Lucy that the girl was not objecting to Ed's seizures but only to his driving. Lucy nodded and said that she could understand that. Yet, Ed should tell the girl that nobody is perfect and that one can make mistakes and not repeat them. She made quite a speech, saying that in fighting with another person one has to be able to say, "I'm sorry," and to give in. She added with a smile "and don't think we didn't fight before our marriage," and then said, "Ed, why don't you write to her? Maybe she'll listen to you."

> Group worker is sensitive to Ed's feelings and his incapacity to express them. She protects him without hurting his pride.

Ed nodded and said that he would try, but he could not see how he could make it clear to his friend. He had "learned his lesson, but it was awful not to be able to drive."

W said that driving actually seemed to mean more than just driving a car, didn't it? Joe nodded and said that it made one feel so strong. *W* said that it really meant to all of them being a whole person. At that point Ed said with great effort: "I did not tell you the whole story, but I almost killed a boy in my accident. I dragged him along. It was terrible . . ." At that moment there was a strong, warm feeling in the group. Joe said that he could understand Ed's feelings, and he knows he should not drive. He only wished he could have the feel of the car once again. Maybe he could drive if somebody else was sitting right beside him. Ed said that once more after his accident he had driven a car. This happened when he had met a friend who had come from Korea. They had a glass of beer together, and in the same place was an old man who had become quite drunk. He had felt that the man was worse off than he himself. So he put the man in the car and drove him home. They sat in the car for an hour or two, and the man told him all about himself and about his son who had been killed. Ed added, "Well, after I told the man that I had seizures he felt that he was better capable than I to drive the car. He did not want me to take the bus all the way back to the city." This produced a roar of laughter, a helpful ending to an emotional meeting.

> Group worker helps with some deeper understanding of feelings.

Summary—Third Meeting

In this meeting the group had to face realistically one of the limitations related to their sickness. This was not a limitation imposed by prejudice. We see how one of the group members helped others through his open confession of violation of the limit. The group worker's role was to promote an atmosphere that made this possible. At times the group worker interpreted deeper reasons for feeling, as she did in considering the men's need to drive.

We observe also how the group bond deepened.

RECORD OF FOURTH MEETING (EXCERPT):

Marge called about half an hour before the group started, saying in an embarrassed voice that she had to study for an examination and thought she could not come today. *W* asked her about the time of the examination. Since it was several days off, *W* wondered whether the two-hour meeting might not be all right to take in. *W* could almost hear how Marge heaved a sign of relief and said: "I am actually calling you so late, because I wished I could go, and I am glad that you say it is all right. I might leave earlier if I feel it takes too long." *W* said that she could do that.

This little incident shows Marge's two-way feelings about the meetings: she wants to go and she fears them at the same time.

It also shows another phenomenon, occurring in psychiatry, case work, and group work, named "transference." The client relates to the helping person as if he is someone else out of his past. Here Marge sees in the group worker "mother," who tells her what to do. Marge takes a question as a welcome "order." Group workers are aware of this phenomenon and know that it takes time to work through.

When *W* came into the meeting room Don was waiting. He said that he liked to be early. Lucy was the next one to arrive, and the rest of the group, with the exception of Fern, came very early. Ed had brought his friend, Ray. Ray was a huge man, nineteen years old. He was very tall, broad-shouldered, with great strength in his handclasp. *W* introduced Ray to the other members of the group and there was quick and warm acceptance. The meeting did not start formally because they were waiting for Fern. Don said that since he was now working for his room and board, he did not have so much time to brood, and he felt he had less severe headaches and fewer seizures. Marge sat on the couch between Lucy and Ray. Don remarked how well Marge looked, and Marge glowed with pleasure. At that time Fern entered. It was apparent how very attractive she was to the men.

The advantages of a coed group!

While *W* filled the cups with coffee, Don asked Fern about her age. Don said that he felt like a grandfather. Marge mentioned that many people had told her that she looked so very old. It was gratifying to her when several of the group said that she did not look old at all, on the contrary, she looked fine. She actually looked now different from the mousy person she had seemed to be the first time. She wore a bright dress and her behavior was more outgoing. She told the group that this was her twentieth birthday but that she had not told anybody else about it. Ed immediately started singing "happy birthday," and they sang for her. For about half an hour there was kidding back and forth, laughing, and a light and easy relationship. It was interesting to observe that Joe, who had been so aloof in the first meeting, was right in the middle of all this, well accepted by the others and joining in the fun. Ed finally said, "Well, we aren't getting down to our purpose." Fern asked whether everybody knew each other's "life history." They said that they had talked about it but did not know too much about Ray. Ray said that he had grand mal, that attacks were serious and frequent. He thrashed around a lot. Fern said she had had hopes for a driver's license, but they were dashed when her seizures reoccurred. Lucy told her that the group had had a discussion about driving and that Ed had been helpful.

W asked Don whether he would like to summarize what was discussed in the last meeting, especially for the benefit of Fern and Ray. Don did very well. Don said the main point is to understand one's own sickness. Once a psychiatrist had helped him with some of this.

Marge said that she too had had psychiatric interviews. They had helped her some and she was satisfied with them. Lucy spoke up resentfully. She had wanted to be referred to a psychiatrist because she felt that she had many problems she wanted to discuss. She had had great difficulties in relationships with her family and people she wanted as friends. Yet the hospital had not referred her. Her resentment mounted when she described how she had talked with her physician and how he had told her that no psychiatrist could help her if she could not help herself.

Such "recreational interludes" are of great importance. They give relief from too much introspection. It is part of the task of the group worker to be aware of the right moment for them and to terminate at the right moment.

This opened up much expression of hostility toward other hospital physicians: "They have too little time for us, they always tell us we should pull ourselves up by our own bootstraps." Lucy expressed resentment towards the fact that the doctor looks at her for five minutes, prescribes the same thing, and yet she has to wait for hours. *W* agreed that this was really hard on patients. The clinic is a large place, and little individual attention can be given. *W* told the group that Dr. Mann (clinic neurologist) would come to talk to them. They should feel free to bring up their questions and complaints.

Group worker's role is explanation of agency procedure. Worker must accept the feelings of hostility yet help the group members to use the services offered.

Don picked up on Lucy's concern with her family relationships. He wanted to understand more about it. Becoming more independent might help. Marge nodded, and even Joe said that he liked to discuss this. Ray began to speak slowly, his head down, not looking at the others. He told them that he had seen a psychiatrist and that it helped somewhat, but he wanted to talk to *them*. He had been such a terrible child. The teachers had been friendly to him, but when he had his first seizure at the age of seven or eight, he felt so resentful and so frightened that he fought everybody. Yet he always was afraid. He knew he was a strong-looking boy but that there was this secret sickness and he could not really live up to the way he looked. He did not do his school work. Finally he was thrown out of school. Ray spoke in a slow hesitant manner. It was amazing to see the patience of the other group members. (This included Don, who usually was not patient.) They listened with compassion, agreed, disagreed, smiled, and nodded.

We see how fear is hidden by aggressive and other unacceptable behavior.

Ray continued telling how he moved from one school to another, always feeling that everything was futile. He said, "I dreamed of becoming a pilot; all my life I was around airplanes—I even started to build them. But now I know that this is impossible."

He was now in vocational training, but he often missed school. He knew it was only partially due to the seizures. He always felt mad at the world. His seizures had become much more serious. Recently he had experienced a very serious one and had fallen down two flights of stairs. His mother had found him badly bruised. He added with great feeling, "She had just left the house for two minutes. She hardly dares to leave the house when I am around." Don said that he, too, had found himself

Being with "fellow sufferers" allows for a quick feeling of confidence. With confession comes relief. This gives the first possi-

falling down several flights but strangely had not hurt himself. Lucy said the body seems to be relaxed during seizures. Ray went on in his halting voice, filled with emotion, saying that his seizures were actually getting worse and worse, and then he added, "All right, since we are all in the same boat, I am telling you something, but I don't want it to go out of this room. I am drinking heavily." Several of the others, especially Lucy, Fern, and Joe, said with great compassion, but rather firmly, that he must not do this, that alcohol increases seizures. Ray said, "I was told this, but I did not believe those doctors." The others laughed and Ray added, "I guess I have to believe those fellows now, because I have seen how the seizures follow the drinking."

bility of working on the problem. Group members set limitations for one another.

Fern leaned forward and said to Ray, "How does the drinking make you feel, Ray?" Ray: "Well, it makes me feel good inside." Fern: "You don't really crave the stuff, do you? You don't even like to drink so very much. It makes you feel like a normal person, like others, doesn't it?" Ray: "My goodness, what a smart deduction!" Everybody laughed, but everybody nodded. Lucy said, "That is it. Fern is right, we always feel we are not like everyone else, and we try to forget it one way or another. The way I have done it is to withdraw into myself. I was such a big girl, and I did not dare to meet others." Ray: "When you drink, you seem to forget that you really are not worth much." Don said that Ray was worth something. He was supported strongly by Joe.

Insight of one group member helps the other one.

W said that they were right, but that one needs time and help to learn this. Ray nodded and said, "Maybe it helps talking with all of you about it. I don't know." And then he continued, in a monotone, about how he hated himself when he drank. He told of his having a seizure right in the bar. He broke a window. He woke up and looked into the faces of three policemen, who were holding him. He could not explain that he had had a seizure. He repeated this several times, demonstrating how he tried to raise his head to explain and could not do it. He was taken to a hospital and locked up. He told of the feeling of shame and futility. Don suggested that epileptics should carry a dog tag indicating their sickness.

During all this discussion Ed was very quiet. It was obvious that he had wanted this opportunity for his friend, and he was glad he was talking. He always encouraged him. When Ray said, "Should I tell you?" Ed nodded, "I told a lot last time, don't worry." When Don suggested the dog tags, Ed agreed that this might help, but one should try not to get into such a situation. Ray nodded seriously. He then continued, "I know Ed here says that he is not ashamed of having seizures, but the truth is I am, I am ashamed." Lucy: "You see, Ray, we all felt that way, but you have to learn to live with this, and actually it is nothing that we can help, nothing that we have done. You don't have to feel ashamed of this. Don't you have any friends?" Ray said that he had a few friends, but lost them easily. Once he was driving with some of them. He must have become unconscious or fallen asleep, but they dumped him out of the car, and went on without him. The reaction of the other group members to this was extremely strong: Those were not real friends. They had done a terrible thing to him. Why was he so stupid to consider them friends?

High group identification.

W asked Ray whether he was trying very hard to make friends. Ray said, thoughtfully, that he never believed anybody could be his friend and perhaps he was trying too hard. When they hurt him, he would hit them. Fern said, "And if you would not lick them, you would feel that you are not worth anything, would you not?" Ray said, "Sure. I am just a coward inside." Fern said, "You are not a coward, you are just so darned insecure because you don't think that people will like you." Lucy said to him, "Why do you think that you have to be so afraid and desperately look for friends? You are such a fine-looking fellow. You really look wonderful, you don't have to be afraid." There came Ray's pathetic and quiet answer: "Well, that is not the way I look at myself."

Group worker moves in the direction of more insight.

Worker's question has led into discussion of Ray's inner feelings of worthlessness.

Ray's answer is most significant. Our "self-image" (what we think we are) seldom coincides with the way others see us and our *real* being. Yet every human being feels more at peace if those two pictures fall together. It is one of our goals to help people to achieve some true self-knowledge.

Fern was sitting beside *W* and whispered in a low voice while the others were talking: "You know, he needs help, more than any one of us; we must help him, he really needs it very badly."

Ray went on to say that it helped him when the teacher in his class told him that he should meet another fellow who also had seizures. He had never known anyone else with seizures. When the teacher told him that it was Ed, he simply could not believe him. Ray said, "You know I thought it would be Fred." Ed: "Yes, he looks like a little insecure runt." Ray: "Or perhaps Roy." Ed: "Well, he looks quite secure." Lucy: "See, Ray, you think a person who has seizures must look like a terribly insecure little person. You don't look like this yourself." Ed: "You see, Ray, you never believed I could be the one who had seizures. You don't look that way yourself. To everyone but yourself you look like a fine fellow. Maybe you can believe it now." Ray looked to the floor and said in a low voice, "Well, it really is amazing, all of you don't look that way. . . . It sure helps to see this and talk about it."

Increase of self-confidence through identification with others.

While they were getting up, enthusiasm about this meeting was expressed. Marge said that she was glad she had come, this was the best one yet. Joe agreed. Don said, "Every one of us is so insecure, perhaps with the exception of the social worker." *W* laughed and said they probably *all* had that in common, although it might be related to different problems.

Group worker must appear almost unreal because her problems are not discussed. It is important that the group feel the focus is on them.

Ray said, "You know, it is amazing how I could talk to all of you today, and you know why? It is because we are in the same boat. We have something in common, and when I talk to you, I know that you know what I'm talking about. It was good to talk to the psychiatrist, but it took me twelve meetings to find out what I had in common with this guy."

Awareness of the help that comes from group interaction.

Joe and Don talked excitedly about the meeting. Joe said, "You know, this is simply marvelous. Well, this is more powerful than any medicine I ever had." Don: "That it is. My goodness, you don't feel relieved just those two hours we sit together, it somehow works on you the whole week and you feel better." Joe: "And there is always the next meeting to look forward to. It is good to come regularly to every meeting."

Comment—Fourth Meeting

This one was a very significant meeting. The new group member gave the others an opportunity to focus outside of themselves. Yet his problems were close enough to their own so that they could identify highly with him. His own realization that he had taken on the prejudices of society about epileptics and his astonished relief that not all epileptics were really ugly was an experience that had much meaning to all of them. The feeling of belonging broke through in this meeting. There was little recording of the worker's role. The meeting was so alive that the worker's presence was necessary mostly to give security. The discussion would not have been possible without somebody present who made the members feel that it was safe to be so frank. At times a question by the worker led into some more insight.

Fifth to Eighth Meetings—Summarized Accounts

In subsequent meetings, the group moved into discussion of the problems of everyday living. At one meeting the chief neurologist was invited to answer questions about their disease. He was frank and gave straight answers about symptoms, possibilities of treatment, and the kind of regimen they had to keep to diminish seizures. His visit was followed by half an hour with the group worker alone when the members repeated and reconsidered some of the problems they had discussed with the physician; they expressed their feelings about following a diet.

In another meeting the counselor from a vocational guidance bureau visited the group members, and they learned from him about work opportunities. His visit also gave them an opportunity to interpret to a stranger their own condition and to learn how to explain it to him or to an employer. After those two meetings Lucy asked the group again whether they would allow her husband, Ted, to participate. She felt that this experience was so important to her that it should be shared by him. She also wanted him to see other seizure patients because she felt that this experience had given her so much security.

RECORD OF NINTH MEETING (EXCERPT):

Lucy said little. Joe looked so much better and calmer than on the other days. Lucy said that she felt more relaxed. Ted spoke up emphatically. He insisted that all that Lucy needed was to feel more relaxed, that drugs were not worth a thing. He, Ted, was against drugs and thought that there was no use in taking them. *W* asked what the others thought about it. Joe said that they had learned from Dr. Mann that drugs do not do miracles but are helpful. Ed said that medication was important

Here is an opportunity for the group members to tell an outsider what they had learned about their sickness.

even if emotional feelings played a part in their sickness. Marge described how her prescription had to be changed to follow her needs. She now had only petit mal attacks. Grand mal attacks might reoccur, if she left off the medication.

Don and Ray agreed with the others. *W* summarized by saying that they had learned that body and soul belong together. Medication and understanding one's emotions can work together. Ted seemed impressed by the fact that others, who had the same sickness as his own wife, agreed with the medical profession. He said that he could accept medication for Lucy. He only wished she were less upset. She was especially upset each time she had had contact with her own family. This time the content of the meeting focused mainly on Lucy. Lucy told that her father and mother were separated. When she spoke with her mother she felt she had to defend her father, and when she spoke with her father, she felt she had to defend her mother. She hated her stepmother, the woman her father married after his separation from her own mother. None of her present and former family had ever been warm towards Lucy, and her father preferred the stepsisters. With mounting emotion she declared that she could never forget the day her father was leaving the family. She was a little girl, and she had tried to hold him back. She held tight to his pants and screamed that he should not leave the family. He had slapped her across the mouth and flung her across the room. Although she felt that she could never forget it, she had never talked about this before.

W asked the others whether they understood what had hurt Lucy. Joe said that what had hurt her most was that her father seemed not to care for her. It must hurt to see that he now cares for others. Don said that she was jealous of her stepmother. *W* said that it was hard for Lucy to realize that her father liked others. She had been hurt by the man she loved first in her life. The hurt had occurred at an age where every child is dependent on an adult. Don added, "I think she really dislikes her father, but she *thinks* that she dislikes her stepmother."

W explained that in spite of Lucy being now an adult woman, her feelings were those of the little girl who cried for love and was pushed away. This made her resentful when she saw her family. It also made her afraid of other relationships. Ted nodded

Group worker uses the interpretation of the other members. She summarizes and explains some deeper meaning.

Interpretation given.

and said that Lucy was afraid of liking people. *W* asked, "What about friends, Lucy?" Lucy said, "I always think I will lose them, and I hold on to them and then lose them anyhow." *W* nodded and said that she was hanging onto people just as she hung onto her father. She was afraid of the rejection that she expected.

Marge suddenly cried out, "Now I understand myself much better, it is the same with me. This is the way I have always acted with friends, and I have never known why. But I know now because my mother and father were fighting with each other, and I was always between them. One day when I wanted to prevent my father from hitting my mother, he hit me. I have always felt guilty towards my mother, because I felt I had not protected her. Oh, I understand so much better now." Ray nodded thoughtfully and said, "Sounds familiar. I never saw my old man." At this moment he frowned; he was having an attack of petit mal. Attention was turned back to Lucy.

Insight into the feelings of one individual in the group produces insight in another one.

W summarized what had been said. She added that Lucy needed to feel that she was no longer seven years old and did not depend now on this person who had rejected her. Ted said, "She still looks for father." *W*: "And yet she can't make Ted her father." Ted: "I would not want to be her father." Lucy: "And I would not want Ted to be my father, I think I want him to be my husband. I think it helps to realize this." *W* said that it often helped to learn what makes us tick. Perhaps Lucy could relax with the knowledge that she now had her own life, her husband, a child, another on the way. Those children were now dependent on her.

Don said that only two months ago he had been so dependent and resentful towards his family. Yet leaving home, getting on his own feet, and having the group had made all the difference in the world. Lucy: "How can I relax when each time I visit the family they discuss their problems with me?" Ted said gently, "Maybe it is also my responsibility to take Lucy away from these worries about her family. We should do more things together, things she likes, like having picnics." Ted also talked about his own father and that he did not have a very good relationship with him either. At least his father had not abandoned the family. His mother was a kind woman. He, Ted, now realized that Lucy had been

Movement toward health does not go in a straight line. Lucy returns to her fear of family conflict.

Ted has gained understanding and is able to be less resentful of Lucy's tenseness.

hurt more severely. Ray said that we must understand that the people who have hurt us are human too. He wanted to try to look at his "old man" that way. Somebody asked Ed why he was so quiet. He only smiled and said that he did not have much to say. Joe added, "That is usually my role, isn't it?"

Joe begins to "cover up" less. He is aware of his reluctance to participate.

Comment—Ninth Meeting

This time another member of the group, Lucy, was in the spotlight. She introduced the problem of family relationships and the impact childhood experiences have on the adult. The worker's role in this meeting was a more active one. She moved towards more interpretation than she had given previously.

Tenth Meeting—Summarized Account

The tenth meeting was not a discussion meeting but one in which the group tried to exercise some social skill. They had supper together. Then the evening was spent in learning a new skill, dancing. None of the group members with the exception of Ed had learned how to dance. The experience was an unusually liberating one. The group members were first anxious and hardly dared to move. Under the skillful leadership of another group worker, who showed her sensitivity by starting with simple, uncomplicated steps, everybody became involved in dancing. When during the evening Ray, the giant, started dancing with the tiny Marge and finished by lifting her up in the air while the rest of the group stood in a circle and applauded with joy, one had the feeling that the group members had made an important step toward healthy relations to others and toward self-confidence.

RECORD OF ELEVENTH MEETING (EXCERPT):

Ed was concerned with the question of what set off the seizures. Ed had felt sick this morning. He had not gone to school, but he had had no seizure. He wanted to understand better what emotions have to do with seizures. His seizures recently came mainly at the time of large dances when he was anxious not to have seizures. He felt he was not afraid of those dances, but he was nonetheless more comfortable in small groups. He was tense with many people around him. *W* asked Ed whether there were other moments when he had felt similar fear. He de-

Ed had given the impression of great security, as long as the others were very insecure. Their movement toward health allowed him to admit more of his problems.

scribed his feelings when he stood on the stage. He said he felt so terribly frightened when he knew that all those people were looking at him. He trembled and felt dizzy and was very surprised that he had had no seizure. Ray said, "You had stage fright."

W wondered what they thought stage fright was. Marge said that it was fear of not doing the right thing, when everybody watched you.

W agreed and added that we are afraid of being a failure. *W* explained that we must learn not to make a *whole out of a part.* Failing on a stage did not mean being a total failure. Tensions come often from high standards that we are not able to live up to. Joe said that he understood that very well. He had changed schools but failed in courses he usually could handle. It was especially bad when someone else produced good work.

Group can now take interpretation of feelings early in a meeting.

W said that feelings of competition are strong with many people. They start with rivalry with brothers or sisters and get transferred to other people. Marge said that much of her feelings of rivalry related to her sister. Ray commented that Marge must have overcome some of this since she seemed so different from the first day when he had seen her. Ed said that he began to understand some of his feelings. He added that he usually was not afraid of dances. Only right now he had no girl. Ed said that his seizures had been worse in January, at a time when he drank much and before this group met. Now he was drinking far more moderately. It was significant that Ray, who had previously told about his own drinking, said that this moderate drinking was perhaps too much for Ed.

Joe said that he could not understand the whole discussion. His seizures always appeared when he was contented, and he had nothing to complain about. This was said with an unhappy and solemn facial expression. He said his last seizures occurred when he was fishing with a friend. One of the group members asked Joe whether the person with whom he was fishing was a good friend. Joe said, "Yes, and it was our last meeting before he went into the army." Ed said that that must have made him sad. Joe shrugged his shoulders.

Later Joe asked the group worker for some time alone with her. He said the group meant more to him than he could describe, only he was still inhib-

Group workers must be able to conduct individual interviews. This is Joe's

ited. He then spoke freely of his school failure, in spite of his high intelligence, and of other unhappy experiences.

step toward showing his true feelings. He must do this first in an individual contact with a person he trusts, before he can do this in a group.

We must allow for such individual differences.

Comment—Eleventh Meeting

In working with people, we learn that development never occurs in a straight line upward. Though the group had had a happy experience, new doubts assailed the members. Those members of the group who in the beginning had a great need to cover up anxiety and to pretend that they had no problems now felt freer to bring out their doubts and fears. Ed and Joe appeared at this meeting with their problems. Joe was still very reluctant to talk but did not keep up his pretense of indifference.

Many of the problems presented were the problems of all young adults and not only exclusively related to their sickness. The worker's role was to be understanding and to give support, information, and some interpretation.

Twelfth to Fourteenth Meetings— Summarized Account

In the next meetings, some of the problems, especially those of Ed and Joe, were worked out. Fern had been able to accept a job. She was supervising some young women and training them for sales work.

RECORD OF FIFTEENTH MEETING (EXCERPT):

Fern showed up after missing several meetings. She spoke up immediately and said that she had a problem. She was the supervisor for the women at work and felt, therefore, "that they had to look up to her." Unfortunately, the other day she had had a seizure when the women were present. With much feeling she described her fear that they might stare at her and question her. What should she do when she went back to work? She had stayed away from work for a day. The manager had known about her seizures.

Fern returns to the group in a moment of real crisis.

W threw the question back to the group. Ray said she should say nothing. W wondered whether that was the best approach. Marge said that that was not the best way because the women would always wonder what had happened. If Fern said nothing she

An opportunity for the group members to use their own newly won insight.

made it seem like something one must not talk about. Ed wondered whether she should ask the manager to explain to the women. He added that he thought, though, that Fern should be able to do it. Had we not tried to work on ourselves to be able to do this? *W* agreed, but did Fern feel comfortable? Joe said that Fern felt afraid because she felt she had lost status. Fern nodded. Marge said that she thought it not right for the manager to explain. It looked like an apology. *W* asked the group whether they felt that Fern had to apologize for something. Fern said that she would like to apologize for the commotion she had started but not for having seizures. She asked whether she should start by saying, "I'm sorry for what happened." Joe said that he felt that she should not say that she was sorry but start out by explaining what happened.

> Group worker reminds Ed of the *reality* of feelings. We cannot always do what we *should* do.

W asked whether Fern had some idea how the women felt. Marge thought the women were probably quite curious and somewhat frightened. *W* asked the group whether they thought being frightened would be natural. They realized that a seizure was frightening to those who had never seen one. Marge suggested that Fern might say she was sorry for the inconvenience she had caused. She should explain to the women that she had felt no pain and that they need not be afraid. Fern asked what she should do if there were more questions. Marge said that people usually do not ask too much. They want to understand, but they do not ask for a whole medical lecture. *W* agreed to this and suggested that Fern should give added information only if asked. *W* also suggested that Fern could tell the women that it might help them on their job to be informed. They might meet anxious parents who have children with seizures and the women could help them to understand better. Fern was delighted and relieved by this idea. If she could make this experience a part of the training, she felt that she could now face the women.

> Notice Fern's anxiety, also the change in Marge, who has become more secure and outspoken.

Comment—Fifteenth Meeting

The excerpt of this record shows the importance of immediate help with a very real problem. The group presents a source of security and learning. The group members, identifying highly with one another, cannot yet look at their sickness objectively; the group worker supplies the more objective aspect.

Sixteenth Meeting—Summarized Account

The sixteenth meeting was again a "reality tryout." The group met to eat in a public place. They went to an exhibit together.

The seventeenth meeting was the last one for the group. It is important that ending not be done abruptly. Ending often intensifies feelings of fear and rejection. If necessary, some hope of other support must be offered. The group worker had prepared the members for some time previous to the last meeting for this ending. She planned the meeting as one of conscious evaluation to help the group members to be aware of their own development and to give them strength to increase it.[39]

RECORD OF SEVENTEENTH MEETING (EXCERPT):

W suggested the group members do some evaluation of the group experience. What had the group experience meant to them? Fern, as in the first meetings, took the lead and said that the group had helped all of them to gain a great deal of self-confidence. She said that though she had not been present all the time, she felt that she was able to explain her sickness to others and she herself did not feel as badly about it. Ted spoke up and said that self-confidence showed in one's relationships with other people. Several of their acquaintances had commented on how very different Lucy was. She was more relaxed and seemed to be more friendly with people. Lucy was a little embarrassed and quite flushed. *W* said it was nice to get such compliments from one's husband. Lucy nodded and said that she felt it was easier for her to talk with people now.

W said the gaining of self-confidence was one of the major aims of the group. Were other aims accomplished? Did the members understand their sickness better? Several group members did say that they realized that their sickness was not a mental sickness but partially physical and partially emotional. They would have to work on both those aspects. Fern said that the most important thing she had learned was that this sickness was a reality. There were limitations that this sickness imposed on them. She had a friend who was crippled by infantile paralysis and he too had to accept this. Marge said that she had learned about the impor-

[39]Alfred H. Katz, "Applications of Self-Help Concepts in Current Social Welfare," *Social Work* 10, no. 3 (July 1965): 68–81; and Henry Wechsler, "The Expatient Organization," *Journal of Social Issues* 16, no. 2 (1960): 47–53.

tance of liking oneself. For a while she had almost hated herself and had not wanted to continue to live. The group had helped her to see that she was actually as good as everybody else, even if there were limitations. Ed added that one must know that there are many more people in this world who have difficulties, even if one cannot see them.

W added that the limitations imposed on them might not be static; medicine was trying to learn more and more about this kind of sickness. There might come a day when they could go swimming unattended or drive a car.

Group worker adds realistic hope.

W reminded the group that they had discussed their relationship with their families. At their age everybody had to deal with his feelings of wanting to be independent. Their difficulty was that their illness had increased their dependency. They had expressed a great deal of resentment towards this in the early meetings of the group, and it would be helpful to see where they thought they were now.

Lucy felt that she had to learn a great deal more about her feelings towards her family. She did not feel as badly any more, but knew she was not yet calm.

Marge said she had gone a long way towards independence and that she felt she could have never done it without the group discussions. She now lived without her mother, but it was not always easy.

Joe said that he had not had as much difficulty with his family as the other members of the group but had learned not to run away from his feelings. He too wanted to become an independent human being. He felt he could be more on his own and be more secure in his learning.

Ray was more hesitant than the others. He felt dependent upon his mother. She still prepared his medicine, and so on. He said that he was trying to be more independent about it but could not quite achieve independence.

Fern said that a younger sister had asked to live with her. If one knew about their previous relationship one realized Fern's progress. *W* asked her whether living with the younger sister would be very hard. Fern felt that it would be very good for

Group worker wants to prepare for the possibility of conflict.

her, and it would improve general family relationships. Some difficulties that might arise were discussed to prepare her for them.

Ed said that he still felt quite dependent on and guilty towards his family. He had hoped for a summer job but could not find one.

Another goal of the group had been to increase the members' capacity to look for and hold a job. Fern said that she had been very happy on the job but was not sure she could hold it. Perhaps this position was too strenuous for her. She also mentioned that Don had recently called her and had sounded happy because of his work. She felt the group had given Don the confidence to take a job. Joe joined in and said that it had helped him when we had made him talk in the group. He was now able to do well in school, and he would soon finish his course. After this he would look for work. Later on he might consider returning to study. Marge felt very happy. She had a job for the summer and a regular job in the fall in a home for the aged.

The fourth goal had been improvement in social relationships and skills. Lucy felt this to be her greatest achievement. She and Ted considered joining some church or neighborhood house group. Fern and Ed had had no great difficulties. Ray had not improved much and was anxious for the group to meet again. Joe had recently joined a church group for young people and was proud of his active participation.

Comment—Seventeenth Meeting

The worker was consciously more directive in this meeting. She instigated the evaluation, and she asked the members of the group questions in relation to the points where they needed help and where they had to continue working on themselves. She carried through an additional responsibility of the social worker—namely, suggestions for referral to other community resources. The latter served to give the members support and also hope.

At the end of this meeting, the group members decided to meet by themselves during the summer. They also suggested that they would give help to any other group that would serve seizure patients. It was agreed that the worker could be contacted if serious problems arose and that *she would refer them to appropriate resources.*

Summary for the Group of
Seizure Patients

In following this group, we have seen how the group process worked in helping individual members. Group interaction, group discussion, and reality testing were helping agents. We saw the role of the group worker as one of giving support, of giving information, of helping with some insight, and of referral to other community resources. We recognized as the basic goal in this group a reestablishment of self-confidence in individual members, a giving of security through a sense of belonging, a testing of skills, and a beginning of insight into oneself by understanding better one's relationships with parents, family, and job.

Having seen a group in action, we will now use excerpts of records that will show specific aspects of the group work process.

Help with the Process of Decision Making

Example: (A group of early adolescent girls in a settlement house.) The group worker consciously used herself in group meetings to help the girls become less upset by opposing opinions. This necessitated helping the girls gain a feeling of group strength in a majority choice, overcoming the insecurity they felt in planning when they were pressured by a few domineering members. Here is an example:

> The girls had made plans for a sleigh ride during the meeting. Plans were extensive, and the girls were all set to go. At the next meeting two girls came in saying they wanted to go on a bus party; a sleigh ride was no fun.
>
> Vivian said, "How many want a bus party instead of a sleigh ride?" Three hands went up, and Mary said, "A bus party it is." Worker said, "Just a minute, I think this is something that should be discussed further." Vivian said that a majority had voted for it. Worker asked how many girls would go if there were a bus party. With worker's support, Betty, Elizabeth, Lois, Rosalie, and Betsy said they wouldn't go.
>
> They moved on to plan the sleigh ride. The following week, as they began to talk, there was an undertone of "bus party." Worker asked how the plans for the sleigh ride were going. Grace said, "Let's have a bus party." Vivian chimed in. The others looked unhappy and obviously turned to worker to see what she would say. Worker said, "Well, I thought you had agreed on a sleigh ride. A lot of the kids can't afford a bus party." Rosalie picked up, "And you can always have a bus party, but not a sleigh ride." Betsy commented on the fun of a sleigh ride. Betty called for a vote. Grace and Vivian lost out. Grace assumed a carefree expression of "Oh, well." Vivian said she wouldn't go. Worker said we all wanted her to go, so we hoped she could.

This was a stepping stone in helping the group move in the direction of more democratic control. Democracy is not learned or exercised by putting a voting ballot into a box. It means thinking through matters, discussion, and the courage to withstand pressure and accept conflict. The group worker helps in this learning process in day-by-day group decisions. In this case, the group worker realized that the group's use of a vote was frequently a very unsatisfactory method of group control. The members were quick to call for a vote in order to avoid a difficult spot. It was the role of the worker to sense the readiness of the girls to accept a decision formed by a vote and to use herself to prevent the vote's misuse by stimulating constructive evaluation and discussion of conflict.

Balance of Self-Determination and Help

Example: (A neighborhood house club of fifteen-year-old girls.) In the twentieth meeting the girls came to the club in a very anxious mood. Sharon was suggested for membership. This precipitated the strongest split among club members all year. During this meeting, the girls were unable to verbalize their reasons for not wanting this girl in the club and could not explain to worker why Sharon had been voted out of the rival clubs. Half the group defended Sharon, saying she hadn't done "it." The others held that the other club would be angry if they elected her. (A projected reason, for they were not able to say they felt she was guilty.) Because of the heat involved, worker helped the group to decide to put voting off until another time. Before the next meeting, worker arranged to discuss the situation with the visiting teacher and school nurse; she found the situation was this: Sharon had been accused of stealing a sweater downtown. This had been substantiated by members who were also involved. The situation was being handled by the school authorities. Sharon had been accused of trying to get others in trouble by reporting false rumors about them anonymously over the phone.

The next time only seven girls came to the meeting. A rival group had threatened to beat up the members if they voted for Sharon. Worker had used individual conversations to feel each girl out on the issue; as the meeting got started, she told the girls that she felt that there were some important things to talk about. Worker pointed out that she realized the importance of the group to each one of them and felt that they should really think through what accepting or rejecting Sharon would mean. During this meeting there was a "hair letting down," and the girls discussed in a sincere way what they wanted from the group. From this came a greater understanding of variety in people. Worker wanted to help the girls make a decision that would be acceptable to them and to prepare the way for their evaluating the situation for themselves.

Worker asked the girls to consider what it would mean to them should the charges (they had described what they had heard) be true and should

Sharon become a member. The girls felt that she was their friend, and they wanted her in, for they could not believe the stories. If the stories were true, the girls would vote her out. Worker asked the girls what they would feel like if they made a mistake and the group voted them out . . . wouldn't they want to be sure that including Sharon in the club would mean they liked her even if she had done something wrong?

It was decided that should they vote Sharon in, they would want her to stay. They felt a friendship responsibility toward members they accepted.

Sharon was accepted by a 4–3 vote. The decision stood.

To achieve a balance between letting the group make its decision and yet helping them to accept other human beings with their difficulties is one of the skills of the social group worker. It involves skill and self-discipline to feel comfortable in handling such a problem, the worker neither letting the group simply reject another human being nor so identifying herself with the rejected person that she imposes her own intentions on the group.

Recognition of Unexpressed Needs

In a run-away facility tensions mounted daily. Overt complaints related to craving need for some drugs.

Two boys expressed this sharply in a group discussion. John attacked Eric for having induced him to come to this place. We suggested that John might want to leave—no fences. John broke into tears meaning "I can't." Arms went around him. Eric said, "We don't need drugs, but friends."

Individualization in the Group Situation

To exemplify individualization, the authors will present short summaries written by the social group worker after two weeks of observation in a camp for handicapped children.

Jim is a twelve-year-old boy who shows some difficulty in meeting the group living situation. He appears extremely shy and withdrawn when he talks with an adult for the first time, but he is also the instigator of much horse-play in his cabin. In the group situation, he is very resistant to adult suggestions. Alternately he is pathetically withdrawn and very aggressive. He is fearful of the water but boasts about his swimming ability, which he has never proven. The counselor will have to give much encouragement to Jim without prodding him into activities.

Bud is a six-year-old boy who shows great behavior difficulties. He is kind and helpful to younger children. Yet when they show some independence, he becomes very hostile and attacks them viciously. He cannot be reached by reasoning. He is completely fearless physically and climbs up into places that can be dangerous. Without provocation he will attack adults. During a bus ride, he sat beside the counselor, watching the landscape. Without any obvious provocation, he suddenly turned and began to spit at the counselor. He disturbs the other children in their cabin.

More observation of Bud is needed. It is suggested that he get individual attention while the other campers have afternoon naps or just before going to bed. There is need for knowledge about the home situation and for psychiatric observation.

Mary is a twelve-year-old girl who in the beginning made fun of others because they worked on their physical therapy. In one of the group discussions she revealed a deep resentment of her mother who had not cared about her and had done nothing about the birth injury that now handicapped her. She expressed her feelings of being so ugly that there was nothing that could help her. The group worker showed her what beautiful eyes she had, and another camper seemed to help her by pointing out to her that she, the other camper, was not pretty either but had nice hair and took good care of it. Later Mary asked the counselor to fix her hair and was very proud of her changed appearance. Mary needs help in personal appearance and an opportunity to talk about her unhappiness. Coed activities at the camp will also motivate her to take better care of herself.

John is a thirteen-year-old boy who first gave the impression of being an extremely frightened child. Whenever an adult approached him, he shielded his face as if to ward off a blow. He wet his bed at night. He had difficulties in joining in any activities because of his extreme fear of animals and of other children. In the course of this week he has shown some aggressive behavior towards some of the women counselors. It seems that John is an especially repressed child who will probably go through a period of aggression. It will be important that his male counselor establish a good relationship with him and that the program allow him the expression of his hostile drives and give him some self-confidence to overcome his fears.

Lily is an eight-year-old girl who is very silent. Lily participates, but only as a follower. At night she wets her bed. Even during games she carries in her hand a small prayer book and never lets it go. It was only once that she allowed the counselor to hold this book for her. Lily will need much warm acceptance and opportunity to talk or play out some of her fears.

Constructive Use of Limitations

Example: Twelve-year-old Jerry seemed shy and almost frightened when he appeared in camp. He needed much encouragement to participate, and he showed constant fear when a counselor approached him. Only slowly did he seem to understand that he was wanted. Yet after about two weeks he suddenly turned all his suppressed hostility against those children who were weaker and smaller than he. He bit them, kicked them, twisted their arms. The children were afraid of his sudden attacks. They could not retaliate directly, but they showed him in other ways how much they disliked him.

It was understandable that this boy, who had been full of fears, needed some outlet for the sharp negative feelings he had. Yet there were two reasons for helping him accept limitations: (1) the safety and mental health of the other children—they could not live under the threat of being tortured by somebody stronger than they, and (2) the mental health of Jerry himself. The attacks gave him an outlet, but they made him guilty and fearful of retaliation, actually increasing his old fears instead of relieving them. He also became an isolate in the group, although he was yearning for acceptance.[40]

The group worker, therefore, had to help Jerry understand some of his difficulties. This was possible through the good relationship developed between them and the trust that had grown. The worker had to provide Jerry with some constructive outlets for his feelings, which he managed by intelligent program planning. Jerry learned how to swim, an energetic kind of outlet as well as a real contribution to his self-esteem, and Jerry participated in a play where he could be an aggressive outlaw but had an opportunity to change in the play.

The group worker had to help the other members to feel that it was all right to stand up against Jerry, and he even had to support them when Jerry started his torturing, but he also helped them in a group discussion to understand why Jerry did this. Jerry was part of this discussion and learned that *understanding* did not mean that anyone *liked* his behavior or would let him do it.

Use of Program in Relation to Needs

Example 1: (A group of nine-year-old boys.) The boys were stimulated after their discussion and appeared restless. The group worker suggested food at this time. As they were sitting together, Peter went to the sandbox and was soon joined by Bob. They began to throw sand at each other and soon there was a free-for-all. Peter began throwing sand in everyone's face. Worker initiated a game of bombing a target with the paper plates used for refreshments, and this siphoned off considerable aggression.

[40]See also: Lewis Yablonsky, "The Delinquent Gang a Near Group," *Social Problems* 2 (Fall 1959): 108–17; Scott Briar and Irving Piliavin, "Delinquency, Situational Inducements, and Commitment to Conformity," *Social Problems* 13 (Summer 1965): 45 ff.; Fred L. Strodtbeck, *Group Process and Gang Delinquency* (Chicago: University of Chicago Press, 1965); and Glasser, Sarri, and Vintner, *Individual Change Through Small Groups.*

The group worker related not only to the individual needs but to the mood of the situation. Instead of forbidding, she used a game to limit the boys' aggression.

Example 2: (A church group of teenage girls.) There was much conflict between this group and their parents. The girls resented their parents' demands to conform to standards, and the parents considered the girls unreasonable. The group worker suggested to the girls a meeting where both the young people and the parents were present.

A stage was improvised, and the girls were asked to present in a play the way they felt their parents were treating them while the parents sat in the audience. Lucy and Carla presented very stern parents who were nagging them continually. They presented the mothers asking too many questions when a girl returned from a date. The girls were very reluctant to answer.

After the girls had finished their presentation, the parents were asked to go on the stage and present their version of the situation. This time the girls were in the audience and saw their fathers and mothers presenting teenagers who were sullen and uncommunicative even when the parents suggested something kindly. They saw their fathers nervously pacing the floor when the clock had struck one in the morning and they had promised to be home by eleven o'clock. During the two presentations, there was much laughter because of the amusing way in which the roles were presented. After this there was a serious discussion. They had seen each other's views in a more vivid light than if the situations had only been discussed. Out of this meeting grew better understanding and some disagreement between children and parents.

Example 3: (Nine- and ten-year-old girls in a day camp program.) Joyce, a nine-year-old girl, said that she was surprised that Rita did not go to church on Sunday. Joyce said that Jews are bad. Rita started to cry. Lucy kicked Joyce and said she was mean to say such things. Joyce said that her mother said this too. The group worker asked the girls whether they knew what it meant to be Jewish. None of them could explain. The worker asked Rita whether she could tell the group something about the Friday evening services. The worker put her arm around Rita's and Joyce's shoulders. Rita began to tell of the lighting of candles, and some of the others remarked that that was similar to candle lighting in their church. The worker then gave a simple explanation about the origin of different religions and how they all believed in one God. She also promised the group to bring a book that had pictures of the services of different religions to the next meeting.

It is very clear that religious or racial prejudice will not be eliminated by one such incident. Yet learning occurs by repeated experiences of this kind. It occurs not only on the intellectual level but also on the emotional level because of the example of the adult who accepts everybody equally and because the youngsters begin to get to know each other. It is very important that the children are not prevented from expressing their hostility, that instead they talk about it freely in the group so that it can be handled and worked through.[41]

Programming in group work is as large as life itself. What it *really* demands of the group worker is a high degree of creativity and sensitivity to individual, cultural, and group needs. It means a constant keeping up with interests of specific age groups, which change with changing technologies and political and economic circumstances. It includes knowledge of the interests in different social strata and of individual needs.

Much of the present-day programming is probably outmoded. Young people growing up in a technical age will need a different program than was appropriate only ten years ago. Interests of different age groups change. Television has introduced a wide range of knowledge and skill. Activities that previously were appropriate for twelve year olds can now be carried through and enjoyed by eight year olds. In an institution for delinquents, I observed the boredom with which fourteen- and fifteen-year-old boys used crayons. The picture of this group, the satisfaction they received, the contentment that came with accomplishment changed considerably when a more creative group worker got an old broken-down car and let the boys take it apart, learn about the mechanics, and fix it up as much as they could.

We sometimes forget that programming also includes a discovery of new areas of knowledge and enjoyment. Fulfillment of the adventure spirit can be found in trips and in seeing new places and also in the discovery of art appreciation and of new and different people.

A program must also be related to the setting in which it is found. One of the prisons recently initiated the use of certain prisoners as air-raid spotters in regular exercises for civilian defense. The confidence placed in them, the regularity of the assignment, and the feeling of comradeship that developed among the group chosen was of real help in rehabilitation.[42]

Mental hospitals have a long history of little activity for patients. In the past the patient was usually confined and received some psychiatric treatment, but the rest of the day he was left to himself or among other

---

[41]Kurt Lewin, *Resolving Social Conflicts* (New York: Harper, 1945); William Schwartz, "Toward a Strategy of Group Work Practice," *Social Service Review* 36, no. 3 (September 1962): 268–79; and Charles Garvin, "Task-Centered Group Work," *Social Service Review* 48, no. 4 (December 1974): 494–507.

[42]Paul L. Crawford, Daniel I. Malamud, and James R. Dumpson, *Working with Teen-Age Gangs* (New York: Welfare Council of New York City, 1950); Walter B. Miller, "The Impact of a Total Community Delinquency Control Project," *Social Problems* 10, no. 2 (Fall 1962): 168–91; Spergel, "Selecting Groups for Street Service"; and Robert E. Knoll, "Social Group Work in Juvenile Corrections: A Synthesis of Clinical and Group Dynamics Principles," *Social Service Review* 48, no. 2 (March 1974): 87–95.

patients without guided activities. This has changed in recent years. We find in many mental hospitals occupational therapists and some recreation programs. Social group work has only recently entered this field. The specific function of the group worker in these hospitals is to help patients to move slowly into more realistic relationships with others and to try this out constantly in their present situation, by helping them to actively relate to other patients. This can be done only through some common endeavor, either in an activity or through discussions.

Media must be chosen according to the stage in which the patients find themselves. Solitary, frightened patients need a long period of slow introduction to others. They cannot be coaxed and forced into a fast ballgame, for instance. But a patient can sit quietly listening to a music program, just "feeling" the presence of others, then perhaps start a checker game with only one person (sometimes the first one must be the group worker himself), until the patient can join in some project with two or more. There might be no discussion for a long time. Patients in another stage of development might be anxious to talk and need group acceptance and group reassurance. Some such groups have been formed by group workers around the experience of treatment that was frightening to patients, such as shock or insulin. Here the patients could talk out their fears, gaining reassurance from the group worker or from a psychiatrist who was invited or from the fact that others felt the same way.

When such a discussion group was ready to move into some other activity, such as the planning of a ward dance, the group worker had to be ready to accept this change of direction, if it was considered a helpful trying out of new reality. If it was only a running away from discussing some of the more painful aspects of confinement, the group worker had to help the patients to understand that a little more time was needed before moving into the next step. These kinds of considerations are usually discussed among all members of the staff who work with the patients so that each activity becomes the most helpful one. "Program" is not a mechanical device but closely related to treatment, and demands again the knowledge of individuals, group readiness, and imagination.[43]

Only in recent years have we begun to learn that our "old-age" population is not only increasing but is not as we had pictured it. Very few want to "sit and rock." The feeling of being moved out of the general stream of life, of not being needed, of just waiting to die is one of the most desperate ones. A group worker beginning some work in a home for the

---

[43]Jean M. Maxwell, "Group Services: Well-being for Older People," in *Social Work with Groups* (New York: National Association of Social Workers, 1960).

elderly was struck by the unhappy quiet that lay over the place. People living in the same room did not know each other's names: "It was no use." They just sat and stared into space. There had been "entertainment" from time to time, children coming to sing for them at a Christmas party, gifts being distributed. Few realized what an insult such "entertainment" is to people who have led an active and self-respecting life.[44]

How different became the atmosphere in the home when the group worker began to learn—first individually—from some of the inhabitants about their interests. Some of them formed an art group, doing some painting and reporting to each other about some great masters and their various ways of using color and form. This art group became almost a small college course, issuing invitations to experts; finally an exhibit of the work of the group was shown. Another group was more interested in journalism and reported daily events in the home as well as summaries from radio and television. Others did some sewing. During the activities there were lively exchanges of experiences and opinions, not always without conflict, but this made the situation so much more lifelike than its former graveyard conformity. A resident committee discussed special problems among themselves and with management and helped some of the inhabitants to accept more individual help when they needed it.

IV. THE GROUP WORKER AS
TEACHER AND SUPERVISOR

> Volunteers are to Democracy what circulation of the blood is to the organism. . . . The health of a democratic society may be measured in terms of the quality of services rendered by citizens who act in "obediance to the unenforceable."[45]

One of the characteristics of social group work in youth-serving agencies, in settlement houses, and in institutions for children or adults is that the group worker frequently is not doing the direct work with the members of the group. His skill lies in helping others to do the direct group work. We have not yet decided clearly enough when this is appropriate and when it would be better that the group worker do the actual group work. Recent experience shows that groups with difficult psychological or social problems must be handled by the trained group worker, because of the constant need for quick diagnostic skill. This applies, for instance, to

[44]See also: Walker, "The Decision-Making Superiority of Groups."
[45]Edward C. Lindeman, *A Fantasy*, 3rd ed. (New York: YWCA, 1952), p. 4; and William Schwartz, "Social Group Work: The Interactionist Approach," *Encyclopedia (1971)*, pp. 1152–63.

groups in clinics, hospitals, and treatment institutions, and to work with gangs in the community.[46]

There is positive value in having volunteers doing some of the direct group work. In recent years in social work, we have sometimes forgotten that it is one of the basic needs of individual human beings as well as of the society that people have the opportunities to learn to help one another. We have often taken such opportunity away from the volunteer. This has not helped clients or strengthened the spirit of cooperation in our communities. Our young profession, realizing the need for professional approach and understanding, must not forget the importance of the cooperating citizen. The clearer our knowledge becomes, the more we will be able to teach others to carry some of the helping functions.[47]

This will not diminish social work's professional aspect. The professional authority and importance of the medical profession have not lessened with the development of many auxiliary services. The major professional aspect of social work lies in its capacity for *psychosocial diagnosis* of the individual, the group, and the group's situation.

Some groups call for the skill of the fully trained social group worker only, but in some groups this skill can be transmitted to others. The group worker, in order to teach and to enable another person to help, must have a keen appreciation of adults with a view towards their capacity to be helpful. Making use of volunteers or untrained workers is not just a matter of taking anybody who offers his services. It includes careful selection and evaluation of each volunteer's capacities; it means deciding where these capacities best can be used.

The volunteer needs regularly scheduled conferences with the group worker. Such conferences are sometimes conducted in groups and sometimes on an individual basis. The purpose of the conference is not to check up on those who do the direct group work but to help them gain additional skill and insight into their own capacities and weaknesses and to strengthen self-confidence.

---

[46]See Eva Rainman and Ronald Lippit, *Team Training for Community Change: Concepts, Goals, Strategies, and Skills* (Riverside, Calif.: University of California Press, 1973); and Alfred Jacobs and Wilford Spradlin, eds., *The Group as Agent of Change* (New York: Behavioral Publications, 1974).

[47]Leslie Button, *Discovery and Experience: A New Approach to Training, Group Work, and Teaching* (New York: Oxford University Press, 1971); Eva Schindler-Rainman, "Are Volunteers Here to Stay?" *Mental Hygiene* 55, no. 4 (October 1971): 511–14; Thomas L. Woods, "The Study Group: A Mechanism for Continuing Education and Professional Self-Development," *Clinical Social Work Journal* 2 (February 1974): 120–26; M. Hausman, "Parents' Groups: How Group Members Perceive Curative Factors," *Smith College Studies in Social Work* 44 (March 1974): 179–98; and Martin Wolins, ed., *Successful Group Care: Explorations in the Powerful Environment* (Chicago: Aldine, 1974).

Example 1: (Conference between the social group worker and a camp counselor.) We discussed at this conference mainly the question of participation. What is meant by this in practice? Does it mean that if a child does not want to participate we just tell him he can do what he wants to? Sometimes this would be perfectly all right. Not all children like to do the same things at the same time. Yet sometimes there are children who need to get the taste of participation and they actually yearn for help in trying it out. The word *help* has important meaning. Just leaving the child alone might mean rejection. But we also do not want to coerce him. Helping does not mean a gentle prodding either. It is done in terms of the other person and in terms of his particular need. We discussed this in relation to Katie (age eleven). She was in a "no" stage. She would not participate at all but if left alone would feel very unhappy. The counselor found that if she says to her, "You don't have to do this, but I can do it with you," then Katie enters into the activity. The group worker helped the counselor to understand why children at this age will easily say "no" while inside of themselves wishing that an adult would help them.

It was also discussed in this conference that the cabin showed some sub-grouping. The counselor was worried whether this would start "cliques." The group worker helped her see that this development was not necessary even if some youngsters related closer to each other. She helped the counselor to realize that we must not expect all children to love each other to the same degree.

Example 2: (Conference with another group counselor.) The counselor worked with a group of thirteen-year-old boys. He came to this conference very concerned with the fact that he did not seem able to handle the boys, who were quarreling with one another. The group worker started to discuss what the counselor expected of the boys. From the counselor's description it became clear that he had a great need to hear from the boys that they loved him and that they liked everything. The group worker helped the counselor understand that all people feel "two ways about many things." Children can like a camp and still not feel happy about everything. It is all right for a child to think that home, too, is wonderful and feel some yearning for it. The counselor realized that it was chiefly his own insecurity that made him worry if the children did not continually express their happiness.

The group worker and the counselor then discussed the relationship of thirteen-year-old boys to one another. All people at all ages have difficulties adjusting to a new group, especially if it involves a twenty-four-hour living arrangement. At this age, personality begins to be formed, often with much pain, and one's contemporaries are often quite disturbing even though one wants them. Quarreling among boys of that age is to be expected. The question is whether it has become a constant state or whether there are times of real satisfaction and mutual appreciation. This led into the discussion of different forms of programming appropriate to the needs of this age group.

It is part of the education of the social group worker to learn to teach others who do the direct work and to do this in a simple language.

Most of the settings in which social group workers work cannot afford and probably will never be able to afford only trained workers in all the positions needed. This applies to youth-serving agencies as well as to mental hospitals, institutions for dependent and disturbed children, and correctional institutions. Group services usually serve such a large clientele or are spread over such a long period of time—as group living situations—that much staff is needed. It is because of this necessity that supervision becomes such an important tool. In supervision and in in-service training, the social group worker must combine teaching skill with understanding of the individual and the group. Volunteers feel abused and rightfully so if their capacities are not used to the best advantage and if they feel they are treated as second-class workers. Actually, they bring to a program something that no professional can bring: they give patients or group members the feeling that the lay community is interested in them. They can give this only if their efforts are channelled into worthwhile and acceptable work.

Even more important is supervision of personnel in camps or in institutions. The living situation needs to be permeated by a deep understanding of human development and of relationships between those in this situation. It can be the most therapeutic and growth-producing situation. In treatment institutions, it is not enough that children have conferences with caseworkers or psychiatrists. These contacts are exceedingly important, but they must be supported by constant relationship to adults who understand changing moods, deep inner needs, and fears. These adults must also understand the impact of group pressures and the need for privacy and for a balance of activity and relaxation. These daily requirements are difficult to fulfill, and houseparents or counselors need the supportive help of a supervisor as well as a constant learning and rethinking of their own role in relation to the children.

It is one of the problems of education for social group work that in his first assignment the group worker usually is thrown into the role of supervisor and teacher.[48] On the other hand, this makes his work an extremely challenging and responsible task. The curriculum taken by the social group worker, therefore, includes a heavy schedule; besides learning the direct group work method the worker needs classes in supervision and in-service training.

An interesting research project involving the skills and experience of group work methods has been conducted under the auspices of the

[48]Lilian Ripple, ed., *Innovations in Teaching Social Work Practice* (New York: Council on Social Work Education, 1970); Louis Lowy, Leonard M. Bloksberg, and Herbert J. Walberg, *Teaching Records: Integrated Learning and Teaching Project* (New York: Council on Social Work Education, 1973), pp. 85–107.

School of Social Service Administration of the University of Chicago.[49] This project introduced group work methods into the field of public assistance operations by the creation of "work groups" under the leadership of a social worker with a professional degree instead of single caseworkers. In view of the increasing separation of financial aid from social services and aid to families with dependent children, this project seems of special importance because it enables a trained supervisor of a work team to apply his professional knowledge and skills in guiding less well trained workers in public assistance operations. In addition, in cases where an assistant worker may not recognize all the client's needs, a supervisor can help secure the best social services.

Another significant application of social group work skills has recently been made in West Germany. There the lack of an adequate number of university teachers and assistants led to the introduction of small study groups under the leadership of advanced students who were known as "tutors." The work of these small student teams was guided by the methodological principles of social group work and proved successful in preparing both the tutors for advanced academic work and the students for scientific methods of learning and research skills.[50] The principles of social group work developed insight and scientific thinking in students and leaders.

V. GROUP WORK AS A PART OF SOCIAL WORK AND AS A PART OF SERVICE TO HUMANITY

> Social work should not be evaluated, as is sometimes alleged, by a self-liquidating test. Its purposes, historically based, are still concerned with making love instead of hostility effective in human relationships.[51]

In Gisela Konopka's room hangs a picture painted by a young artist that seems to be the symbol of our profession: a street lamp throws a dim light on a wet pavement, bleak tall houses stand in the background against dark

[49]Edward E. Schwartz and William C. Sample, *The Midway Office: An Experiment in the Organization of Work Groups* (New York: National Association of Social Workers, 1972); for another example of a similar project see Sheldon D. Rose, "In Pursuit of Social Competence," *Social Work* 20, no. 1 (January 1975): 33–39. See also: Jacobs and Spradlin, eds., *The Group as Agent of Change*, pp. 365–407.

[50]Ernst Bornemann, "Zur Arbeit mit kleinen Studentengruppen" [The work in small student groups], in *Report of the Twenty-Seventh Congress of the German Psychological Society in Kiel, 1970*, ed. G. Reinert (Göttingen, Germany, 1971), pp. 265–71.

[51]Gordon Hamilton, *Theory and Practice of Social Casework* (New York: Columbia University Press, 1940), p. 371; and Dorwin Cartwright and Alvin Zander, eds., *Group Dynamics*, 3rd ed. (New York: Harper & Row, 1968).

leafless trees. A lonely man hunched against the rain walks on the road. All human beings carry in themselves this loneliness, this feeling of having to walk against bleakness. All human beings have both times of hopelessness and the capacity to fight it. This occurs whether one is three or thirty or sixty years old. Sometimes one can work through this by oneself, but human companionship and understanding are always needed. Sometimes happiness will come through friendship. Often there are outside forces or those in the human being himself that prevent this happy experience.

It is at these moments that the social worker offers help. The moments can be dramatic as they seem in the record of the group of seizure patients, or they can be the simple, everyday occurrences in a teenage group. Whenever they occur, the group worker must muster up all his feelings of sympathy and all his latest knowledge of human beings in society. Again we quote from Gordon Hamilton:

> Social work lies midway between the healing and educational professions and draws on the insight of both. It offers both social treatment and psychological education, depending on human needs.[52]

The borderline between social work and other professional skills can never be drawn tightly. There will be overlapping between the social group worker, the teacher, the psychiatrist (if he does group therapy), and the clergyman. Yet the specific role of the social group worker is to focus on all the needs of the individual in the group and on helping the individual function to the best of his capacities. The group worker must be able to accept the contributions of others, but he is the one who should accept the group situation as a whole and have the skill in either handling it or helping others to handle it. The worker must be the one—not separated from others but in a common endeavor with them—to understand both the individual and the demands made by the group and by society as a whole. He must have the capacity to do social psychological diagnosis and to deal with people individually and in groups. The worker's knowledge and skill involve the understanding and capacity to work with sick and healthy people, with conflict processes and group tensions. It is a big order. It involves much knowledge, skill, and self-discipline. The worker must become something more than a skilled craftsman, something more than a well meaning idealist. . . .[53]

---

[52]Gordon Hamilton, "Helping People—The Growth of a Profession," in *Social Work as Human Relations*, ed. Cora Kasius (New York: Columbia University Press, 1949), p. 5.
[53]Eduard C. Lindeman, "Science and Philosophy: Sources of Humanitarian Faith," ibid., p. 221.

SELECTED BIBLIOGRAPHY

BACK, KURT W. *Beyond Words: The Story of Sensitivity Training and the Encounter Movement.* New York: Russell Sage Foundation, 1972.

COYLE, GRACE. *Group Work and American Youth.* New York: Harper & Brothers, 1948.

DIMOCK, HELLEY S., and TRECKER, HARLEIGH B. *The Supervision of Group Work and Recreation.* New York: Association Press, 1949.

HARTFORD, MARGARET E., and COYLE, GRACE L. *Social Progress in the Community and the Group.* New York: Council on Social Work Education, 1958.

HENDRY, CHARLES E., ed. *Decade of Group Work.* New York: Association Press, 1948.

————. "The Advance of Group Work." In *Social Welfare Forum*, National Conference on Social Welfare, Columbus, Ohio (1955), pp. 35–47.

JACOBS, ALFRED, and SPRADLIN, WILFORD, eds. *The Group as Agent of Change.* New York: Behavioral Publications, 1974.

KAISER, CLARA. "Social Group Work Practice and Social Responsibility." In *Proceedings of the National Conference of Social Work* (1952), pp. 161–67.

KLENK, ROBERT W., and RYAN, ROBERT M. *The Practice of Social Work.* Belmont, Calif.: Wadsworth, 1970, pp. 157–223.

KONOPKA, GISELA. *Therapeutic Group Work with Children.* Minneapolis: University of Minnesota Press, 1949.

————. *Group Work in the Institution.* New York: Whiteside, 1954.

————. "Requirements for Healthy Development of Adolescent Youth." In *Adolescence* (Roslyn Heights, N.Y.: Libra Publishing) 8, no 31 (Fall 1973), 291–316.

————. *Social Group Work—A Helping Process.* 2nd ed. Englewood Cliffs, N.J.: Prentice-Hall, 1972.

————. *Young Girls: A Portrait of Adolescence.* Englewood Cliffs, N.J.: Prentice-Hall, 1976.

MERL, LAWRENCE F., ed. *Work with Groups in the School Setting.* New York: National Association of Social Workers, 1965.

MIDDLEMAN, RUTH R. *The Non-Verbal Method in Working with Groups.* New York: Association Press, 1968.

NORTHERN, HELEN. *Social Work with Groups.* New York: Columbia University Press, 1969.

PHILIPS, HELEN U. *Essentials of Social Group Work Skills.* New York: Association Press, 1957.

REDL, FRITZ, and WINEMAN, DAVID. *Controls from Within.* Glencoe, Ill.: Free Press, 1952.

ROSS, SHELDON D. *Treating Children in Groups.* San Francisco: Jossey-Bass, 1972.

SAROYAN, WILLIAM. *The Human Comedy.* New York: Harcourt, Brace, 1945.

SCHWARTZ, WILLIAM. *New Perspectives on Services to Groups.* New York: National Association of Social Workers, 1961.

SCHWARTZ, WILLIAM, and ZALBA, SERAPIO R., eds. *The Practice of Group Work.* New York: Columbia University Press, 1971.

TRECKER, HARLEIGH B. *Social Group Work Principles and Practice.* Rev. ed. New York: Association Press, 1972.

VINTER, ROBERT D. *Readings in Social Group Work Practice.* Ann Arbor, Mich.: Campus Publishers, 1967.

WILSON, GERTRUDE, and RYLAND, GLADYS. *Social Group Work Practice.* New York: Houghton Mifflin, 1949.

WOLINS, MARTIN, ed. *Successful Group Care.* Chicago: Aldine, 1974.

CHAPTER FOUR

COMMUNITY ORGANIZATION AND SOCIAL PLANNING

Genevieve W. Carter

I. INTRODUCTION

Our emerging new, postindustrialized society is extremely diversified and pluralistic, but the segments are closely interrelated. We do not need a great master plan from the White House. Rather, we should have a process, a number of planning mechanisms at different levels and in different institutional sectors of our nation. These ideas are paraphrased from Alvin Toffler,[1] author of *Future Shock* and a later work, "The Eco-Spasm Report." Toffler's fluid ideas explain the hazards from too heavy a reliance on centralized, national planning where distance and the mixture of diversified groups increase the potential error. Unless you have feedback coming in from the millions of ordinary people whose lives are affected and unless these millions have something to say about correcting and altering these plans, conditions can be created for economic and social disasters far surpassing anything we have yet experienced.

---

[1]"The 'Future Shock' Man Sees More Drastic Changes Ahead—Interview with Alvin Toffler, Author" *U.S. News and World Report*, May 5, 1975, pp. 53–54.

The startling nature of the above theory causes us to reflect and ask questions about the kind of planning processes we have that may be more damaging than no planning at all. Traditionally, to further paraphrase Toffler, planning is dominated by professional experts and governmental bureaucrats. It's based on the notion that plain ordinary citizens are dumb and passive. Toffler goes even further and adds that our social planning (and certainly the economic planning) is elitist and is consequently subject to capture by powerful interests.

Our student groups today are future oriented, and we can expect an increasing interest in their encouragement of participatory social and economic planning. There is, however, a fine line we must draw. How can we develop and enlarge this citizen participatory base and at the same time intelligently use the planning knowledge and technology of the seventies that offer the rational component to planning decision making? There is no possibility of stopping the clock and going back to the rural community meeting halls or to the completely left or right wing for simple instant solutions that may have been recipes for the past. The societal context for industrialization and an ever-growing gross national product can hardly serve as the best context for the next phase of national development.

Social planning, community planning, and community development are the specializations in applied social work that are most sensitive and responsive to the social, economic, and political contest.

We cannot readily substitute the term community organization for social planning unless we quickly incorporate the concept of participation, i.e., community organization processes. There can be social welfare services program planning and design, but the degree or potential for participation of those to be affected is found in the concept of social planning. The ordinary citizen does not need to have the expertise for designing a multifunction social service delivery system in order to have a planning input or to have an opportunity to alter the plan. The more he exercises his participatory role in social planning, the more knowledgeable is his base for expressing his decisions and desired directions.

Student discussions about the evolving practice of social planning and community organization will inevitably lead into issues of what goals should be pursued in intervention into social changes and *what* social objectives should be considered in social planning. The social action enthusiast will have to answer for the methods he uses because the ends, per se, do not justify the means. Means, like goals, have a value or moral context. The social work profession has its common value system for professional behavior and ethics. There is also a common commitment to advocacy for the poor, the disadvantaged, and the unprotected. At the same time, there are certain hazards along the way to consider—helping one group of disadvantaged in the community can bring serious damage to another group. An unwariness of this kind of conflict is irresponsible.

It is good to remember that the professional aspects of community organization practice contain both the technical skills and knowledge as well as the social goals and the value stance.

The present trend in social work education, which educates for generalized social work practice, will, in most schools, offer students ample opportunities to develop and express their social attitudes, values, and goals for today's society as well as for the future unfolding of a better society. In addition to desiring economic stability for all, most students of social work have hopes for a more humanistic society. Community organization, social planning, and social policy will be important determinants in this future.

The sections that follow are practice focused. They are intended to offer a generalized "how-to-do-it presentation," limited to a chapter length. The first main section, "A Developing and Changing Professional Practice," offers a brief review of the literature, pointing out selected books in the field, each of which has contributed a special thrust to practice development. Special attention is called to the enrichment of practice choices over the past decades.

The second section, "Components of Practice," presents a scheme of seven practice components, explaining each and showing how they interrelate in practice.

The third section is called "Profiles of Practice" and is comprised primarily of two practice illustrations. So many pieces make up a case example in community organization that only excerpts from short sequences of practice can be presented within a section of one chapter. Continuing in this section, the writer then attempts to relate the practice components described earlier to the profiles of practice. It should be mentioned that there are similar schemes to this one used for organizational analysis or systems analysis, indicating a feedback loop. One important difference lies in the fact that unlike a management process, which is generally an integral part of a structured social institution or business organization, a community organization process changes launching pads, arenas of operations and casts of characters as planning projects are completed. The arenas shift when new problems are defined, new sets of objectives posed, and another planning thrust or social issue becomes the target for social change.

We will first turn our attention to the changes in concepts and methods in a developing professional social work practice, found in the first major section of this chapter.

II. A DEVELOPING AND CHANGING PROFESSIONAL PRACTICE

Ever since the rapid development of community chests and planning councils in the 1920s and 1930s, there have been several efforts to conceptualize community organization practice, social planning in particular. One persisting central theme has emphasized the improvement of health and welfare service programs and the balancing of community needs and resources. This approach generally led to a series of community need surveys and social agency program inventories. Health and welfare agencies were assessed, and service gaps and unmet needs identified. Attempts were then made, primarily through health and welfare planning councils, to adjust social agency programs to the exposed needs and service gaps. It is interesting to note that survey techniques of community need assessment have not changed much since their development in the 1940s and 1950s. New knowledge has introduced new concepts such as institutional barriers to service utilization, client access to service, or organizational constraints. These notions have added some new dimensions to the traditional community need surveys. In turn, these new and broader concepts have influenced the practice of community organization.

A. Changing Concepts

Most of the early concepts are still relevant, but the range of concepts has broadened. Social planning has continued to be emphasized as a rational approach to more effective use of available resources. Many of the new concepts stem from improved technology for health and welfare planning. Information systems, for instance, have produced more usable data on population characteristics, health information, and service distribution.

Social policy, based on federal legislation for new social programs, has incorporated requirements of a planning phase and a proposed program design that has involved citizen participation. In the early sixties, the nationwide delinquency projects under federal authority included guidelines for community sponsorship, for local participation, and for programs planned on the basis of presumed casual theory, i.e., opportunity structure theory. A few years later, the antipoverty programs, as well as the model cities programs, called for a local target area planning phase before the initiation of the several programs. More recently, the new public welfare social services legislation (Title XX of the Social Security Act) has included a section of law, "Services Program Planning," which provides specific criteria for the process that a state must go through in developing its state plans. This also includes public participation—which is yet to be defined.

As planning concepts move from the voluntary agency platforms to the public organizations and become written into law, we become sharply aware of the changes that are taking place in the social planning arena.

One of the important differences in contrasting our former concepts with some of the current theoretical notions is the broadening of the focus and scope of the planning operations. The Health and Welfare Planning Council of the earlier years was concerned with programs of organized professional health and welfare services as a primary tool in alleviating social problems and social ills as well as individual and family deficiencies. Developing new social services, improving the quality of services, and the coordination of service programs were paramount.

Added to the concepts inherent in these more traditional planning and organizing activities are the more recent interests in a social problem approach as a means of marshalling a range of services as well as effecting community change. Social policy advances are also generally linked to social problem areas and concepts or theory about causation.

Institutional change concepts are now usually included in remedial program plans as well as the services to change or correct individual deficiencies. Institutional change concepts are especially helpful in understanding how certain institutions (hospitals or agencies) tend to reinforce deviant behavior in the young delinquent or the mentally ill rather than alleviate the individual disfunctioning.

Another early conceptual theme was phrased as strengthening the community through citizen participation. This notion has continued to be heavily based on democratic ideology or philosophy rather than on rationally tested concepts. Earlier objectives for community organization practice were directed toward creating and identifying opportunities for strengthening democratic participation in decision making and planning. This notion is still a sound one, but objectives today are more likely to center on end products rather than the process.

A revival of the citizen participation theme was found in the "maximum feasibility" concept of the antipoverty program guidelines.[2] Citizen participation in program planning and agency policy was also a requirement in the Model Cities programs.[3] Participation of the poor in local

[2]The term "maximum feasibility" appears in section 202(a)(3) of the Economic Opportunity Act of 1964. This section defines the Community Action Program, in part, as being one that is "developed, conducted, and administered with the maximum feasible participation of residents of the areas and members of the groups served."

[3]Section 103(a)(2) of the Demonstration Cities and Metropolitan Development Act of 1966 requires that a Model Cities program provide for "widespread citizen participation" in the program.

decision making was viewed as one way of helping the poor gain more control over their own destinies. Opportunities for leadership training at the neighborhood level were budgeted items in these programs. There were concerted efforts to search for and find potential local-level leadership. During this period, the welfare mothers were developing their Welfare Rights Organization. Child care centers financed by federal funds required parent-consumer representation. There have been a few studies on the effectiveness of citizen participation, but none have produced knowledgeable answers because usually we are not clear as to what we expect citizen participation to accomplish. The shift in our concepts of citizen participation from the Planning Council Community Organization period is again one of change in breadth. Formerly, the citizen participation concept meant volunteer participants from upper- and middle-income groups who had a sincere interest in helping those less fortunate. Later, as public services increased, other power elite were added to the citizen participation notion. The more recent inclusion of consumers from poor minority groups, slums, or low-income groups has again changed the earlier concept of citizen participation in community organization. Practitioners in urban development and community development methods have also struggled with the implementation of the citizen participation concept. To their dismay, even the remote, poorest villages frequently have lost the first enthusiasm of broad participation, and the real decision making has been captured by a few village leaders.

It is becoming more clear in neighborhood work that the important decisions are being made further up the bureaucratic stream. The villages in developing countries[4] find that the ten to fourteen governmental services available to them are predetermined products from higher level bureaucracies. The urban areas in industrialized countries find that the federal or state guidelines have already tightly defined the conditions for use of the program funds.

Overall, we have probably accomplished more in the use of rhetoric about the effective participation of the poor (or the consumer group) than we have in finding avenues for the poor to influence decisions about the services that they are expected to use. The use of the phrases "citizen participation" or "local decision making" has actually obstructed clarity because we use these phrases as philosophical notions rather than operationalizing the concepts in behavioral terms that might tell us: At what levels and about what issues are the citizens expected to make decisions?

[4]For instance, both Egypt and India are reexamining the village as the basic unit for organizing rural populations. Clusters of villages are being explored as a more viable unit. As governmental services have become more separated from local interest, new research demonstrations are being developed to reactivate citizen participation as an influence for making these services more responsive to village needs.

What are the options, if any? Which citizens are eligible to decide? Do we expect citizen reaction or action? These and other questions are needed to clarify the vague ideas of citizen participation.

Closely associated with citizen participation is the notion of representativeness, often discussed in the earlier literature on citizen participation. Representativeness was perceived as convening delegates of the welfare services community (agencies, universities, related public institutions, lay leaders, etc). Implementation of planning results depended on involvement of those who were to carry out the plans. Again, this concept has utility and has been the basis of social planning practice principles. Now that most social welfare programs are under governmental auspices, the older concepts of representativeness are inappropriate. There is a recognized distinction between the legislative policy makers who are elected representatives of the people, the technical planners, and the various representative groups of geographic interests. Second, we seldom approach a planning issue with a vision of a total welfare community that operates through a central planning vehicle.

Some of the former concepts have merely changed labels rather than meaning. The concept of readiness has been incorporated into broader descriptions of tactics and strategies. Readiness is a central component in community development .strategies. Readiness may be included in the formulation of feasible goals and subobjectives. Concepts of community need or group needs have changed less, but as technology provides better measures of health and welfare conditions, we do not rely as much on such general terms as social or psychological needs.

An increasing reliance on the developing social science body of knowledge has resulted in the greatest change in use of concepts in community organization and social planning. Advances in social change theories, systems theory, organizational and interorganizational theories, and others have braced the knowledge base for practice. Practice has advanced and become diversified as we have borrowed from the social sciences. The advanced practitioner is not too concerned about a personal practice theory. Rather, he wants to incorporate the available social science knowledge about the phenomena with which he must interact. The theory sources in this area are rich, and the work ahead for theory development lies in the transmission of relevant theory pieces for social planning or community organization practice.

One of the most obvious conceptual changes over the past twenty years has been the gradual weaning away of the community organizer from the caseworker model. No longer are there strained attempts to make casework concepts fit. There is a nostalgic ring to some of the earlier phrases borrowed from casework, such as, the community is the client, the worker's primary role is to facilitate the enabling process, or we must respect the rights of self-determination by the appointed representatives of the planning committee.

B. Major Strategies or Approaches

1. PROCESS ORIENTATION. In the background of practice development in community organization and social planning, the conceptualization first presented by Murray Ross of Canada represents an early landmark.[5] Murray Ross was one of the first exponents of organizing communities for the purpose of strengthening community participation and integration in order to build cooperative relationships and develop experience in groups and organizations for working together on common community problems.

This impetus on process and relationships came at a time when Community Chest and United Fund had established a successful money-raising organizational pattern modeled after a military structure—from the top level strategy engineers to the captains of residential volunteer workers. As planning councils separated form the Community Chest structure to become independent community planning bodies, the emphasis on committee processes and interrelationship between social agencies became a primary approach in social service planning. The Ross-process orientation was opportune and gave planning councils a stronger basis for becoming independent organizations with more distinct methods and goals. The early lessons of the importance of a planning process and community experience in working together on common problems cannot be ignored. This is still an important ingredient in planning and organizing.

When an experienced practitioner goes into a new community, for instance, to direct a new planning agency for the aging, his first step is to assess the participation level and experience of his assigned area. If the community or target area has had little or no experience in working together on common problems, then the substantive program goals must wait until some gains have been made in developing a process, a commitment to the cause of helping the aged, a structure for establishing relationships and communication. Process and structure become the goals for the initial effort. As this phase is accomplished, the process goals achieved become part of the means instead of an end result. Then the primary effort becomes centered on tasks or program objectives. In a small town or unsophisticated rural area, the strategy may take the form

[5]Murray G. Ross and Ben Lappin, *Community Organization: Theory, Principles and Practice*, 2nd ed. (New York: Harper & Row, 1967). The original book by Murray G. Ross, published in 1955, is considered the landmark book in community organization.

of a successful limited task of constructing a first service directory for older people. Such a resource directory for senior citizens serves two process purposes—working relationships are established through a common interest and a short-term project can be successfully completed without conflict or problems of authority. The process and relationship goals may be more important than the service directory product in the initial organizing phase of a long-term community organization project.

As we look at the practice field in perspective, we see that the proponents of community participation and integration as process goals were not proposing a special school of community organization. Rather, this component of community organization was identified and emphasized. If this approach occupied the full attention of the practitioner, we can predict that the completed tasks, jobs completed, or planning outcomes achieved would be minimal.

2. PLANNING COUNCIL NEEDS—RESOURCES APPROACH. Health and welfare planning was earlier defined as balancing community welfare needs and resources. This was the central thrust of the community organization practice described in most of the early professional literature. Every health and welfare agency in the area was expected to be a planning council member. About three-fourths of all social workers in community organization took their field work placements in planning councils or federation-type agencies. This kind of practice represented the community organization and social planning of that period in this country. By the middle of the 1960s, other perspectives of social planning had developed.

As far back as the Lane report,[6] the balance of social welfare resources and human needs has been a central purpose of social planning agencies. The voluntary agency effort in much of the industrialized countries (especially with Christian and Jewish religions) has preceded the establishment of government services and government-sponsored planning. The first service planning efforts were voluntary. A central health and welfare planning organization (with branches or area councils in large cities) was assumed to provide the planning arena for hundreds of agencies and organizations of all types—from hospitals or juvenile probation to dental clinics or city golf courses and swimming pools. Planning activities were generally service or program centered, not problem or issue centered. Although there were a number of large community surveys of needs and health and welfare resources of all types, the magnitude of the planning effort usually resulted in surveys by fields such as family and child welfare, group services and leisure-time activities, and

---

[6]Robert P. Lane, "The Field of Community Organization," in *Proceedings of the National Conference of Social Work*, National Conference of Social Work (New York, 1930), pp. 495–511.

health and medical care resources. Later, more divisions of services were made, but planning issues or the use of a social problem focus are of more recent origin.

One must not discredit the contributions made to the development of social planning and community organization in this country by the Community Chest-sponsored voluntary efforts. These settings offered the first professionalization for the practice as well as providing the origins for the use of social research in social planning. Planning councils today offer well-paid positions and interesting planning functions. No longer do the planning councils supported by United Fund attempt to hold the central planning responsibilities for all the agencies. Their scope is more directed to the voluntary sector, including the large number of volunteers who can be forceful in affecting public social policy.

Unless the contributions made toward professional development in the past are known and are part of the body of knowledge available to social workers, as well as policy makers, there will be continued efforts to rediscover "the whole." Some illustrations of these reminders from the needs-resources planning period follow:

The planning councils introduced the use of target areas and a neighborhood approach to defined, needy geographic areas.

—Indices of need, ratios of service distribution, beneficiary service surveys, high urbanization-rural indices, demographic analysis of planning areas, and criteria for program subdistricts are other examples of planning tools in use today.

—Decentralization of planning activities and decentralization of service delivery followed the pattern of urban sprawl. Most large councils served as the city resource for population analysis.

—One-stop, multiservice centers for veterans returning from military service in the early forties and integrated service centers in poor areas bringing public and private services together under one roof were examples of integrative service planning.

—There were numerous experimental multiservice centers. Results have shown that voluntary arrangements for integrated service centers, where there are no financial rewards for loaned staff or the agency, will hold together only about two years. The initial enthusiasm wanes, the decentralized staff still have their career rewards based in the parent agency, and the agency administration decides it has lost its identity in blurring its service with other related services.

—The so-called "elite citizen participation" of the Planning Council period of community organization continues to marshall leadership, raise money, secure commitment to causes, and get things done as they implement their plans in promoting new welfare services, environmental programs, arts and cultural programs, or major civic changes. We social workers have tended to be so concerned about the changing issues that have been neglected or avoided by these citizen groups that we have sometimes forgotten to enlist citizen support for important changes based on common cause.

—There was only passing attention (except in Settlement House programs) given to consumer reaction to services provided, rights of so-called charity clients, participation of the poor in planning or policy making, and advocacy or challenge against bureaucratic barriers or constraints and only selective actions to effect broad changes in the civil rights picture. In the latter, educational means constituted the primary tool for assisting minority groups.

—A number of lasting principles were established, such as: (1) a service planning organization should avoid combining direct welfare service operations with its planning and coordinating functions; (2) decentralization of services must take into account which services are generalized, more commonly used, or needed by most of the people and which services are specialized and should remain as central or regionalized services; (3) services only for the poor are likely to be poor services unless the recipients have support for grievances or monitoring standards; (4) planning participants receive greater satisfaction when the activities are task centered and there is a concrete output that indicates completion of a phase or project; (5) planning participants of all income or educational levels develop with graduated experiences. It is a disservice to all when the unsophisticated are thrown into committee work with the experienced citizens who represent leadership models beyond the new participants' present potential for interaction; (6) leaders trusted by their peers can repeat the very same words spoken earlier by the professional who is an "outsider," and the peer group will hear what they did not hear before.

3. TOWARDS ADVOCACY AND SOCIAL CHANGE FOR DISADVANTAGED. A third community organization perspective is represented by the writings of Charles Grosser, who terms his position a contemporary view.[7] He turns the social work focus from helping the disadvantaged through organized health and welfare service (Planning Council Community Organization) to an institutional view that sees an individual's inability to cope successfully as a function of social disorganization. He urges the profession to expand its definitions of practice to accommodate the dissembling political behavior connected with social change. In fact, Grosser labels this action for bringing about equity on behalf of the disadvantaged as "social reordering."

Social reform is seen as the primary purpose of the community organizer-planner in social work. Grosser suggests that the total community must be made aware of the social problems as well as of the options for their resolution. He points out that racial discrimination, employment, education, and housing affect the affairs not only of the poor and disadvantaged but also of the total community. That is, poverty is everybody's problem, not just a problem of the poor. Grosser emphasizes social goals as a matter of public responsibility and maintains that the

[7]Charles F. Grosser, *New Directions in Community Organization—From Enabling to Advocacy* (New York: Praeger, 1973).

elements of a good life are the on-going objectives and commitment of professional social workers. The political and social developments of the 1950s and the 1960s are pointed out by Grosser as having special or revolutionary implications for social work as well as for the field of community organization. Changing from a view that focuses on helping individuals overcome their personal inadequacies to one that believes that the inequities in human functioning are due to the inequities in the functioning of our institutions brings about a profound difference in the approach to social planning and community organization.

The Grosser book does not offer much help to the practitioner on how to make the changes, but the author does bring to focus some social change and institutional change issues. He also brings to surface some of the dilemmas and problems facing the practitioner involved in social change goals. This perspective by no means can account for the total range of community organization practice. It makes its impact because of the contrast with the earlier thrust of the processing, integrating, enabling theme that dominated practice for a time. The book reviews some of the early social action so effectively carried out by social workers during the Settlement Movement days. These concepts add flexibility and richness to the range and purpose of social planning and community organization. The professional tool kit of the practitioner offers more choices for selection of a course of action or a manner of practice behavior that best fits the situation and the skill of the worker. The variety also adds to the complexity of what is called social planning and community organization. This is why an advanced curriculum sequence in social work will divide this broad subject area into separate courses: Social Planning I and II, Social Policy I and II, Neighborhood Work, or Working with Institutional Change. Another cut is to combine Service Programs with Social Policy, such as Social Welfare Sequence in Child Welfare or Social Welfare Sequence on Problems of the Aging.

Not only is there the range in substantive content for the formal education of the community organization worker, but, as Grosser emphasizes, there is increased variation in worker roles. His view of social work makes only a passing reference to the casework or therapeutic function of a social worker. By variation of worker role, one infers that more overt action and assertiveness are expected than generally ascribed to community organization roles by other writers. One of the roles emphasized is the social worker acting as broker, where the social worker aggressively functions as negotiator on behalf of client groups to overcome the barriers that prevent or discourage access to services. When the case-by-case method is too slow, then an aggregate solution to benefit the whole class of persons is indicated as a responsibility for the community organizer.

Class action as a major strategy is stressed as one of the tools for social change. Social worker interest in this area of social change is being reflected by educational experiments in joint social work and law degrees as well as by social work graduates who are pursing law degrees. Other roles of advocate, activist, ombudsman, or proponents of nonviolent action are discussed and encouraged as professional components to be considered for enlarging and strengthening the scope and choice of strategies in community organization practice.

Recently, this writer reviewed an interesting doctoral thesis by a young, creative public administration student titled, "The New Guerillas: Public Administration in the New Industrial State."[8] This rather unusual change model draws its organizational change concepts from guerilla warfare tactics. This piece of research from public administration is mentioned because it indicates the variety of social institutional change strategies emerging in related fields.

This section on advocacy and social change stresses the self-generated and assertive concern of the social worker in community organization. Unanswered questions for this type of aggressive practice include issues such as: How does the organizer justify his involvement in attacks on the agency that pays his salary? What are the practice principles that guide the worker in activities (during or after his work day) that border on civil disobedience or may be in direct conflict with his employment conditions? What clues does a worker have for staying sensitive to his continued acceptance by the oppressed group as their advocate? Is he willing to learn the political game rules before he tries to function in the political change processes?

4. SOCIAL PLANNING AND SOCIAL POLICY. In this review of an emerging community organization practice, this writer has omitted a long list of authors in the field. The purpose of pointing out certain contributors is to call attention to a particular practice emphasis. You will recall that our first practice orientation was the process approach where the role set of the community organization practitioner was passive, helping, and enabling. At one time, this approach or general strategy was considered proper for the community organization worker. That is, an enabling process approach was the only way for professional practice in social work for those following the pathways of analytical casework.

During the Planning Council period, the enabling approach was still strong, but community studies, fact finding, and surveys of needs and resources were considered an important component in community organization practice. With this emphasis, the beginnings of increased rationality in the planning process were initiated. The voluntary agency

---

[8]James A. Marshall, "The New Guerillas: Public Administration in the New Industrial State" (Ph.D. diss., U.S.C. School of Public Administration, 1973).

movement dominated the social welfare scene compared to the slowly developing public agency social welfare programs. Social planning and citizen participation were considered as indigenous characteristics of the voluntary agency sector. Social policy and an expanded view of social planning did not influence practice until tax-supported social welfare programs expanded. The professional vigor in the earlier days of social reform and social action dwindled with the increasing youth services programs in the Settlement and Center agencies. As health and welfare public programs increased and gained importance, so did social policy and public agency gain influence in planning.

Although a number of writers had written articles and speeches, Alfred Kahn can be credited with placing social policy and social planning in a position that warranted special attention in the community organization field. In his *Theory and Practice of Social Planning,*[9] he emphasized the rationality in planning and social welfare programming and decision making regarding the options available to policy makers. He called attention to the expert role of the community organization worker, where knowledge of program designs, social policy systems, and social welfare institutional arrangements was central to practitioner efforts in community planning. Kahn's point of view represented a much needed push at that time to move away from the heavy absorbtion in planning committee process agency coordination and the overburdening community planning structure. In a sense, this approach tended to legitimize the special academic and intellectual competence of the professional worker. Social planning practice was developing a social planning expertise whereby the competence might be transmitted through consultation or alternative plans might be analyzed for decision makers, not only for community-based people but for administrators or legislators who were also recognized as social policy makers.

Kahn does not attempt to delineate the planning roles of the community organization worker, the planning organization, or the legislative participants. In fact, the dynamics of the social planning processes are played down as is necessary for some planning structures where participants are to be involved. Kahn does not focus on the practice behavior of the practitioner or how the planning expertise is developed. The social policy analyst is presented as the author's perspective. With the thrust of social policy as a planning approach, a flow of social policy literature has followed. Richard Titmuss,[10] the British social policy leader, has had considerable influence on social planning philosophy, especially in our

[9] Alfred J. Kahn, *Theory and Practice of Social Planning* (New York: Russell Sage Foundation, 1969).

[10] Richard M. Titmuss, "Essays on the Welfare State," in *The Social Division of Welfare,* ed. Richard M. Titmuss (Boston: Beacon Press, 1969), chap. 2, pp. 34–55.

eastern universities. Rein,[11] Krammer,[12] Wickenden,[13] Morris,[14] and others were contributors (even before Kahn, but their writing was not as comprehensive or as integrated).

The impact of this attention to social policy and social planning has been reflected in the curriculum of all graduate schools of social work in this country. International interest in this thrust was taking place a few leaps ahead of the American scene. This is illustrated by the fact that the International Conference of Social Welfare in The Hague had as its organizing theme, "Social Welfare and Social Policy."

Social policy positions of the various countries influence the organizational arrangements of their social welfare institutions. In general, public policy is concerned with reallocation of national or state resources. Welfare and economic policies are closely interwoven with cultural and political values. This accounts for differences between countries and for different emphasis between political administrations in this country. Public social policy development then becomes the most powerful planning tool to affect social change. That is why this section on social policy and social planning adds another dimension to the development of professional practice in community organization and social planning. With this new awareness of social policy as the power center for macro changes, some of the futile committee exercises at the local level are understandable. At the same time, there is a new frustration and a new challenge. How do social workers organize their resources to make an impact on social policy issues? What constitutes intelligent policy analysis? How do students learn to form a stance about policy and about policy positions taken by their professions? Planning goals, then, emerge from clear social policy position statements.

Social planning and social policy will most likely remain as significant specializations for the community organization worker. This is one reason why this writer prefers to keep both terms together for the present period. Social planning and community organization are not the same, but they belong together. The community organization practitioner, the c.o. worker, is a familiar label to keep for the social worker in community work.

[11]Martin Rein, "Social Planning: Welfare Planning," in *International Encyclopedia of the Social Sciences* (New York: Macmillan Co., 1968), pp. 142–54.

[12]Ralph M. Kramer and Harry Specht, eds., *Readings in Community Organization Practice* (Englewood Cliffs, N.J.: Prentice-Hall, 1969).

[13]Elizabeth Wickenden, Hunter College, New York. Prepared by Wickenden for Social and Rehabilitation Service in connection with the United States Committee Report in Social Welfare Policy; Helsinki Conference, 1969.

[14]Robert Morris and Robert Benstock, *Feasible Planning for Social Change* (New York: Columbia University Press, 1966).

5. COMMUNITY ORGANIZATION AND SOCIAL PLANNING. This fifth selected episode in the development of community organization practice is selected because the writers Robert Perlman and Arnold Gurin have attempted to balance the relationship of social work practice and organizational setting with other emerging technologies and rational strategies. Their book *Community Organization and Social Planning* and the companion volume, *Community Organizers and Social Planners*, by Joan Levin Ecklein and Armand Lauffer,[15] represent a landmark because of the broad base from which the material was developed. This is both a blessing and a problem. The Perlman and Gurin textbook lacks an integrating posture, and there is a haunting, persisting plea for a research-based theory that will bind the pieces together. It is rich in what has been known about our practice and leaves the range open for the variations in community organization so essential for differences in goals, organizational and political settings, or practitioner specialization. The universality of community organization practice suggests a basic societal approach needed for all changing societies or for those backward and unable to change. In this country, c.o. workers are organizing in slum areas, in isolated rural sections, or in state legislation lobbies. In other countries, c.o. workers constitute the main stream of social work intervention because the issues and change objectives are broad ones, contrasted with an individual approach. The Perlman and Gurin textbook resulted from several years of field work inquiry sponsored by the Council on Social Work Education under a grant from the Social and Rehabilitation Service of Health, Education, and Welfare. The reader travels over a broad spectrum of practice, service agencies, the voluntary associations, planning organizations, and comprehensive planning including new towns and concludes with a prospect for the future again calling for an integrated, research-based theory.

There is a depth of understanding offered in the text about the relationships of the c.o. worker to his employer agency. The illustrations about social agency adaptation to social change are realistic, with considerable explanation as to "what to do about it." Perlman and Gurin give the community or planning context a good balance of discussion, pointing out how such influences shape the role and the aims of the practitioner.

The authors consider the agency setting for the planning or the organizing work to have the most powerful influence on facilitating or constraining the social action activities of the c.o. worker. Goals and tasks

[15]Robert Perlman and Arnold Gurin, *Community Organization and Social Planning* (New York: Columbia University Press, 1974); and Joan Levin Ecklein and Armand Lauffer, *Community Organizers and Social Planners* (New York: Columbia University Press, 1974).

are mentioned, but Perlman and Gurin do not come to terms with the c.o. worker's skill in assessing the congruence between action objectives of the particular planning project and the agency mission. For example, voluntary agency goals are notoriously vague and appealing. This serves to rally the needed constituency and keeps the unifying umbrella of social purposes flexible. When the goals are made operational, the conflicts surface. Goal and value conflicts of parent agencies are predictable.

One of the rewarding themes that runs through the Perlman and Gurin text is the continuing reminder of the social work base of c.o. worker practice and the commitment to building a better society, the alleviation of social problems, and the attainment of larger goals of social justice and individual self-fulfillment.

This fifth approach was selected not because it called our attention to a neglected area or an emerging thrust of practice, but rather because it attempted to call the whole community organization family together for a well-rounded review.

III. COMPONENTS OF PRACTICE

To some extent, this section follows the generic, broad perspective of community organization and social planning as described in the Perlman-Gurin textbook. Since this account is limited to only one section, there was the choice to carve out one service field as a specialization, such as mental health, aging, and child welfare, or to cut across the community organization field at a level where there are basic understandings that have meaning for all specializations. It is this latter course that this section has pursued.

The writer's position about the search for a research-based theory of community organization follows along this line. There is not likely to be any integrating theory for community organization practice now or in the near future. We can expect to advance in theory-based tactics and techniques at the middle-range level, where theory pieces give guidance to tactics and techniques. For instance, some theory-based tactics flow from communication theory, some from organizational behavior, numerous ones from social change theory. Defusion theory also offers other useful notions to guide action in effecting change in operations. There is no likely road map that will stake out a course or sequence of decisions that will identify the techniques the c.o. worker should select to use at each particular instance.

At one time it appeared as if practice models might be developed that would be characterized by a central purpose. For example, Jack Rothman has described each of three models of community organization practice in terms of a twelve-dimension scheme, such as the nature of the problem, the power structure to be used, the type of target client group, etc.[16] The practice model for locality development (similar to community development) would serve as a predictable model to be followed in working with a situation where the population was homogeneous and where there was considerable goal consensus.

In practice reality, there is seldom a planning or organizing situation that can be contained in any one model. A developmental approach model may be appropriate for a first phase. When events change, some parts of the second model, community planning, may be more appropriate. It is also possible in the same endeavor to carve out a piece of action that would borrow some parts of model three on social action, where resource alteration and changing power relationships are strategies employed.

The infinite possibilities in community organization situations have defied an integrating theoretical approach for practice. The predictable ordering of events or consequences is found in the body of theory about the social phenomena. Choices of change strategies or tactics can be inferred, but there is not likely to be any typology of social problems or planning situations that can be matched with prescribed sets of roles, strategies, or tactics for the community organization worker. If the uniqueness of the individual, as well as of the therapist, deters generalizations in the study of clinical practice, the variations and numerous possibilities of a neighborhood unit and especially larger targets for social change are progressively more complex.

In accepting this general viewpoint about the futility of the integrating-theory search, it is possible to view the practitioner as a linking agent who works from research-based knowledge at times and from inference and discretionary decisions at other times. He orchestrates the essential ingredients that are brought together in the best possible proportions at appropriate times. These components or essential ingredients of practice can be posed and described. Professionals may use differing nomenclature or even different divisions in identifying the elements, but the meaning or intent of the components will be understood by almost all practitioners.

A simple-appearing schema is presented here to illustrate how the seven components we selected interact in community organization practice. The community organization worker is placed in the center of the orbit because he draws from each component with varying intensity and frequency. Circular lines are used because the sequence in practice

[16]Jack Rothman, "Three Models of Community Organization Practice," *Social Work Practice* (New York: Columbia University Press, 1968). Copyright National Conference on Social Welfare.

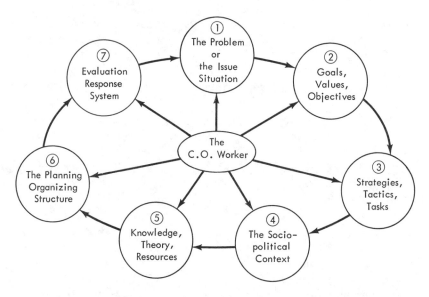

Figure 1   Components of Practice

progression is not linear. It does not always move from step one to step two in order. The components also have varying weights at different times.

The seven practice components listed around the orbit are: (1) the problem or issue situation; (2) goals, values, and objectives; (3) strategies, tactics, and tasks; (4) the sociopolitical context; (5) knowledge, theory, and resources; (6) the planning, organizing structure; (7) evaluation-response system.

After a brief explanation of the proposed seven components of practice, we will illustrate these component parts using a simple, uncomplicated community organization situation. Following the short example, we will try out the schema at a practice level that is more sophisticated and that utilizes each one of the practice components.

The number sequence for the seven components of practice may represent a pattern of the most typical order for a continuing community organization or social planning project. Component number one is the essential starter. Without a problem, an issue, or a social concern, it is difficult to imagine how an organizing or planning process could get off the ground.

1. THE PROBLEM SITUATION OR SOCIAL CONCERNS. This double label implies that there are social planning or community organization activities that are not always focused on social problems or malfunctioning. For instance, there are numerous citizen efforts to improve the qual-

ity of life, to enrich the environment, to provide developmental activities, to initiate prevention programs, to offer equal opportunities to women, or to recruit minority leadership.

Social concerns are a part of the value system and often change as time passes, such as concern about the sale of alcoholic beverages on Sunday or concern about neighborhood interference with the use of police helicopters with their bright floodlights.

A social problem or a community problem is never without its situational context. Textbooks on social problems redefine and reorganize social problems with each new edition. Labeling of concepts changes over the years. The child abuse problem has been separated from the former child welfare problems of dependent and neglected children. Giving birth to an illegitimate child, with its long history of moral overtones, is now generally considered a social problem only for the poor because it is an added tax burden. For those who are affluent or famous, illegitimate children may be considered part of a new life style for the single-parent family.

There is no universally accepted list of defined social problems because the boundaries differ as technological, economic, and social trends change and as public opinion and the political climate shift. For example, the list of poverty-related problems has faded from the priority position held in the 1960s. The recent "crime on the streets" programs represent a rephrasing of a social problem that was defined by some groups as the right for legal equity and social justice. Similar problems are formulated differently depending on the social context. Delinquency as a social problem may be emphasized during a period when middle-class fears are aroused about school-age drug abuse. Mental illness may continue to be recognized as a social problem because of the on-going mental health educational programs.

Social problems or dysfunctioning situations do not emerge as clearly identified and defined problems. They begin as areas of concern —something is wrong, people are worried, or people want to see some changes in a troublesome situation. From this area of social concern or as part of a larger problem, a problem for planning focus is finally roughly described.

Community problems emerge more sharply when there is a crisis, an event that draws attention, or an expression of anger or fear from irate citizens. A problem situation is reinforced, i.e., twenty-three elderly patients burn to death in a firetrap institution, ten runaway youths are identified in a mass sex murder, a bus loaded with elementary school children is hit at a blind crossing. Experienced organizers are always alert to timely events that create a crisis and generate a high energy level for quick community response to a long-neglected problem.

The target for the planning process, i.e., organizing attention, may be limited to one aspect of a problem. For example, a lack of public awareness and education regarding the poor nutrition of older people may be the part of the aging problem that is initially selected for attention. If lack of public awareness is one aspect of the aging problem that seems to have first priority, then community organization practice may follow an educational approach. If the focus is on service integration for the aged, the community organization practice would likely lead to a plan for coordination of services where the organizing efforts are directed to more effective linkages between several streams of service for older people.

Community or social problems, like individual problems, can readily be partialized so that one or two manageable aspects can be handled at a particular time. Rather than having work go off in all directions at once, an action focus that is within the resources and capabilities of the worker and participants is often defined. Sometimes the partialization of the problem situation is based primarily on consensus; that is, readiness of participants and the community (or constituency) to join together in collective efforts. Other times, such factors as the urgency of a crisis situation, astute political timing, or the expertise of the worker may influence the focus of the problem. Sometimes an organized action group may begin with the portion of the problem that has high appeal to a group of participants only to find out later that they must back up and start over again because of the disclosure that expected necessary power or support will not be forthcoming.

Social problems stem from multiple causation; they are complex and interrelated with other social problems. Usually both institutional changes (including policy) and individual case changes are involved. The potential for partialization is limitless. The success potential for the piece of action selected depends on how the problem situation is formulated and what resources and power are within the reach of the sponsoring organization, the worker, and the participants.

A redefinition of the problem situation to be pursued generally must adapt to available power and resources. In turn, the objectives are redefined as the problem is reformulated. Choices of strategies and tactics then must fit the objectives for the changing problem situation. Sending a letter of protest to the county welfare director about the new mandatory employment registration for AFDC mothers illustrates use of inappropriate strategies and an inappropriate selection of the problem focus. It also indicates that neither the objectives nor the means (strategy) were carefully considered. Action aimed at county level for changing federal level policy shows that there was an insufficient analysis of the forces causing the problem and forces needed to change the situation.

A problem situation becomes a target for change in a defined, desired direction. The interplay between (1) the problem situation, (2) the goals and objectives, and (3) the means or change tactics is closely interwoven. When one of the three components is reformulated, the consequences for the other two must be immediately reconsidered.

2. GOALS AND OBJECTIVES. At a high level of abstraction in the context of an implicit value system, we have what might be called societal goals. Human service agencies will have generalized goals expressing character-developing objectives, the enhancement of family life, building informed citizens for tomorrow, or fighting mental illness or tuberculosis. These broad health and welfare goals are always compatible with common societal goals. They serve as an umbrella to cover an area for a social course and a common commitment. Governmental organizations also make pronouncements of goals, usually in the form of a mission statement. The board goal statements seldom arouse conflict. It is only after some of the particulars are known that the controversy starts. Expansive program objectives may shrink considerably after eligibility requirements are announced, after funding constraints are exposed, and after the level, type, and amount of benefits are described.

We can recall instances of extravagant goal descriptions by agencies starting a new program. For example, goal interests are described for combating some rare disease where statistics are given on incidence, death, or a lack of research attention for the cure. After an explanation of the importance of the work that needs to be done to prolong the life of those afflicted with the problem, the program offered is found to be limited to an educational and information service staffed by volunteers who have a personal or family interest in that type of health problem. The point made does not intend to discourage parents and family members who organize services on a common-interest or shared-problem basis. Rather, the point is that while the objectives of the services are legitimate and helpful, in no way would the services offered reach the ambitious goals attributed to the program. The formulation of program goals and objectives that are out of reach of the resources available may initially attract attention, but public donors, as well as taxpayers, are becoming increasingly sophisticated about overly ambitious program goals.

The community organization worker also must help to keep goals and objectives at a feasible level; otherwise successful achievement may never come. Organizing goals are often vague, with pleasing rhetoric. But as soon as plans for action begin to be operationalized, the objectives have to be made plain enough to guide behavior or to suggest alternative plans and steps toward accomplishing something. A blackboard or newsprint can be used to pose tentative, concrete objectives. Often the c.o. worker formulates two or three immediate objectives and perhaps a longer range one on a portable blackboard. The objectives are tested out for consensus. After the c.o. worker has demonstrated the technique of writing concrete objectives, very soon other participants are ready to formulate objectives that can be expressed in operational terms. The formulation of planning objectives requires learning and practice.

Let us take an example of an objective statement that is too abstract and at too high a level to be practical or useful to a group of planning participants. "For those children without homes of their own, our purpose is to secure permanent homes in adoptive families so that these children may develop into self-sufficient, productive citizens." This goal statement promises self-sufficient adults whom the public will not have to support with tax money—an ultimate goal that can hardly be tested even fifteen years from now. This type of goal statement does not give guidance for immediate efforts. If we restate the goal in concrete terms to guide our activities, it may read to this effect:

To organize a countywide planning commission known as MARC (marshalling adoption resources for children) in county government-sponsored foster families

To enlist support and cooperation of agencies and other resources, particularly legal services, to be involved

To conduct a screening survey of the foster children case load, which is estimated at 970 children

To select (or "cream off") the first ten percent of children's cases most ready for relinquishment and adoption and begin the project with those cases

To organize needed integrated community resources by using a team approach for each child (social worker, lawyer, doctor, other)

To identify one lead adoption agency to accept all the children who are relinquished or to refer to other appropriate adoption agencies

To transfer the adoption resource and relinquishment activities to an ongoing adoption agency in the community

To disband the county commission known as MARC as soon as this transfer is completed

A series of operational objectives can readily move into a work plan and time schedule for completion.

Goal attainment means we are working toward an expressed outcome and that all concerned will know what this goal is and when the goal is reached.

We expect to have three home-care team units in the field by January 1975— providing integrated home services to one hundred aged homebound. By January 1976 we will have ten units in operation, considered as the optimum for cost effectiveness.

In the first year of our project on drug abuse education for school-age youths, we will have completed a report on the nature and incidence of drug abuse by youth in our town. After our study commission has discussed our report with the board of supervision, we will set new objectives.

Our goal in improving public housing opportunities for the poor is a modest one as a first step. Our objective is to retain the level of housing now available and prevent the sale of Woodland Gardens to a private firm, which would reduce public housing for the poor by 350 family units.

Our objectives the first year of our efforts will be to provide a forum for exchange of ideas or to explore what could be done about the increasing numbers of out-of-school, unemployed youths. At the conclusion of our first phase, we will sponsor a joint workshop or conference with the involved agencies, youths, and other community leadership.

In our organization, we have a five-year goal, but our first steps will be to establish a direct linkage between our agency and our state-level legislators. At the same time, we will offer legislative workshops so we can learn first hand about the political processes involved in state and federal legislation in the welfare field. Our third immediate objective is to develop an assembly made up of interlocking membership for other civic and social action groups with special interest in welfare reform. These three objectives should move concurrently during the first twelve months. Later we will consider federal-level connections. The terms *goals* and *objectives* are frequently interchanged. In using the construct of a *goal hierarchy*, the term *goals* is used at the higher abstract levels and the terms *objectives* and *subobjectives* are expressed in progressively more concrete and operational language.

Without goals and objectives, there are no structures for integrating the plans and participants. Participants can tolerate only a limited amount of ambiguity about what they are trying to achieve. When the action is task oriented and goal directed, the community organization process leads to an outcome, one of the milestones of completion or ending for that phase or episode.

A decision about the selected problem focus, the goal or level to be attained, the time structure, and other essentials of structure cannot take place in committee discussion unless there is an input of information on which to plan the efforts. The quality of the planning discussions and program designs depends on available knowledge on, for instance, drug abuse alternative-treatment programs. Theories of causation, statistics on incidence, new demonstration, and research results must be available to the planning specialists and/or the decision makers. Planning participants and other specialists in the community or region bring resources to bear in formulating goals and objectives that can guide the planning efforts. When the c.o. worker does not have the resources himself, he knows where they are and possible ways of bringing them to the planning situation.

3. STRATEGIES AND TACTICS. You will note the interchange of terminology in the community organization literature as to the activities of the community organization (c.o.) worker. Some writers are careful to use the term "professional social worker," which distinguishes the for-

mally trained from the untrained. Others will use a more lengthy phrase of "social worker in community work." This supposedly is a broader term that includes all the organizing activities such as neighborhood work, social planning, social action, community development, health, education, and such. Different localities and different position classifications use different terms. There is no standard nomenclature, and the title of who does the organizing does not tell us very much about what was done or what is being accomplished. In this section of the book, terms will be used interchangeably, and there is no intent to offer an official glossary of position titles.

What is being done by the c.o. worker should have more importance for understanding practice than *who* does it. What gets done or what has been achieved is the most important matter, yet too often it is neglected. Attempts to isolate the activity units that make up the domain of community organization practice activities have not been very successful. A task is considered the smallest activity unit that has a beginning, an end, and a purpose for the action. When tasks are quite concrete or readily replicable, there can be standards for performance levels and work output expectations. Tasks that are primarily prescribed (there is a rule for the task or an accepted way of doing it) can be observed or described. For example, there may be a rule that says, "Notice of the next board meeting and the minutes of the last meeting must be mailed to members ten days in advance of the meeting date." Mailing out the notice constitutes a task that the secretary usually handles for the c.o. worker because it is a prescribed task. The secretary may have notes or tapes for the c.o. worker, who has the task of preparing the minutes for distribution. A task increases in complexity as more professional discretion is needed. Minutes of meetings can be limited to a standard format where only formal actions are recorded. Preparing minutes that are thoughtfully written, selectively checked for accuracy with certain of the participants, and prepared as an educational tool for subsequent meetings and policy development constitutes a task of a high order. Some ten to fifteen decisions on the part of the c.o. worker may have to be incorporated into the preparation of the minutes of a meeting.

With the task viewed as the smallest meaningful unit of c.o. practice activity, strategies or major approaches are, by contrast, the macro units of practice. Sometimes a strategy may be formalized as a model where key concepts to be used are identified and where certain key elements of practice are systematically defined and the interrelationships are known or assumed. The use of models for direct service delivery is more prevalent than models of practice because organizational structure, program design, and target groups are generally concretely described as part of the model. Some professionals may use the term "the role of the c.o.

worker"; others may say he is using an educational model; others use the language of major approach or major strategies. There is some overall rationale that guides the selection of alternatives in how one gets started, what the first step will be, what time limits might be imposed, if the worker's style will be heavy on leadership out front, if he will be an assertive actionist, or if he will enter the planning scene as the supportive technical resource for facilitating the actions of several well-established community leaders. The variations in situations are many and almost endless if we attempt to include all possibilities. Fortunately, two kinds of development reduce the complexity of the decisions to be made by the individual c.o. worker on the job. Fairly early in practice, the practitioner learns about his own natural abilities, his interests, and in what areas he receives the greatest professional satisfactions and development. Second, at different age periods, c.o. workers change interests and seek employment that allows more leeway for their special competence; as a c.o. worker becomes specialized, the range of decision-making requirements becomes more narrow. Seldom is a c.o. worker highly effective in local-level action and advocacy and also equally effective as a legislative lobbyist in social welfare at the state or national level.

The general strategy or general approach of choice must be within the stretch and competence of the c.o. worker. Some c.o. workers have a wide stretch for role changes. Others learn their role limits and skillfully develop participants who can fulfill the requirements of the major approach that best fits the situation.

Examples of major strategies have been mentioned, i.e., a process-oriented approach to develop motivation, integration, and communication among participants; a crisis-theory approach that utilizes aroused-citizen energy; an educational approach that brings a message to potential citizen participants; an aggressive civil disobedience strategy where publicity and attention appear to be necessary for social reform; a highly rational approach with social planning alternatives, relative costs, and such.

Below the level of broad strategies or approaches, there are tactics and techniques. These are middle-range activities, tools in the professional tool kit. These tactics often have theory prices or predictive hypotheses behind them such as "doing it this way, in this type of circumstance, usually results in this kind of consequence or this expected outcome." Some samples of tactics and techniques based on concepts are:

Reinforcement—as planning participants make gains, achieve results, and identify courses for certain social problems, the worker may strengthen this process by using tactics of rewards (awards, press notices) and tactics of encouraging expressions of praise and overt agreement by peers. The c.o. worker may set a model for praising accomplishments that is followed by praise from a peer group—the best of the rewards. Appropriate reinforcement often alleviates competitive tensions and conflicts among participants, particularly organizational representatives.

Shared objectives gained through the use of consensus and common commitments to a cause, a deadline, or a level of achievement. Group commitments are stronger than individual objectives or promises. A management-by-objectives system involves staff, boards, or related leadership to jointly formulate goals, to set their own time limits, and to decide on the level of performance needed to create a climate of commitment where everyone works to get things done.

Partialization tactics to gain a focus on an action problem or set of planning objectives by selecting a manageable piece of a larger area of concern. Some parts of large problems are amenable to change; some parts require resources of power that are out of reach, and some aspects of the social problem area cannot be handled until certain legal issues are settled. In these latter or similar instances, partializing the problem not only sets a focus that makes the plan for operations more clear but also allows for objectives for some successful outcomes that are feasible.

Later in this chapter we will return to the tasks, tactics, and strategies in the practice of community organization and social planning. As one moves from the problem or area of social concern to the practice component termed "goals and objectives" and then to the component called "strategies and tactics," it becomes apparent that these component parts are closely interrelated. Each one affects the other. At first observation, the scheme on page 176 looks as if there might be an orderly progression from steps one through seven around a smooth oval pathway from Social Issue to Evaluation. It is already quite apparent that this is not the case. The social issue to be selected for focus may resist clarification until there has been a "once around" assessment for each of the seven components. In brief, the c.o. worker (and participants) look over the warehouse shelves to find out what there is to work with before starting the action. On the other hand, sometimes the c.o. worker can be asked by the city council, for instance, to take on an organizing task. After exploring only one component, the social-political context, the worker decides before starting that this is no time to become entangled in a political fight with city council members.

4. THE SOCIAL-POLITICAL CONTEXT. This component influences community organization practice at every level of decision making, from organizing a tenant's committee in a public-housing project to testifying as a witness before House hearings on health care resources available for the senile aged. The influence of the political, economic, and social context in the shape of community organizations and social planning is

more readily understood when observing social planning in other countries. Social planners in this country do not have much to say when c.o. specialists in other countries worry about such issues as how to narrow the income distribution range between the rich and the poor, or how they can get a higher priority of available national resources for the growing urban aging population from their national social planning commission.

We, in this country, do not have a national social planning body. We do not have a national planning structure to develop or propose direct measures for redistribution of income in this country. If there were such a structure, the issue of income redistribution would not be compatable with a competitive free-market society. We do not overemphasize government-supported employment (government-created jobs), nor do we overtly plan for a full-employment policy. When we are asked by c.o. specialists in other countries why we have no social development programs or why we do not promote social development goals, we quickly recognize the contrasts in the political-social context of the various countries. These different national settings result in different institutional arrangements and value bases for special welfare undertakings. Human needs are quite universal, as indicated by various cross-national studies on foster children, mentally retarded, rehabilitation, the aged, working mothers, or university student revolts. Institutional patterns for meeting these common needs vary according to the social, political, and economic contexts of the country.

Because we are so much a part of the community context in which we live, we are not sensitive to similarities and some of the differences between neighborhoods, towns, counties, states, or nations. The community worker must be able to detach himself from his own set of values and beliefs or he will fail to recognize significant value sets in other communities or population groups. This means more than mere tolerance for other points of view or other social welfare arrangements. Such understanding of other value situations should have an effect on the worker's mode of operating, on his choice of words and the tactics for the planning and organizing activities.

Increasingly, we find that differences in religious preference have little influence on value sets held by population segments. Age of adults and age of children indicate sharp differences in priorities for planning attention. Young families with preschool children will be active in the community for purposes of child care, recreation, safe traffic, and immunization programs. Older, middle-class parents with teenage children are anxious about drug and alcohol abuse, the generation gap, gang activities, sex education, and flexible vocational and other educational programs.

There are "bible belts"; rugged individualism sections; conservative, suspicious regions; and population pockets of insulated minority groups. There are communities where all decision power is centralized in three families, or communities where decision centers are entirely different for different planning arenas—this group runs the schools, this one is active in the opera and other cultural arts, or that segment is the only place to find a ready interest in social welfare issues.

Economic changes at various times also affect the social planning context. There is a greater tolerance for assistance payments to welfare mothers, extension of unemployment insurance, or food stamp programs when people are worried about the possibility of the economy slump reaching their own income source. When most working people are holding their own, there seems to be a greater hostility toward welfare issues. The strong beliefs in this country about the ever availability of jobs for those who really want to work are quite constant and usually change only for those who have lately had some first-hand experience. Because of the variations in the intensity of social value beliefs, certain social programs will be acceptable in some places and not in others. The expression "a hand-out program" reflects feelings about individual responsibility and the importance attached to working for what you get.

As public programs continue to dominate the American scene, the social welfare institutional arrangements for the major resources within a state are quite similar around the country. Federally supported programs do differ as to how they are structurally arranged. Some states will have superstructure arrangements attached to the governor's office. In most states, the local control is primarily at the county level, and county leadership is strongly active at the capital, where legislative changes take place.

The new c.o. worker in a community needs a crash education program to learn the whereabouts, the history, the line of authority, and the inner workings of the major public resources to be involved in the organizing activities. Demonstration and research funds are generally identified with federal government regional offices. Having the information about funds and resources for program expansion or experimentation is part of the c.o. worker's professional tool kit.

The effects of political context and location of power are pervasive throughout most planning and organizing work. The growth in personnel and budget over the past ten years for governmental units at the state and county levels attests to the developing local power and public services planning. The several levels of government affect the various public programs differently. Changes at the state level nearly always have an impact on welfare service programs within the limits possible under Federal Financial Participation (FFP). Partisan political changes in federal government administration can have dramatic effects on decreases or increases in human services programs, as well as on other, related public social policies—tax relief, school scholarships, home ownership. Increasingly, social planning prospects in some areas of human needs are closely tied to the political climate and to party platforms.

At a less complex level, the c.o. worker may enjoy an entry into a small farming town on the Mississippi River where he gets to know his way around in a few days. Under the introduction and guidance of the Farmers' Cooperative Council, he is given a welcome tour and orientation. There is quick consensus by those concerned on the organizing project and objectives that can be achieved within the existing time limits and resources. There are numerous c.o. efforts, where events at international, national, state, or county levels do not impinge on the community organization objectives that are feasible and contained within the resources of a locality.

On the important human survival issues, such as food, clothing, shelter, jobs, and health care, the political climate and federal-level support control the needed resources. Social policy then becomes the all-powerful tool for social planning on the big issues.

5. BODY OF KNOWLEDGE. The community organization and social planning practitioner draws from a body of knowledge that is research based, as well as from knowledge segments that are based on varying degrees of validation. Social intervention programs that are established and stabilized are not easily responsive to rigorous research measurements. Innovative and developmental service programs are even more difficult to evaluate or analyze because of the changes that must be introduced and because newly organized services adapt to meet desired objectives. Keeping abreast of relevent current information about program demonstrations or innovations is part of the job of the c.o. practitioner. This constitutes one important source of professional knowledge, even though the methods used and the effectiveness of such experience have not appeared in the literature. If practice were limited only to research-validated knowledge, we would exclude the many opportunities for trying out the new and untested approaches or tactics that later become hypotheses or assumptions for research testing.

The knowledge base for practice on "how to do it" constitutes a different order of facts and ideas than the body of theory and literature about the social phenomena with which we work. In this area of theory and research about social problems, social structure, or social institutions and organizations, there is a rapidly growing pool of social science knowledge.

Let us first examine the available knowledge pool from which we seek c.o. practice guidelines. There is a closer association with the social service knowledge that explains the social phenomena with which we work and the knowledge on "how to do it" than is at first recognizable. It is primarily from enriched understanding of behavior of people, organizations, or communities that the practitioner derives clues and guidance for his line of action. For example, inferences for action can flow directly from understanding of organizational behavior.

Without research-based knowledge, the practitioner follows principles or assumptions that are really ad hoc hypotheses. We are saying: given this kind of situation, if I act in this way, I should expect this type of consequence or result. The practitioner's behavior is not based on what he feels like doing at the moment, but rather he consciously directs himself according to the requirements of the situation. Some of a worker's behaviors are practiced until they become internalized, and this learned behavior appears to be a part of the person. Other self-directed practice behaviors are unique for the situation, guided by the best knowledge available to the practitioner.

The most comprehensive attempt to systematically connect available published findings having a close relationship to the choices of practice behavior is found in the Jack Rothman book *Planning and Organizing for Social Change.*[17] Rothman also points out that most of the original studies that he reviewed were about the social phenomena, not about mechanisms as the processes that constitute social intervention or the "doing" of community organization. Rothman does not attempt to pose an integrated role theory framework, but rather uses theory pieces such as principles guiding practitioner role sets or dynamics of role performance. This writer has referred to similar concepts as the approach used or major community organization strategies. The categories used by Rothman may differ from those posed by other writers, but the meaning and intent of concepts with differing nomenclature are readily understood. Those who are veterans in this practice field will find considerable reinforcement in reviewing the action principles that Rothman has enunciated. Many of the principles drawn from repeated studies with the same conclusions are the familiar principles (or truisms) that have emerged from pragmatic practice experience and have been seen to work.

For beginning practitioners, the use of the action principles will likely require some interpretation from faculty or a fieldwork supervisor, who can assist the student in linking the abstract generalization to the reality of the practice situation. Learning the practice may be facilitated more by bringing in the bits of practice from the field and linking the action with Rothman's guidelines. It is the playing back and forth of what is happening in the actual practice and the rationality of theoretically

---

[17]Jack Rothman, *Planning and Organizing for Social Change* (New York: Columbia University Press, 1974).

based action principles that furthers the development of professional competence.

Rothman's book results from systematic application of research findings on practice to one thousand studies from thirty journals over a period of six years. Journals in sociology, political science, applied anthropology, psychology, social psychology, and various practice fields were reviewed. The other major source of knowledge for practice comes from textbook publications that offer social science explanations about phenomena such as social change, social problems, or community behavior. Authors of such books generally process and integrate what is known in a selected area within a chosen framework. A book of readings is another approach to offering the reader a number of perspectives or related aspects within a selected focus. Some have been prepared specifically for community organization practitioners, and others are directed to students of major disciplines. Sociology, social psychology, anthropology, and economics are examples of disciplines that are closely related. Education, law, psychiatry and medicine, and public administration are examples of interrelated practices that often share knowledge interests. The problem that faces the teacher student, or expert practitioner is one of selectivity of literature and criteria of relevance. For the latter, there is the translation problem. Out of all the interesting findings, what will enrich our practice or improve practitioner decision making? What action can be inferred from this understanding of the social phenomena with which we work? How does this piece of action or validated action fit in with the overall sequence of activities in which the practitioner is engaged?

As mentioned earlier, the practitioner learns much from ongoing demonstrations, new patterns of reorganizing service delivery, or service innovations introduced for testing. States, localities, or communities are continually alert to new ways of more effectively conducting human service programs. Often there are political pressures for change, usually to save tax dollars or to respond to the public clamor for a decrease in crime.

Some of the typical social welfare demonstrations or organizational changes of which c.o. practitioners are often expected to be informed are the following:

1. A neighboring state has launched a reorganization by establishing an umbrella human services superstructure. It has been in operation for a year. Staff training and development have been merged for all programs, i.e., vocational rehabilitation, public welfare social services, mental health services, and juvenile delinquency programs. A similar proposal is under discussion for this state. Local communities want to be informed and make recommendations to their state assembly.

2. Two rural counties in the state have been experimenting with a mobile team unit for integrated social services to individuals and families. The director of the Rural Community Development Project in this county has been asked to assist in developing a similar plan or some other new method that would bring services to these outlying areas.
3. The welfare commissioner of the state has called together a group of county directors to discuss the feasibility of having the local level comply if the state welfare department is required to participate in a Planning Program Budget System (PPBS) now under consideration. The local county director wants some briefing before he goes to this conference—where else is PPBS used, does it work, and what kind of data would the county be asked to produce from its welfare files?
4. The chairman of the evaluation committee of the demonstration project wants the c.o. worker to brief him about social indicators. Can they be used for program evaluation? Why don't we use them? How or where do they work? Is there an expert on this in the community?

There is no practitioner who is an expert on all the possible tools that might be used in social welfare planning and programming. Techniques used by management are becoming better known to c.o. practitioners, especially those who are close to social welfare planning, program design, and evaluation. Fortunately, the practitioner does not need to know everything, but he does want to know where to find the resource expert with the knowledge.

Finally, one more area of knowledge that must be mentioned in this brief overview of knowledge as a component in community organization and social planning practice is information about the social welfare arrangements. These institutional arrangements must be known on the federal level in order to understand what constraints or goals are predetermined before the state, county, or locality begins to assess its service provisions.

Social work practice, social welfare programs, and social policy are closely related but represent quite different orders of phenomena. Social work practice is the doing, the intervening, the helping. Social welfare programs are the institutionalized forms or mechanisms for channeling human services to eligible groups of recipients. Social policy is a rule, a procedure or social plan written into law by legislation, sometimes confirmed by the courts or introduced through administrative order. It serves to govern program implementation or further decision making in the same area.

Social Welfare Institutional Arrangements includes that body of knowledge more commonly called Fields of Social Welfare, as illustrated in the Friedlander text *Introduction to Social Welfare*[18] or in *Research in the*

---

[18]Walter Friedlander and Robert F. Apte, *Introduction to Social Welfare*, 4th ed. (Englewood Cliffs, N.J.: Prentice-Hall, 1974).

Social Services, edited by Henry Maas.[19] The latter includes primarily research-based knowledge about fields of social service.

For the planners, or c.o. practitioners specializing in the areas of public health, mental health services, the aging, drug abuse, or alcoholism, there is an essential, comprehensive body of knowledge. The c.o. worker will share similar practice skills but, for instance, the c.o. specialist in the field of aging or mental health will have a depth of knowledge about the historical development of the issue, the disciplines involved (law, medicine), the professional leadership in the field, the research literature in that area, or the variety of service arrangements. In specialized fields it is necessary to learn about the nature of the aging process, for instance, or the various viewpoints about causal factors in alcoholism.

Another important knowledge segment (besides the general pattern of social welfare arrangements for the nation, state or local area, and the c.o. specialized field of practice) is the existing social policy structure and the current social policy issues and conflicts. It is not always possible to be informed in a number of policy areas, but it is possible to know where to go for the information as it is needed.

Professors of social welfare policy in schools of social work have a unique body of knowledge about social welfare policy not generally known to faculty in other schools or departments. Major governmental health and welfare programs at the local level have personnel who are policy specialists. The federal government, particularly the Department of Health, Education, and Welfare, has ten regional offices across the country for the purpose of decentralizing governmental policy interpretation as well as for monitoring compliance of policy and regulations.

Of all the seven components of community organization and social planning practice discussed in this chapter, the one that most quickly distinguishes the professional from the untrained practitioner is the level of competence developed in the knowledge component. Natural ability, personality style, and previous experience will support the practitioner only so far; when new or different situations occur, the educated practitioner can draw upon this body of knowledge for theory, generalizations, principles, and concepts. The details of each life experience in community organization work create a ponderous load to carry from one situation to another. Assumptions, theoretical notions, concepts, principles, or knowledge segments are light footed and travel quickly from old situations to new.

6. ORGANIZING STRUCTURE. This component of community organization and social planning practice is usually considered in the context

[19]Henry S. Maas, ed., *Five Fields of Social Service Review of Research* (New York: National Association of Social Workers, 1966); rev. ed., *Research in the Social Services: A Five Year Review* (1971).

of auspices—i.e., public, voluntary—rather than according to the function it is to serve. Increasingly we are questioning the capability of organizations to perform the functions required by their objectives or missions. Typical bureaucratic organizations are longitudinal in structure so as to fit the bureaucratic model of a line of authority or chain of command. Client access to service delivery systems that are highly bureaucratic in structure is considerably more difficult than access to service organizations that are more horizontal in structure. A current example of a horizontal-type service organization would be the free health clinics, which first began in the so-called "hippie" neighborhoods. Estranged youth are hard to reach, and the informal walk-in approach for medical aid without the routinized intake channels offered an acceptable entry into the service system. Some program specialists would say that the strength of this type of horizontal organizational structure, where lines of authority are so informal as to be unclear or negligible, proves also to be its primary weakness. Sufficient time has elapsed to warrant a systematic study of this attempt to make medical care service organizations more responsive to patients' acceptance and service utilization.

Less attention has been given to innovations in planning and organizing structure. Formerly, social planning was considered to be the domain of voluntary health and welfare planning agencies, with participation primarily by professionals and middle- or upper-middle-class volunteers. The present role of government in state- or community-level social planning has emerged only in the last ten or fifteen years, coinciding with increases in government financing.

Area planning councils and neighborhood planning councils have been in existence since the days of the neighborhood settlement house. Neighborhood planning has generally focused on an issue or a community problem to be solved. Therefore, the structure required was ad hoc and attached to the parent agency. The planning committee was easily dissolved after completion of the project.

The literature on the history of the Settlement Movement and the Community Chests and Councils includes numerous references to the desirability of having a planning substructure that is community centered attached to an operating parent agency. Many of the arguments were about the independence or dependence of the health and welfare community planning councils attached to United Funds. The planning concepts during the high points of Planning Council activities were based on notions of centrally planned change or communitywide comprehensive health and welfare planning. With these broad aims, the organizational structure attempted to accommodate decentralized geographic substructures as well as ongoing health and welfare service segments. The planning emphasis on social services called for a continuing structure with division and units, such as hospitals, children's institutions, or a public recreation unit. When planning councils became social-problem or project centered, the organizational structure became more time limited, and it was possible to dissolve a committee or commission after a task was completed.

Hospital planning and coordination probably created the first community service field to initiate what has been labeled segmental, or sector, social planning. The availability of government funds for hospital construction legitimized separate planning platforms for specialized areas of health services. Social planning activities have continued to move in line with the funding sources because of the accountability requirements in fund allocations and because central planning of all fields became too unwieldy.

A second trend that relates to changes in planning structure is a more recent thrust to encourage service integration and more flexibility between the various streams of federal money. Multiple funding, multiple grants, and voluntary fund matching with federal dollars have created new demands on planners, organizers, and administrators.

It is practically impossible to engage in community organization or social planning without some organizational structure. There must be a place or a platform for interaction of the relevant action and public communication if there is to be any semblance of an open planning system. It is possible for an expert or a team of experts to develop and deliver a set of plans for health and welfare programming without any planning structure. It is possible for the planning and evaluation experts now located throughout the federal government to develop program designs and health and welfare service plans for innovations or changes as the basis for FFS (Federal Financial Support). Although a government worker in a human services department in Washington may use the same knowledge, skills, and techniques that a c.o. worker in a social planning organization uses, the former is creating social program plans, while the latter is engaged in social planning processes—an open system, responsive to continuous inputs and corrections from various sources. Social plans and social planning processes are not the same.

When the government allocates funds, such as revenue-sharing money to be disbursed at the community level with provisions for public participation and local planning decisions, some planning mechanism must be developed. County government staff may be able to develop excellent social program plans based on research and other rational supports, but it is not social planning at the local level. There is no provision for participant interaction or communication about the plans in progress.

One more example of the social planning organizational structure follows: This writer has over a number of years acquired a certain competence level as a practitioner in social planning. Although a private consultant to state administrators or an expert preparing a report on some new social service plans for the secretary of the Department of Social Welfare use the same storehouse of social planning skills and knowledge as the present writer-practitioner, neither the consultant nor the expert is engaged in social planning. Social planning is linked to community organization practice.

Because bureaucratic-type organizations are engaging in social planning, attention must be given to organizational patterns that will accommodate and enhance these planning functions.

One of the common approaches in setting up a planning platform is to establish a citizens advisory commission to the board of supervisors, which is the governmental body directly responsible for fund allocation. In one west coast city, a group of individuals, agencies, and organizations interested in the basis for allocation of local revenue-sharing money were brought together as a sponsoring ad hoc group. A committee was formed in order to have a continuing channel of communication to the board of supervisors while negotiating for a satisfactory solution. We should hasten to add that this board of supervisors had already experienced the endless frustration of trying to deal individually with some forty-five different organizations and interested individuals who were demanding some consistent rules and accounting on the use of revenue-sharing money by the county.

The aim of the organizing efforts was to develop a social planning mechanism for the county that would be trusted by the social welfare public as well as by the elected officials of county government. An appropriate planning commission was established, and the recommendations of the commission have been followed by county government at least 90 percent of the time. As long as the supervisors delegate this 90-percent level of authority and a continuous budget for the advisory commission and as long as the commission can function with the support of its community segment, the social planning mechanism should continue to be effective.

Another type of social planning structure attached to a government body occurs when a planning project or demonstration is undertaken. The aims of such planning projects are usually to effect an impact on the sponsoring governmental body and/or the community of agencies. Government agencies frequently have direct service projects attached to their organization but seldom build in community planning structure as a part of the bureaucracy.

One of the illustrations that follows in this chapter is a case example of a community-centered social planning structure developed and supported by a governmental direct service agency. This represents a reverse twist of the earlier periods, when voluntary agencies developed planning structure for the planning of public services.

7. EVALUATION RESPONSE SYSTEM. With an emphasis on the formulation of goals and the operationalization of the organizing and planning objectives, outcome evaluation, and the assessment of planning progress become more possible. Those who are involved in planning processes within or between organizations have found that early declaration of tentative goals and objectives serve to improve both communication and human relationships. This is one reason why some form of a management-by-objectives system seems to improve staff morale in governmental as well as industrial organizations. The guessing game about what is really going on in the organization as to priorities, work allocation, or planning objectives fades out as staff participates in developing common objectives. Group awareness and cooperative commitment to shared goals and objectives make it possible for each participant to be alert about evaluation. When the direction and the targets are clear, there is more concern about time limits and economy of effort. Contrary to some of our traditional ideas, efficiency in the social planning arena is not necessarily destructive to democratic processes. Time structuring for planning processes enhances group effort as well as improves the chances for the end products to be ready in time to be of use. A planning report that is ready the day *after* the important decisions are made not only "misses the boat," but the satisfactions of achievement for the participants are lost.

Social research has always been considered essential for social planning. The rationality of planning is primarily based on a research or factual basis for decision making. This rational basis would also include site visits or systematic observations of what is being done in other localities in similar situations. Social planning processes include layers and sequences of decision making. One of the important contributions of the c.o. practitioner is to facilitate the linkage of the planning participants to the rational resources or experiences that improve decision making.

Social research, statistical analyses, or simple fact gathering will never tell decision makers what they ought to do. Information about the history of a social problem in this community, what has been done previously, the magnitude of the problem, what is known about causation of the problem, the possible direction if something is not done, plans and designs of intervention that have been tried elsewhere, alternative plans or actions, costs, sources of funds, or other related data may help to improve the basis for the decisions about the best possible course of action. This supportive factual basis develops informed decision makers but does not make the decisions.

Getting the right experts together to pool information is one way of building the rational component in social planning and community organization. The analysis of available statistical data and research results provides the most frequently used source for planning. The conducting of special research projects or surveys serves to provide the most relevant information about a particular planning situation, but money, technical resources, and time limits often preclude these special inquiries when action on a problem is already pending.

The best planning research (often called policy research) is that which can be done during the period when there is both an increasing interest in the issues and a chance of completing the study before decisions must be made. Good social research methodology is the same for all forms of applied social research, but the research questions must be policy oriented, and the timeliness of the research results for social policy or social planning issues is highly important. Unfortunately, the "truth" does not always have the greatest power to sway decision makers and social planners. A sympathetic political climate and a heightened anxiety or social concern about a current problem situation will likely result in action quicker than a good research report. But when the research results are marshalled in concert with the heightened public anxiety, the combination practically guarantees successful planning outcomes.

The terms "research," "evaluation," "feedback loop," and "correction" have become jargon from systems languages, and this continuous input into the planning process is essential for evaluation. Without evaluation and an assessment of progress toward goal attainment, there can be no new learning or improvement. Response or correction comes from receiving the message that you are off course. It is possible to have a continuing good evaluation mechanism in place and functioning effectively, but if there is no communication that directs this evaluation information into the administrative or decision-making centers, no adjustment can be made. If there are no signals or warning bells to call attention to mistakes or to planning efforts that are running off the track, the planning process becomes a closed system. Messages of reassurance and positive results are equally important.

Computerized information systems are important technical aids for ongoing planning efforts if they are developed for that purpose. Most of the evaluation and feedback in social planning or community organization activities are through human interaction and through exchange of information or material. In earlier times, the king or the leader was likely to dispose of the messenger who brought bad news to him. Even today, it is not so easy to feed back bad news or new facts that indicate that a change of strategy or tactics is needed to improve the planning efforts.

Planning departments of organizations that work on a closed-system basis are generally as successful as the degree of authority and resources given them to implement their own plans.

Evaluation and research come to play at two levels in social planning. The first is the use of research in assessing client groups, social program effectiveness, and program costs for alternative programs. As social workers become more involved in formulation of social policy, they are becoming more sophisticated about projected costs of services and comparative costs of programs. We have found that carefully computed cost information, posing alternative programs or options, enhances the credibility of the social planning proposal. Too often, legislators and decision makers have an image of social planners as dreamers who know nothing about financing their schemes. Research and evaluation about social programs constitute an important resource for planning.

The other level at which research and evaluation come to play in the planning process is in the evaluation process, which becomes one of the new inputs to improve planning decisions. Now that planning objectives are becoming more explicit, it is possible to assess goal attainment at the desk of the c.o. worker as well as of others involved in the planning. With some objective fact gathering on planning or organizing progress and with participatory evaluation as a principle, all who have been contributing can cooperate in goal setting as well as evaluation and assessment.

IV. A PROFILE OF PRACTICE

The preceding section on components of practice offered a conceptual scheme or framework for sorting out the pieces involved in the practice of community organization and social planning. It was emphasized that these practice components were *not* to be considered as a strict linear sequence where one would proceed in an orderly manner from step one to step seven. Rather, the framework of components included those activity areas most typical in a planning project of a year or so duration. In real life situations, the community organization worker first does some explanatory work and would likely give most attention to an analysis of the problem situation and *why* this problem seems to be important to *which* people. He or she considers the possible client groups to benefit and the present and potential community sponsors or initiators. As the c.o. worker explores component four—the social-political context he begins to infer some planning or action objectives (latent or manifest) as described in component number two. He says to himself, "I will worry about strategies, tactics (number three), and the constraints and organizational problems (number six) tomorrow. Right now, I must do some further exploring and testing to confirm or adjust the hunches I have about the general focus of the problem and how much of a consensus can be expected among the possible participants."

This brief introduction to section IV of this chapter illustrates some of that portion of community organization practice that goes on in the thinking processes of the c.o. worker as he relies on professional discretion in talking about his immediate plan of action. The worker's behaviors that follow from this analytical process may be performed at a skillful level, or the c.o. worker may blunder along for awhile. The interaction of the worker in the early planning situation with the initiators of the planning problem will unfold clues and ideas for the next sequence of worker behaviors. These exchanges will be continuous throughout the planning process as the c.o. worker interacts with participants and the planning context.

There are many variations of this initial interaction process. In the early exploratory phase, much depends on whether or not the social worker is initiating the action as part of a planning agency program and if there is a carefully developed project. For example, there may be a planning proposal where funds and time schedule have been already approved, or the future may be as vague as some general instruction requesting the social worker to go for six months into a troubled marginal farming section where a new power plant is unexpectedly scheduled for construction.

When this writer was a beginner in community organization practice, the illustrative story of the juggler who was keeping five balls in the air at one time appeared very amusing. Later, the comparison seemed quite appropriate when observing the different social worker roles in individual therapy, small groups, and community planning.

The c.o. worker initiates or interacts within several community arenas at one time period. For example, in adoption plans for handicapped minority children, there may be five or more community sectors, such as: minority groups, the courts and lawyers, the private sector, public resources, county or state government, and professional associations.

Social workers in community organization, social planning, and welfare administration share work activities in sustaining a number of relationships at the same time. Neighborhood organization work, for instance, initiates sets of several horizontal relationships. We would expect the c.o. worker in social planning to handle a much larger scope and number of relationships. If it's a social policy issue, there would be several vertical level interactions—state, regional, or national.

There are generally three dimensions in the dynamics of worker relationships that determine the professional complexity of the practice. The sheer number of relationship sets involved is one determiner. By sets or sectors we mean that the relationships are usually in a context, i.e., a professional association, a group of social agencies, federal-level advisors, a student council, or a civil rights or minority leadership group. Second, the rational-technical requirements constitute another dimension of complexity because program design, research, policy, or other expertise may be needed in order to carry out the objectives. The third dimension of complexity lies in the planning constraints that must be faced, such as impeding or punitive program regulations, heavy political pressures, strong conflicting value positions, or perhaps unexpected changes in time and money constraints. Sometimes we plan within the given constraints, and at other times we may invest the resources to modify the constraints when feasible.

Planning for the Aged—A New Agency

This first practice example is considered uncomplicated because the c.o. worker enters the social planning situation with a number of existing supports, all positive in this instance except the time cycle.

There are prescribed tasks to be accomplished in the first six-month planning phase. The problem or issue situation will not require a tedious developmental period.

A board of directors, committed to the new agency, already exists. During the preparation of the proposal for the planning grant for needs and services of the aging, a climate of community readiness was developed. In other parts of the state, similar planning agencies are being developed under this government grant source. This usually offers a supportive association with similar agencies.

Operating facilities have been arranged, and the budgeted positions have already had merit-system authorization.

The new director was formerly a caseworker in public welfare in the largest of the three counties making up this service region. The c.o. worker is familiar with the area. Transportation is no problem in the tricountry area.

Services for the aged are underdeveloped, and the existing service agencies welcome expansion and coordination. There is a newly organized but energetic retired-persons association in the urban county. Minority-group and low-income aged are concentrated in one county and are not organized.

The project budget included additional personnel money for research consultation and interviewing to carry out the proposed survey in the preplanning phase.

There are no serious underlying conflicts. Local government officials are interested in supporting increased attention for the aged, but at this point no one politician is out front to claim the leadership.

The newly formed, tricounty planning agency for the aged was given a mandate by the board of directors to conduct a needs-resources survey that would serve to let the communities know about the new agency and that would also provide a basis for a beginning planning phase.

Mike was the new planning agency director, whose previous experience was as a recreational director and, more recently, a caseworker in the public welfare agency before completing his master's degree in social work. He had completed some special courses in gerontology, and his last fieldwork placement was with a multifunctional institution for the aged where he successfully organized and supervised a volunteer home-visiting program. The quotes that follow are selected to illustrate some of the practice activities in the preplanning phase of organizing a new planning agency for the aged.

July 15: I came on the job two weeks ago and I figured I'd better line up my priorities before I went off on horseback in all directions at once! At the time my new board of directors hired me in May, they also mandated a needs study and resources inventory to be conducted in the first six months. At first I thought my chief worries would be getting office space, employing my c.o. assistant, the office secretary, and managing for some consultation money in the budget. All this has fallen in place rather quickly. Before I completed my graduate work, I came here several times and talked with some ten or twelve people . . . county officials, professionals, leaders. What really bugs me and came as a surprise was the seasonal change. The vacation period for agencies is July–August. Women volunteers (especially middle or upper income) and the school people leave town. Over half of my board members, including the president, are gone for a month or more. It's not just the "pros" and the "elite" . . . even the three leaders of the service recipient group whom I had lined up earlier are away. I can't wait until mid-September to start the preplanning phase. The budget cycle, the due date for a first report, and my time commitment to the board when they hired me for this preplanning phase . . . all these are "givens."

July 15: From this first comment from Mike, the c.o. worker, we pick up several clues. Although he had previously worked in the tricounty area, his perspective about leadership leaving town or being unavailable in the July–August period is quite different when he is on the outside coming in. (The tricounty section is "inland," with some severe summer heat.) Climate, as well as politics, can affect the social-economic behavior in a planning context. (Component four—the social-political context.)

Mike is unnecessarily building some heavy pressures for himself about his time schedule and does not fully recognize the early progress made in gaining the advance lead time for organizational structure, physical facilities, budget adjustment, and personnel. Initiating a planning structure at neighborhood, county, state, or national level is a critical and time-consuming process depending on the breadth of participation sought, the expertise, power, and resources needed. Sometimes a c.o. worker falls heir to an inappropriate planning structure. In this case example, the worker was fortunate.

Note that Mike does not explore possibilities for adjusting the time constraints imposed on the preplanning

And how can I organize when everybody goes about his own summer plans as usual! I feel deserted, like the captain on a sinking ship.

phase. Mike will later learn more about dealing with constraints in planning situations—some constraints you learn to lean on for welcome support; some are fearfully followed to the letter; sometimes we find great flexibility within regulations that appear as constraints; and other times our resources are directed toward removing or changing the constraint or barrier.

August 1: Sometimes you have to work up some anxiety before you can get launched in the right direction. My problems are unraveling now. Talked to my president long distance and we agreed on a chairman for the survey steering committee—this subgroup will be at least 80 percent of leadership who will be here during the summer. We have now identified better recipient leadership for all three counties. After talking to the social survey consultant, I found out there are more technical steps to go through before and after getting the input ideas from planning participants. Also, I had thought of this survey as a unique kind of information gathering about the needs of the aged in this special tricounty situation. When the research consultant showed me the findings from dozens of needs-for-the-aged surveys, national and international, I was impressed. Makes you think about the universality of human needs. Since we will probably be repeating similar findings already in the literature, we will cut some of the more general needs questions and focus on the local situation. We will conduct group interviews with the "pros." Most of them are in the urban county. The resource inventory won't be such a problem because the Tri-County United Fund has just completed a revision of the Health and Welfare Directory. We plan on using a workshop approach for analyzing community needs in relation to available and accessible services. Looks as if the response will be greater than we

August 1: Mike gives little attention to component one, clarifying the planning problem or issue. In this instance, a prescribed preplanning phase is designed for that purpose. He will maintain a fluid position about alternative planning objectives, priorities, major strategies, etc., until after the tricounty workshop on the aging, which will mark the conclusion of the preplanning phase as outlined in the grant proposal. The planners will set directions for long- and short-term planning objectives and priorities after a more careful analysis is made as to what some 200 participants have said or did not say.

With these brief clues, we can infer that Mike has covered the circuit of involved professionals and has identified local expertise for supporting and sharing management responsibilities for the coming workshop. At this point, his focus seems to be reaching agency and organizational support. The contacts on the new community services directory from the Tri-County United Way may lead to some of the unorganized, low-income, older population groups. Informal and voluntary services attached to churches or neighborhood organizations come to surface in the search for specialized resources.

thought—maybe over a hundred from the urban county and fifty each from the other two. Mrs. Hamilton is our chairman with terrific experience on handling conferences. I have learned more from her than any book could tell me about how to put on meetings.

September 15: Everything is beautiful. Our first board meeting is on September 24, and it looks like a full attendance. The aged-survey steering committee will have a good report, and there are several real meaty issues for the board to discuss and make some decisions on. My associate is working on the resources inventory, but we haven't decided just how we will present this material. A directory of service agencies serving the aged is not very original. Maybe we can come up with something different that is not so traditional. Just diagnosed the board membership and the two committees. So far, 45 percent are over sixty years, but there is a lot to be done to improve a three-county representation.

October 10: We set some agency performance objectives at the board meeting. For instance, our workshop date should be before the Christmas holidays—around December 12 to 15. We have three committees going now—the social survey steering committee, the resource inventory committee, and a new program development committee. This last one will serve as our linkage from the workshop outcomes into the initiation of our agency's planning objectives and prioritites. I think of this core committee as the beginning of the real planning action where the broadened base of participants starts. Right now we are having reports on program designs for the aging—like what is going on at the national level, what are some sources of funds, and so on. Also, they are doing their own site visits to senior citizen centers, nutrition programs, information and referral services, and all that. All I can say now is

September 15: We have noticed that Mike is drawing from organizational management techniques, and if he cannot find the time to trace out some literature on analyzing needs and services, he should seek some advice. We can infer that he is conscious of the knowledge component, and has done some fact finding on aged-population demographics in the three counties. Perhaps he is too far away from the workshop event to think about evaluation of the session. When the program for the event begins to sharpen, then Mike and his co-workers must reach a good understanding on workshop objectives. There can be no evaluation until there are clear objectives—most likely short-term ones in this instance.

October 10: Mike is moving rather fast to extend his planning structure and so far has been building participants around functions or major tasks. For each committee there is a product or outcome expected. His resources are very limited, and it will be necessary to plan ahead for the termination of committee and task force groups as new issues require attention. His brief comments illustrate two more points. Mike may have ups and downs, but 90 percent of the time he enjoys his work and gets satisfaction from his interaction with the communities. Second, he does not seem to have that "great need" to control and smother out ideas of the participants.

that everyone is excited about what we will be able to do. It's a challenging and satisfying c.o. project.

November 16: I felt like walking away from it all yesterday. Looks like things are falling apart at the seams. My problems may not be insurmountable, but what I wasn't prepared for was that when one part of the operation gets out of kilter, everything else is caught in the rebound—like a bullet ricocheting. First, I had some sharp words with my research consultant. He says he has done his last revision of the survey questionnaire, and I say we should have the fullest possible input from at least two other groups. These research people just don't understand the participation process! Then, the community resources inventory is way behind schedule. One reason, but not the main cause, is I had to have more help from my associate to get a full involvement in the survey questionnaire. Next, the last board meeting dragged painfully. The meeting agenda was totally on progress reports, and there was faint praise for progress information. But frankly, I had no momentous decisions to bring before them. Another problem has been created because I started the Program Development Committee going too soon. They are getting committed to their pet program for the aging before we complete our preplanning phase with the survey, the inventory, and our assessment workshop. How do you slow down one part of the planning process that is already racing for the home stretch when the other planning segments are about midway?

December 23: I'm looking forward to some happy holidays. We are going skiing for a rest and to celebrate the successful workshop. Everything gradually came together after a couple of rough months. First, the survey printouts came back from the computer just in time for us to draw up twelve newsprint

November 16: Mike has already given us some good understanding of his current problems. This means he is well on his way to solutions.

In the first problem with his research specialist, Mike will learn (as the social welfare research specialist has to learn) that there is an art to knowing at what point the involvement and input of participation from agencies or community must be closed and at what point the technical aspects in research methods must take over.

On his second problem, Mike cannot expect every board meeting during the starting period of an agency to be ready for important policy or planning decisions. Without seeing the agenda, one would suspect that Mike and his staff associate were doing most of the progress reporting. It takes a while for the c.o. worker to develop his own criteria for deciding when he, as the c.o. expert, must be the spokesman and when communication is better facilitated if participants do the interchange.

Throughout this short reporting from Mike, we get clues that when he finds he does not have the technical knowledge he needs, he knows where to go to get it and he is receptive to adapting and using expertise.

December 23: From this short account, we do not get all the details about the planning and management of a conference or community workshop. That constitutes another set of skills. Mike tells us how the Resources Inventory Committee moved from perhaps fifty pages of agency directory descriptions

charts and some simple tables. Our main speaker really put the needs-of-the-aged story together in our opening session and compared our tricounty situation with other communities. The research consultant and I came to an understanding. I must admit that he was more in the right than I was. The inventory of resources was completed in time to mail out in advance of the workshop. My associate and his committee did a good job. They prepared a glossary of definitions for twenty types of services most often found in communities with well-developed programs for the aged. These twenty types of services were listed horizontally across the top of a spread sheet in three groupings—*necessary* for life maintenance, *essential* for human dignity, and *desirable* for social well-being. Availability of these services was marked with one, two, and three stars indicating the extent of service in ratio to estimated population needs. The vertical column listed the counties A, B, and C. County C was divided into urban and nonurban because of the influence of our one big city. All through the workshop, the participants referred to the service inventory. Everyone, from clients to professionals, was able to use the material. There were over 200 participants in the workshop; our objective was not to expect a program plan to emerge, but rather we had aimed at three outcomes: (1) to initiate a communication channel, or a platform, for the expression of different viewpoints about the aging in our planning area. At the same time, we wanted to assess levels of interest in supporting or taking action on aging issues; (2) to gain a sense of the value systems within the three counties as to which problems seem to have priorities or to have potential consensus; (3) to introduce a rational planning approach that would make use of facts and technology as well as human interests. It is already evident that there are

of services available in the three counties to a one-page spread-sheet format that could be used by participants to assess the status of their communities in providing services to the aging. Too often target areas or communities are involved in surveys and there is a lack of know-how for analyzing the mass of data and for translating the results in a form that can be used by citizen or professional participants.

Getting the research-based information is only the first half of the job. Every good survey should have its completed technical report, and it should be made available. But it takes another step of translation to distill the relevant results for the decision makers.

Mike's objectives for the workshop were good descriptive guides. The committee will be able to provide a qualitative type of evaluation. Later, they may be interested in some measurement, such as scaling the degree of attainment on their formulated objectives. Then the objectives would have to be written in more quantifiable language.

We get a feeling that Mike was quite willing to accept the prescriptions handed down for the preplanning phase but that he was happy to have more freedom and flexibility when this was completed.

Even though there was not much to go on, we can share Mike's last comment. If he, his small staff, and all the participants who will be involved work together the next 2½ years, there should be an important difference in the well-being of the aged population in the tricounty area.

quite a few leaders who have pointed out that more health or welfare services won't help some of the problems that are endemic to our society and social institutions. This means some social policy changes. I forgot to add that the time schedule was extended for our first report to the major funding source of our new agency. A lot of times we think these constraints are impossible, but we don't take action to change the constraints. In this case, it caused no problem; extra time just for the asking after we found out how to do it.

Our planning phase starts in the middle of January. We will have our evaluation of our preplanning phase at our next board meeting. The workshop planning committee takes the lead on handling the evaluation since the planning phase outcomes came together at the workshop. A lot of work went into this preplanning phase, and it had to be done because this was a condition in the approval of the government funds. It worked out right for us, but I could well imagine some serious problems in implementing this requirement in other communities where there was a lot of agency rivalry or other conflicts.

My associate and I were just saying this morning that we feel more free now (after the workshop) in choosing our strategies and tactics. There is more going on in these three counties than we had expected. Older people are self-starters—that is, those who are in the organizing stream. No one seems to know much about the older folks you never see. Our needs survey pointed to the nursing and boarding homes and the groups of fragile, home-bound aged. Anyway, there are some busy days ahead for us, and at the end of the three-year project support, we feel confident that this tricounty planning operation will have made a difference for our older people.

An Integrated Services Demonstration

The following illustration of practice was selected because it is fairly typical of experimental or newly organized programs supported by federal or state funds on a time-period basis. With an emphasis on "new federalism," where local general-purpose governments are the recipients or monitors of service programs, community organization job opportunities will continue to be in demand. Some of these opportunities are entirely within the public sector, and others are under voluntary auspices, under contract for public agencies. Over the past decade and for some time in the future, the voluntary agencies will be considered as community resources or service providers through purchase of service contracts by public agencies.

The range and number of planning or action grant programs are diversified, i.e., area planning for services to the aging, child welfare advocacy programs, community-based mental health services, juvenile delinquency division programs, public participation in planning for social services, planning and priorities for revenue sharing, and other fund resources that have dwindled or new demonstration resources that are yet to come.

Also, most time-limited innovations in social welfare are funded by governmental granting sources with the expectation that if the project is successful, the community will have become involved and will adsorb the costs for continued operations. The history of c.o. agencies or programs in most communities can generally be traced back to a demonstration period in which the program was introduced.

In the case that follows, the announcement of a demonstration grant was received in June just before the end of the federal governmental fiscal year. The funds were not processed or first payment received until August. Staff recruitment and office facilities were so slow in moving through the county government machinery that over five months lapsed before the new director arrived on the project scene.

Janet was the new director, in her mid thirties, enthusiastic, somewhat assertive, but with lively humor and laughter that she generally turned on herself. She had considerable experience and success in a middle-management job in the housing agency and as a c.o. worker in the model cities project area.

The Marlin County project proposal had been put together hurriedly with different sections written by three different staff members. Some of the concepts and principles of services integration were incorporated in the proposal, and descriptions of related health and welfare programs needing integration were included. The proposal set forth a target area that was similar to a previous antipoverty demonstration area, and a comprehensive analysis of population and cooperating health and welfare agencies was listed. The sponsoring agency, Marlin County Human Services Agency, had an outstanding director who was recognized as a leader in developing social services programs and in successfully carrying out several experimental programs.

The countywide Human Services Agency included programs on probation, mental health, outpatient medical care, hospitals, welfare and housing, and vocational rehabilitation.

The Services Integration Project as written was quite vague on what was going to be integrated, how it would be done, and especially how such a project could be attached to this large umbrella agency. The grant, $375,-000 for a three-year period, was approved primarily on the basis of the director's reputation and proven interest in service integration.

The project has now been in operation for 1½ years. The notes that follow are selected from several comprehensive interviewing sessions with Janet, the project director and chief c.o. worker. Janet was asked to discuss the organizing processes and the accomplishments during the first eighteen-month period, using as much as possible the seven practice components presented in the previous section of this chapter. Both questions and answers have been briefed and changed to avoid recognition.

Q. Janet, would you first like to say a few words about the positives and negatives inherent in this services integration demonstration at the time you came on the job?

A. First, I'll begin with myself. I liked the concepts presented in the Services Integration Project Proposal. It had a systems approach, and such concepts as service linkage, integration targets, the agency staff as integrators, and the potential for one central information system to coordinate services data from different human services fields made good sense. It was a chance to do something interesting, innovative. It's a positive to be excited about a challenge on a new job.

Other positives were in the newly consolidated Human Services Agency as a potential for carrying on the integration once the project was concluded. Another positive is my boss—he is a great leader and supporter for this kind of innovation.

There were lots of negatives, but the big one was how to get a workable project revision without recruiting and creating a new project that was not the one that was funded. Also, I'm new in this position, and you don't exactly begin work the first day by telling the Project Planning Committee that the proposal as written is not feasible, especially when one of the members was my competitor for this appointment.

Q. Let's begin with the c.o. practice components as they are numbered. You have read the descriptions, and you have had some time to think about your experiences over the past eighteen months. Perhaps the best way to begin with an assessment as to where you were in this component when you began—what you did about it—where you are now. Would you like to try that approach? Shall we begin with the social issue or problem for a starting point?

A. Frankly, my starting point on the problem focus for the project was lower than zero. It is not unusual for a conceptual-level proposal to be approved. This frequently happens where leadership and experience have been proven. But it is unusual for a c.o. worker to begin to organize a community of agencies, clients, and citizens for unknown goals or ends. It took me some time to realize that integration of services is a means, a vehicle, not an end. So, I hope, we are integrating services for some objectives. We can't integrate some seventy-five to eighty services across the board just for an exercise in coordination or to save money by increasing efficiency.

Because of a lapse in salaries, I have consultation money in my budget. We wanted a contract with our research consultant for an evaluation design, but the first embarrassing question about our evaluation design was, "What are these coordinated services supposed to impact *on?* What goals are to be achieved through better integration of services?" So, we began your number seven, the evaluation component, because of our contract to meet the demonstration requirement of an evaluation plan. Early research consultation forced us to analyze component one—what the problem situation was and what selected objectives or goals we were attempting to achieve. I would say that we rocked back and forth from evaluation to problem, to goals and objectives—an interplay between components seven, one, and two.

Next, the research specialist, who was working on the evaluation plan, agreed to write a working paper for me and my project steering group. It was to be a background "think piece" on a social problem approach. As soon as we began to test out a social problem focus, I knew it would work. The research expert explained that if service integration were focused on selected social problems (or a defined portion of a problem), we could set up measures to assess the change in the problem situation. Then we would be asking what impact service integration is having to alleviate or change this social condition. We would have some boundary lines, and we would be able to define integration as two or more services that are packaged for improved service delivery.

Q. Would you say, then, that you just worked back and forth from practice component one to component two? Then, when you know what the problem issue is, you are able to set up feasible objectives that, if attained, will alleviate the problem situation?

A. Yes, I could see those steps ahead for us. But the first trial run was to see if the people could rally around the social problem idea. After talking with agency staff and service citizen leaders who were helping me launch our first meetings, I rewrote the social problems framework paper more in my own language, which would be understandable to the general public. We began with what social problem we should select, because we do not have the resources or the time within our demonstration period to tackle the whole array of social welfare problems in Marlin County. As soon as I could see a handle for taking hold of a list of social concerns, I was able to offer some leadership. Most social problems have multiple causation, and they cut across programs. If we selected issues within community programs or agencies, that would have divided the agencies before we started. Also, our purpose was to find a mechanism that would require two or more agencies to work together.

Q. You haven't mentioned strategies or tactics yet, Janet. What rationale was working for you to guide your practice activities at the beginning? Let's look at practice component number three.

A. Speaking of practice behavior—mine for the first several weeks was more like a squirrel in a cage, round and round without a purpose. Oh, I made contacts, visited agencies, asked for ideas, and listened. I suppose I would claim that my general strategy was process oriented and educational or promotional. The objectives at this point were simple, to get acquainted, to let others know that the Human Resources Agency would be engaged in a service integration project, that we would want to work together—you will hear more from us later, and so on. For some time I've been active in nonpartisan politics in Marlin County, so I made luncheon and conference appointments with a number of county and city officials; also our state assemblyman.

I'm the kind of person who can make a good presentation when I know what I am doing. Right away, I knew how we could implement a selected social problem approach for demonstrating service integration. From that point on, strategies and tactics began to unfold. Each move I made had some purpose behind it.

Q. If I understand what you have said, Janet, you really began your new job not knowing why a set or mix of human services was to be integrated. There were problems of duplication or gaps or access to services, but these were barriers to delivery or efficiency and not the basic social concerns or needs of people. After a legitimate set of social concerns were identified, objectives and strategies for action became more clear. At the same time, you and your staff began to work with the newly appointed advisory board, which was structured outside your agency. Were you beginning to develop organizational structure at the same time?

A. Well, I was thinking about that before we had this conference. At first, it seems like I was spending over half my time on getting a focus that would work for the project—asking "what are the social issues?" (number one). I didn't worry too much about the goals and objectives because I knew that that would come along after we carved out the social problem areas. We will have some criteria for selection of such objectives. Objectives have to be feasible within our resources because there is no money for new services.

Then as these things have to be done, the need for organizing structure comes to the surface. So we are developing the organizational frame as we go along. See, we already had an interagency project committee, chaired by the boss, the executive of the Human Services (Umbrella) Agency. Then there is a project steering committee, which may get dissolved later on.

We must keep the demonstration project structure flexible so it can be dissolved within the superagency organization, so it can move out in the community as an arm of the County Supervisor Board, or so it could be independent. There is plenty of time—no hurry for final decisions on structure. We have two principles: keep it horizontal and as nonbureaucratic as possible, and keep it flexible for a time-limited job.

Q. We want to keep this recording as brief as possible, but while you are talking about organizing for planning issues, would you explain your task force arrangements?

A. Okay. We had a seminar session with a select group of about 20 people, minority leaders, public officials, heads of other departments, etc., a group that would meet once and communicate quickly. Here we planned for a one-day community forum on Marlin County social problems—a kick-off session. Our one-time meeting group of 20 made a list of 125, including most of the people we would like to see continue with the project. Six priority areas were designated with a preliminary description of six social problem areas recommended for our priorities.

After the big forum, our advisory board named a chairman for each of six task forces. The task force groups had some eight to fifteen members and were kept at a working size limit. Our project has only three full-time professionals, so from necessity the task force groups frequently met alone, keeping their own records. For example, the task force on low-income working mothers and the task force on substance abuse (alcoholism, drugs) started a series of hearings on the status of local problems. Staff would secure the experts, a psychiatrist, a director of a half-way house from a nearby city, a specialist on the school dropout problem, etc. We called these sessions our panel hearings for expert witnesses.

Members visited agencies and covered several site visits where some new things were going on in service coordination. They were well informed and involved by the time their reports were due. The reports varied greatly in quality and complexity. The task force on problems of the aging completed a highly professional report, a credit to any planning department.

Q. Then how did these problem-formulation task force groups move into action or implementation?

A. The reports of the task force groups to the advisory board of the project marked the conclusion of that work unit. On the whole, all reports were accepted for implementation except one on school dropouts that was modified toward a problem more feasible for the schools to handle. It became a career guidance project to be introduced at seventh-grade level. The minority groups wanted something introduced before the high school level.

The newly formed groups became the feasibility and implementation committees. There were some carryover members from the task force membership, but new strength was added with more power as well as commitment for implementation.

Q. And where are they now?

A. Each has a time schedule and work plan objectives—something like a mini MBO system [Management by Objectives]. That was the idea of the Day Care for Working Mothers Committee, and the others took on the same pattern. They are all enthusiastic, but I know there will be some disappointments. Keep in mind, we have no carrot for rewards and no stick to punish with or take away.

Q. I remember attending a big award celebration dinner. It seemed to me as if some twenty people received a "carrot"—press pictures taken, a plaque presented or a standup for cheering and clapping! But one more question on the organizing structure: the Legislative or Social Policy Committee seemed to have a different order of tasks. Would you explain?

A. As you know, we are expecting several social service bills to be introduced nationally, something on special revenue sharing and other legislation at state level. Our committee (really a task force) on legislation has already sent its analysis of two federal bills and will be ready to respond immediately to the state social service plans publication. The League of Women Voters helped us get the group going. The County Bar Association is included and the legal advisor for the board of supervisors also is an active member.

These people are very action oriented, and I really don't know just how this will work out because this committee feels independent of the parent governmental agency—the Human Service Agency for the county. But are they independent? Their tactics are refreshingly geared for quiet action—each member is assigned to a designated staff person for each of our state legislators—affecting Marlin County. This is almost too close for the comfort and assured career future of the c.o. worker!

As the task force moved into implementation, each committee posed its own time structure and performance objectives. Our first year's evaluation report was based on performance objectives—a rating scale. For example, one objective was to prepare an office manual with some working memoranda on bylaws for our tentative organizational structure. It was completed, approved, and in operation by the date we had planned. We were rated high on that achievement. We had one constraint after another on our attempts to get a central information system in the planning stage. Our timing and objectives were overoptimistic.

Q. Thanks for the bit about evaluation and feedback in the planning process. That saves a question. This next question is going to be a tough one. Of the seven practice components, in which one would you say you (as a practitioner) were strongest and in which component the weakest?

A. That is a loaded question, but I think I have my own answer. Others who have been close to the project may not agree with my self-diagnosis. I think my greatest strength is in understanding and identifying the political climate of Marlin County, and I mean politics in its generic sense, not necessarily partisan politics. For example, the big merger of human service agencies has left some battle scars that I well know. A compromise on the part of the board of supervisors left the director without sufficient power to carry out his mission of administering a large multifunctional agency. I know which agencies are nervous about further steps in service amalgamation. I am very alert for conflicts and other consequences if we bypass minority leadership or get too far out of line with the social action part of social intervention. As an aside, I am always amused with the acceptance of even avant-garde social programs if the terminology is quiet. You can stand up for your cause and social commitments, but you don't have to attract attention by making unnecessary noises.

On the other side, the weakness, I suppose I would have to admit I could use a lot more of the theoretical knowledge and more about development of social welfare programs. I would not want to get hooked with a vocabulary that would cut down my communication with the average citizen or community leader.

Q. Here is another unfair question. We are interested in today's social work practitioner in community organization and what the future holds for this specialization. Ten years from now, where would you like to be?

A. That question is too specific! First, I have a husband with career ideas, and I really can't say. But, I wouldn't "switch or fight" if it came time for a better balance of women in the political arena who are committed to social goals and social change and who are beginning to wonder if the present change strategies are too slow.

The Practitioner of Tomorrow

Throughout this chapter, the writer has attempted to keep the two terms "community organization" and "social planning" together. It is possible to write several chapters on social welfare program planning and design and never mention participatory processes and organizational structure. It is possible to write a good book on social policy as a form of social planning and focus the practice components primarily on an intellectual scheme for social policy analyses and formulation. In this instance, frequent references are made to the behavior dynamics of planning participants, or organizations or agencies, and of communities. In discussing practice behaviors, we are assuming that this is a specialized area building on a broader base of social work education and training. In the last decade, social work literature has continued to clarify the social science theory base of practice methods, and this advancement has in turn led to distinctions between the value-based socialization for the professional social worker and the knowledge, theory, and skills base of the practice.

The beginning career years of a c.o. worker is likely to be more generalized, cutting across several fields of services, involving local-level government, including community-level participation, and does not require an expertise in program design or research beyond the limits of consultation for simple surveys and evaluation.

The generalized c.o. worker may specialize in child welfare planning and programming, in community mental health, in planning and coordinating services for the aging. There is always the knowledge content for each specialization that must be added to the c.o. skills. Most often these specialized openings come by chance, and the new c.o. worker learns his specialty content in the job setting. His c.o. skills are readily transferable, and he has had his basic social welfare programs in the general social work curriculum.

A forecast for the future of community organization and social planning would predict an emphasis at the local-government level. The county unit is most likely since most of the service delivery boundaries —county health, hospitals, welfare, probation, etc.—are countywide. The c.o. worker must connect with the local, general-purpose governmental unit even though his target area may be an inner-city housing project. The future also will likely find more federal funds being allocated on the basis of a county population formula for distribution, with the state serving more as a conduit. Already this is happening, and the absence of any local planning mechanism to allow for local participation is conspicuous and the source of much complaint. It is not unlikely that county-level government may also begin to initiate an evaluation center to monitor the contracts and grants funneled through county government for social programs. This is an expanding area for planning and community organization.

Although it may appear that a reduction in Federal-level social welfare planning and policy development is taking place, this is quite unrealistic when we consider what policies are made where. All of the life-saving and life-subsistance program decisions flow from the federal level. The less important social welfare issues are left for local decision making. In repeated studies on priority needs of the poor and disadvantaged, the priorities of need come out the same. First is a job—income from employment. If there is no job, then sufficient income maintenance. Then in order come the food, clothing, housing, followed by medical care, i.e., Medicare and Medicaid. Transportation needs loom high in places like Los Angeles, where the unemployed can't get to the place of employment when a job is available. These are the important issues, and the more significant the issue, the higher the decision level and the further this level is from the people seeking help.

When we hear about the new trends in bringing decision making from the federal level to the people at local levels, we must always ask, "What decisions?"

Another avenue for community organization and social planning may be ahead in some ingenious design for a broad participation base as to how national resources are allocated. This is the most important issue of all. Perhaps some kind of participation vehicle that combines the best from the Common Cause members, the Backyard Movement, the National Conference on the Aging, or the past White House Conferences for Children and Youth.

When the feedback to our federal administration, White House, or Congress is limited to the same narrow population samples, we are likely to get a slow buildup of error in general public opinion that can result in disaster. The issue is not one of getting everyone at the local level in on the decision making per se. Rather, it is finding a participation channel that allows for this broad base of opinions, values, and desires to come through to those who eventually make the policy decisions.

Organizing, planning, participation, and decision making are the means, not the ends. Unless it all adds up to a better quality of life for all the people, it will have been merely an interesting exercise.

SELECTED BIBLIOGRAPHY

Interorganization Theory/Organizational Theory

BLAU, PETER M. *On the Nature of Organizations.* New York: Wiley & Sons, 1974.

HAAS, J. EUGENE, and DRABEK, THOMAS E. *Complex Organizations: A Sociological Perspective.* New York: Macmillan Co., 1973.

PRESSMAN, JEFFREY L., and WILDAVSKY, AARON. *Implementation.* Berkeley: University of California Press, 1973.

Management (Technologies) P.A.

LYDEN, FREMONT J., and MILLER, ERNEST G., eds. *Planning, Programming, Budgeting: A Systems Approach to Management.* 2nd ed. Chicago: Markham Publishing Co., 1972.

Information Systems

DUNN, EDGAR S., JR. *Social Information Processing and Statistical Systems—Change and Reform.* New York: Wiley & Sons, 1974.

Social Problems

DENTLER, ROBERT A. *Major Social Problems.* 2nd ed. Chicago: Rand McNally, 1967.

HADDEN, JEFFREY K.; MASOTTI, LOUIS H.; LARSON, CALVIN J., eds. *Metropolis in Crisis: Social and Political Perspectives.* Itasca, Ill.: F. E. Peacock Publishers, 1967.

SHOSTAK, ARTHUR B. *Modern Social Reforms: Solving Today's Social Problems.* New York: Macmillan Co., 1974.

Communication

DAY, PETER R. *Communication in Social Work.* Oxford: Pergamon, 1972.

HAGE, JERALD. *Communication and Organizational Control: Cybernetics in Health and Welfare Settings.* New York: Wiley & Sons, 1974.

KAUFMAN, HERBERT. *Administrative Feedback.* Washington, D.C.: Brookings Institute, 1973.

ROGERS, EVERETT M., and SHOEMAKER, F. FLOYD. *Communication of Innovations: A Cross-Cultural Approach.* New York: Free Press, 1971.

Political Science

HOFFERBERT, RICHARD I. *The Study of Public Policy.* Indianapolis: Bobbs-Merrill, 1974.

JONES, CHARLES O. *An Introduction to the Study of Public Policy.* Belmont, Calif.: Duxbury Press, 1970.

LINDBLOM, CHARLES E. *The Policy-Making Process.* Englewood Cliffs, N.J.: Prentice-Hall, 1968.

Social Change

CAMPBELL, ANGUS, and CONVERSE, PHILIP E., eds. *The Human Meaning of Social Change.* New York: Russell Sage Foundation, 1972.

LIPPITT, RONALD; WATSON, JEANNE; and WESTLEY, BRUCE. *The Dynamics of Planned Change: A Comparative Study of Principles and Techniques.* New York: Harcourt, Brace, 1958.

MAYER, ROBERT R. *Social Planning and Social Change.* Englewood Cliffs, N.J.: Prentice-Hall, 1972.

MORRIS, ROBERT. *Centrally Planned Change.* Chicago: University of Illinois Press, 1974.

ROTHMAN, JACK. *Planning and Organizing for Social Change: Action Principles from Social Science Research.* New York: Columbia University Press, 1974.

CHAPTER FIVE

SOCIAL WELFARE ADMINISTRATION AND RESEARCH

Walter A. Friedlander

I. GENERIC ASPECTS OF SOCIAL WORK PRACTICE

Social work methods in our society are influenced by the fact that social work is a profession. Professions are characterized by a set of criteria distinguishing them from other occupations.[1] Professional organizations assume a moral guarantee of the technical efficiency of their members. They require a test of this efficiency before admitting members, either by standards of education or formal degrees of higher education. Such a test subjects members to an indirect control of their professional knowledge and skills.[2] Professions set up codes of ethics that demand that the confidence of the client be respected, that service be offered whenever and wherever it is needed, that such service be efficient and conscientious,

---

[1] Walter A. Friedlander and Robert F. Apte, *Introduction to Social Welfare* 4th ed. (Englewood Cliffs, N.J.: Prentice-Hall, 1974), pp. 527–29; and Nathan E. Cohen, *Social Work in the American Tradition* (New York: Dryden Press, 1958).

[2] Henry J. Meyer, "Profession of Social Work: Contemporary Characteristics," *Encyclopedia (1971)*, pp. 959–72.

and that the professional person abstain from unbecoming behavior, such as commercial types of haggling, advertisement, and competition. Another characteristic of the professions is their obligation to protect the population against the danger of incompetent practice by unqualified members. Finally, the profession attempts to safeguard the standards and conditions of work and to provide adequate remuneration for its members.

In the professions there is, in general, a relationship of trust between the client and the members of the profession. As in all professions, the services of social work cannot be strictly controlled. They are not standardized but are essentially personal and unique. They are based upon the fact that the professional person gives not only objective skills and performance but also support through his personality.

The practice of social work in casework, social group work, and social welfare community organization is based upon a generic philosophical concept. This concept is that the individual human being is the primary concern of a democratic society, inside of which individuals are interdependent and socially responsible to one another and to the society. This philosophy includes a recognition of the essential uniqueness of each individual, as well as of the existence of common human needs.[3] A pertinent goal of social work practice is to realize the full potential of an individual or a group and to help them to assume their own responsibility for this realization through active participation, which is characteristic of a democratic society. On the other side, social work practice considers it a societal responsibility to provide the means by which the disequilibrium between the individual and his environment may be prevented or overcome, so that obstacles to the self-realization of the individual or the group are removed. These concepts are the foundation for the ethics of social work practice.

Consistent with this philosophy, the practice of social work has the following purposes:

1. To identify potential areas of conflict between individuals or groups and the environment, and to assist in bringing about changes in individuals, groups, and the environment to prevent such conflict
2. To find and strengthen in individuals, groups, and communities the creative forces and possibilities that lead to the fulfillment of the maximum potentialities of each
3. To help individuals and groups to resolve social problems arising from a disequilibrium between individuals or groups and their environment

[3]Charlotte Towle, *Common Human Needs* (Chicago: University of Chicago Press, 1945), pp. 1–3; Charles Frankel, "Social Values and Professional Values," *Journal of Social Work Education*, 5, no. 1 (Spring 1969): 33–35.

Methods of social work practice are systematic procedures designed to achieve these purposes.

The application of social work practice sets in motion a problem-solving process that implies various possibilities of action to accomplish the desired change.[4] The objectives of this social change may be:

1. Change within the individual or of the character of a group in relation to the social environment
2. Change of the social environment in its effect upon the individual (such as the removal of a child from an inadequate foster home and placement in an effective home) or upon a social group
3. Change of the individual, the group, and the social environment in their interaction[5]

Generic professional elements in social work, therefore, require:

1. An organized, thoughtful, purposeful, and scientific approach
2. Professional attitudes toward clients (as individuals and as groups) and toward other citizens and co-workers that are determined by professional knowledge, respect for others, and professional ethics
3. The ability to establish constructive, objective relationships with individuals and groups in the application of professional methods
4. The capacity to develop in individuals and groups an awareness of social needs and insight into possibilities of their fulfillment
5. An identification with a social philosophy inspired by the principle of helping others to further human welfare[6]
6. The ability for a scientific approach in practice, for engagement in evaluative research, and a concern for effective, professional work[7]

In social work practice, the following elements are simultaneously applied, although in varying degrees:

1. *Relationship* is the social worker's responsible and disciplined use of himself in working with an individual or a group. In this relationship, the social

[4]Helen Harris Perlman, *Social Casework: A Problem-Solving Process* (Chicago: University of Chicago Press, 1957), pp. 84–101; and Daniel Hirshfield, "Social Policy and Political Trends," *Encyclopedia (1971)*, pp. 1425–26.

[5]Roland L. Warren, "The Sociology of Knowledge and the Problems of the Inner City," in *Perspectives on the American Community*, 2nd. ed., ed. Roland L. Warren (Chicago: Rand McNally, 1973), pp. 321–41; and Edwin J. Thomas, ed., *The Socio-Behavioral Approach and Application to Social Work* (New York: Council on Social Work Education, 1967).

[6]Charlotte Towle, *The Learner in Education for the Professions* (Chicago: University of Chicago Press, 1954), pp. 234–35; Clair L. Wilcox, *Toward Social Welfare* (Homewood, Ill.: Richard Irwin, 1969); Norman Polansky, "The Professional Identity in Social Work," in *Issues in American Social Work*, ed. Alfred J. Kahn (New York: Columbia University Press, 1959), pp. 293–318; and Daniel Thursz, "Professional Education for Expected Political Action by Social Workers," *Education for Social Work* 9, no. 3 (Fall 1973): 87–93.

[7]Edward J. Mullen, "Evaluative Research in Social Work," in *Evaluation of Social Work Services in Community Health and Medical Care Programs*, ed. Robert C. Jackson (Berkeley: University of California Press, 1973), p. 45.

worker applies professional knowledge and skills guided by the ethical principles we have discussed and by his ability to develop empathy and trust. The psychological understanding of his client as an individual or a group member gives the worker the necessary sensitivity and inventive capacity to make this relationship constructive.

2. *Diagnostic or evaluative orientation* is built upon responsible, systematic observation and assessment of the individual or the group in a given social situation. Careful observation and assessment make social change and treatment possible. The social worker assumes responsibility for his objectivity, and his professional judgment determines the direction of his activities with the client.

3. *Treatment* is based both upon the professional relationship of the social worker to the individual or the group and upon the worker's diagnostic observation and assessment of desirable changes. The social worker seeks to help clients as individuals or as a social group to gain insight into the motivation of their thinking and actions and to find ways for solving social stress and social problems. Treatment may be of short or long duration, but it requires in casework and in group work the professional ability to individualize and to diagnose the social problem and to match it with the community resources.[8]

II. TECHNIQUES FACILITATING SOCIAL WORK PRACTICE

A. Social Welfare Administration

Social welfare administration and social work research are frequently called "indirect techniques" or "enabling methods" because they implement the services that are performed in social casework, social group work, and social welfare community organization. Each of these five fields of social work practice is related to each of the other fields. Each is based on scientific principles and a body of specialized knowledge and experience, and their common, basic purpose is to assist in providing an effective helping service to people in need of economic, social, emotional, or cultural aid. Social welfare administration and social work research both include certain basic ingredients that are common to disciplines other than social work, such as public administration, business management, social science research, and clinical, anthropological, and historical observations and investigations.

As social work is mainly practiced in social agencies or in depart-

[8]See Philip H. van Praag, "Basic Concepts of Social Work," *Social Service Review* 31, no. 2 (June 1957): 183–91; Nathan E. Cohen, "A Changing Profession in a Changing World," *Social Work* 1, no. 3 (October 1956): 12–19; Philip Lichtenberg, "Social Policy: Social Work Contributions to Economic Policy," *Encyclopedia (1971)*, pp. 1426–36; Edward Newman and Jerry Turem, "The Crisis of Accountability," *Social Work* 19, no. 1 (January 1974): 5–16; and Melvin Mogulof, "Elements of a Special-Revenue-Sharing Proposal for the Social Services," *Social Service Review* 47, no. 4 (December 1973): 593–604.

ments and divisions of related health organizations, in hospitals, clinics, courts, schools, detention homes, and correctional and penal institutions, a knowledge of social welfare administration is essential for the social worker. Social welfare administration in public agencies implements social legislation and transforms laws, rules, and regulations into services for people. In private social agencies and other voluntary organizations of humanitarian or religious character, social welfare administration evaluates and puts into action the special goals of the organization. It is "the process of transferring social policy into social services and the use of experience in evaluating and modifying social policy."[9]

The practice of social agency administration is based upon the principles and techniques of administration in general, particularly of public administration and business management, but it is directed to the specific social work tasks of defining and solving human problems and satisfying human needs. A competent executive of a social agency needs to possess a knowledge different from that required for business or industry, based upon professional education and experience in social work. The administrator in a social agency must understand the philosophy, aims, and functions of social work—methods of social diagnosis, analysis, and synthesis of individual or group needs and methods of generalization for change or development in agency goals and functions. The administrator needs to be aware of the human needs of clients and group members and of the complex interplay of client, caseworker, or group worker, as well as the societal function of the welfare agency, its organizational structure, and the relevant resources of the community.[10] The administrator needs to know how the challenge of social work enriches the social worker in his professional and personal life and influences his relationship with clients, fellow workers, and superiors.

In every organization, the administrative process is determined by its particular functions, objectives, structure, and size. In a social agency, the administrator needs to feel with and for the clients whom the agency serves. It is unlikely that an executive without understanding of social work theory and methods would have the necessary insight, imagination, and skill to effectively direct an organization engaged in a helping process for human beings as individuals, social groups, or communities. This is

---

[9]John C. Kidneigh, "Administration of Social Agencies," *Social Work Yearbook* (1957), p. 75; Ralph M. Kramer, *Participation of the Poor: Comparative Community Case Studies in the War on Poverty* (Englewood Cliffs, N.J.: Prentice-Hall, 1969); and Rosemary C. Sarri, "Administration in Social Welfare," *Encyclopedia (1971)*, pp. 39–48.

[10]See Towle, *Common Human Needs*, p. 239; Arlien Johnson, "The Administrative Process in Social Work," in *Proceedings of the National Conference of Social Work* (1947), pp. 249–58; Wayne Vasey, "Should the Administrator Be an Expert?," in ibid. (1948), pp. 451–55; and Michael J. Hill, *The Sociology of Public Administration* (New York: Crane & Russak, 1972).

particularly evident in a small agency where the executive is close to the client level. In a large public welfare organization, the administrator needs to be familiar with operation management, managerial control, finance and personnel administration, and skill in conceptualization.[11]

In the foundation of a social agency, the administrative process calls for the clarification of the agency's purpose and structure and its objectives, functions, and policies in accordance with the goals for its establishment.

The administrative structure of the social agency must be set up so that the policy-making functions of the board of directors are clearly distinguished from the responsibilities of the executive and staff.

Personnel administration has the responsibility for the composition, the number, and the qualifications of the staff, particularly of the social workers who provide the professional services to the clients. It is evident that the quality of the professional staff basically determines the value of the social agency to its clients. Personnel policies as to recruitment and selection of staff, questions of salaries, working conditions, tenure, promotions, supervision, vacations, sick leave, and social insurance protection are important factors for the kind of workers the social agency will attract. These personnel practices also include facilities for in-service training, grievance procedures, rules of dismissal, or retirement.

The administrative function of the agency executive in public or private social agencies calls for imaginative leadership based upon a highly developed social consciousness and a vital understanding of the role of social work in our democratic society. The executive has to enlist full and enthusiastic cooperation of the entire staff; he must have the capacity to share professional ideas with the staff, for improvement of methods and operations, and guide the development of new approaches to the services in the interest of the clients.

The agency executive has to assign to each member of the staff, and frequently also to each volunteer, the specific functions for which each is best qualified as well as determine his own lines of duty and authority. Each staff member should be allowed as much flexibility and opportunity for initiative as his activities permit, so that he recognizes his participation to be of real importance within the operation of the agency for the benefit of the clients.

The establishment of the social policy of a welfare organization

[11]S. Blumenthal, *Managament Information Systems* (Englewood Cliffs, N.J.: Prentice-Hall, 1969); Harold Wilensky, *Organizational Intelligence* (New York: Basic Books, 1967); M. Gruber, "Total Administration," *Social Work* 19 (May 1974): 625–36; and J. S. Aram and W. E. Stratton, "The Development of Interagency Cooperation," *Social Service Review* 48 (September 1974): 412–21.

determines the organization's nature, structure, and functions. This process of policy formation is performed in a public agency by the legislative authority, in a county welfare department by the board of supervisors, or in a state department of public welfare by the state assembly. In a private social agency, social policy is established by the board of directors or by an assembly of the membership, frequently in cooperation with community authorities, such as the municipal or county government. The members of the staff frequently are not immediately engaged in the formulation of social policy, but they indirectly participate in this function because the members of legislative and governing bodies regularly receive from them reports, information, and suggestions.

The main function of social work administration is to put into effect the social policy that has been established for the operations of the agency. In this process, the executive and the staff of the agency convey to the board and to the legislative authority the professional experience gained in the practice of agency operations. These reports may be made in formal accounts, usually given at regular intervals and based upon records, statistics, research studies, and observations, or may proceed through less formal channels of communication. These reports supply the governing body of the social agency with the necessary knowledge of the agency's operations and of their effect upon the clients; and they serve as a sound base for either the continuation or the modification of the agency's social policy.

Since social policy usually is expressed in general terms, social welfare administration in its execution of the policy must continuously interpret and define in greater detail the principles established for this policy.[12] This interpretation in practice frequently leads to a "secondary policy" that implements the legislatively established general policy but does not violate the intent and objectives of the latter. Administrative decisions and interpretations have to preserve the aims of the social policy established for the welfare agency. In this rule-making process of social agency administration, the executive and the staff have to collect and codify these rules and regulations. The executive must inform the staff of these regulations and obtain the workers' active participation in securing the enforcement of the rules, which tend to resolve differences and problems arising during the course of the performance of the agency's social policy.

Social work administration also has to interpret its operations, functions, and social policy to the public to make the people aware of the

---

[12]Charles E. Hendry, "The Dynamics of Leadership," in *Proceedings of the National Conference of Social Work* (1946), pp. 259–68; and Alexander Leighton, *The Governing of Men* (Princeton: Princeton University Press, 1946).

necessity for, and the value of, the agency's work. It uses for this broader interpretation all sources of communication—its official reports; human interest stories; statements and interviews in newspapers, radio, television; and addresses and announcements in cooperation with civic and religious groups, as illustrated in chapter 4.[13]

The mobilization, distribution, and control of the financial resources of the social agency are another important responsibility of social welfare administration. In the case of a public agency, the administrator has to prepare the budget for approval and appropriation by the legislative body, such as the city council, the board of supervisors, the state assembly, or Congress on the federal level. In a private social agency, the executive must not only submit the pertinent financial data for the agency's budget to the board of directors but also frequently justify the agency's needs to the budget committee, the board of the local community chest or the board of a united campaign federation raising the funds for the operations of the voluntary social agencies in the area. It is always necessary to establish a reliable system of records, accounts, and audits for the expenditures of the agency. These documents must clearly demonstrate the correct spending of the allocated funds and must prove the necessity for the expenditures according to the accepted social policies of the welfare organization.

To perform these administrative duties, the executive and his assistants in responsible positions of social work administration need a thorough knowledge of social work philosophy, of the history and structure of the organization, and of the function of social work practices in the community, including the following three concepts:

1. An understanding of the principles of relationship applying to individuals and groups.
2. An understanding of the totality of the process of social work administration with its particular implications for the clients, the community, and the staff.
3. An understanding of the characteristic functions of the individual social agency with regard to the cooperation of welfare services in the community and of the impact of its operations upon its task of transforming the established social policy into useful social services for its clients and the community.[14]

[13]Cf. Peter M. Sandman, David M. Rubin, and David B. Sachsman, *Media* (Englewood Cliffs, N.J.: Prentice-Hall, 1972), pp. 406–11; Alan D. Wade, "The Social Worker in the Political Process," *Social Work Forum* (1966), pp. 52–67; and Charles S. Prigmore, "Use of the Coalition in Legislative Action," *Social Work* 19 (January 1974): 96–102.

[14]H. A. Simon, "The Changing Theory and Changing Practice of Public Administration," in *Contemporary Political Science,* ed. I. de Sola Pool (New York: McGraw-Hill, 1967), pp. 86–120; and Melvin Mogulof, "Future Funding of Social Services," *Social Work* 19 (May 1974): 607–14.

B. Social Work Research

Social work research is the systematic, critical investigation of questions in the social welfare field with the purpose of yielding answers to problems of social work, and of extending and generalizing social work knowledge and concepts.[15] The methods applied in social work research have been to a large extent derived from those used in sociology and social psychology, as well as in history and anthropology.

Since research in every scientific field aims to contribute to knowledge, social work research becomes one of the sources from which social work knowledge is drawn. Important contributions were made by research work in related disciplines, such as medicine, psychology and psychiatry, biology, law, economics, sociology, education, and public administration. In the beginning, social work was hesitant about bringing social science research into the field of social work theory and practice. For this reason, the first working hypotheses of social work research were not rigidly tested by the methods and data used in social science research. Early community studies by social workers of social problems, agency programs, structure, and operations, as well as of the history of social work, and of case material and clinical observations served primarily to prove the need for existing or new social services. Such studies facilitated community welfare planning but did not, in the beginning, contribute essentially to a deeper scientific knowledge of human nature, behavior, and human relations; they proved, however, the need for new social work methods for intensified observations and research.[16]

One of the obstacles to fruitful cooperation between social workers and social scientists in social work research has been their difference in orientation. Social scientists are inclined to separate their values from scientitic theory, to apply rigorous empirical investigation to forces operating according to the law of cause and effect, and to study these forces objectively and disinterestedly. Their research is designed without reference to practical results; it has been called "pure research." Social work-

[15]See Ernest Greenwood, "Social Science and Social Work: A Theory of Their Relationship," *Social Service Review* 29, no. 1 (March 1955): 20–33; Henry S. Maas, ed., *Research in the Social Services: A Five-Year Review* (New York: National Association of Social Workers, 1971); and James R. Dumpson et al., *Evaluation of Social Intervention* (San Francisco: Jossey-Bass, 1972).

[16]See Henry Maas, "Collaboration between Social Work and the Social Sciences," *Social Work Journal,* 31 (July 1950): 104–9; Alfred J. Kahn, "Some Problems Facing Social Work Scholarship," *Social Work* 2, no. 2 (April 1957): 54–62; Ernest Greenwood, "Social Work Research: A Decade of Reappraisal," *Social Service Review* **31,** no. 3 (September 1957): 311–20; Billy J. Franklin and Harold W. Osborne, eds., *Research Methods: Issues and Insights* (Belmont, Calif.: Wadsworth, 1971); and Emanuel Tropp, "Expectation, Performance, and Accountability," *Social Work* 19, no. 2 (March 1974): 139–48.

ers, however, deal with forces in relation to human beings; their research projects are concerned primarily with the solution of specific social problems of the individual, the family, the neighborhood, and the community, and they inquire how the research findings can improve services to their clients. They first took the professional values of social work for granted (see chapter 1) and were inclined to incorporate into the research only elements of pragmatic nature. Social scientists were "research minded"; social workers were "action oriented." Social scientists, therefore, raised questions of reliability and validity of social work research hypotheses and design and were skeptical of their results. In the early period of research, social workers started without sufficiently critical appraisal and were willing to carry on with less rigorous research design and procedures than those required in the social sciences. These differences resulted in mutual criticism, impatience, and misunderstanding.[17]

But, with intensified social work research, social workers have expanded their research to include social theory and diagnostic and treatment typologies. These studies comprehend methodological theory research (such as theory of measurement and sampling), interpretative theory, providing substance to empirical generalizations, research and social work practice theory, operational research, exploring new areas for social work practice and research, research identifying relationships between clients, groups, communities, and social workers, and developing continuity in empirical research.

A social work research project may follow the following procedure:

1. *Selection of subject:* experiences and data of social work practice with individuals, groups, or communities are used to define and formulate the social problem. The research project aims either to clarify a specific problem through the application of social theory or to systematize the various aspects of the selected problem.
2. *Formulation of hypotheses* to clarify and solve the problem in question.
3. *Construction of a research design* that is suited to test the validity of the hypotheses by empirical verification or rejection.
4. *Fact-finding process* including observations, interviews, and inquiries to obtain the facts and data that are required by the hypotheses and the research design.
5. *Analysis* of the collected facts and data in order to determine whether they logically support the hypotheses or refute them.

[17]See John M. Neale and Robert M. Liebert, eds., *Science and Behavior: An Introduction to Methods of Research* (Englewood Cliffs, N.J.: Prentice-Hall, 1973); Herbert Blumer, "Threats from Agency-Determined Research: The Case of Camelot," in *The Rise and Fall of Project Camelot*, ed. Irving L. Horowitz (Cambridge: Massachusetts Institute of Technology, 1967); and Eduard Sagarin, "The Research Setting and the Right Not To Be Researched," *Social Problems* **21**, no. 1 (Summer 1973):52–64.

6. *Interpretation and evaluation* of the research findings and their conclusions to determine whether the findings support a convincing answer to the problem studied and whether they may serve as the basis of further studies.[18]

Other types of social work research are conducted on clinical observations of individuals or groups or on the historical aspects of social work philosophy, organization, and practice.

Classifications of subjects for social work research are not rigidly determined, but the following types of necessary research have been suggested:[19]

1. Studies to establish and measure factors that produce social problems and call for social services
2. Studies of the histories of charitable institutions, social welfare legislation, social welfare programs, and social work concepts
3. Studies of the expectations, perceptions, and situation evaluations of social workers
4. Studies of the intentions, goals, and self-images of social workers
5. Studies of relationships between the social worker's expectations, intentions, and actions
6. Studies of the content of social work processes
7. Studies that test the adequacy of available social services in relation to the needs of the individuals, groups, and the community
8. Studies that test, gauge, and evaluate the effects of social work operations and investigate the competence required for social work practice[20]
9. Studies of clients' expectations, goals, perceptions, and evaluation of situations
10. Studies of clients' behavior in relation to their reactions to social work practice
11. Studies of formal and informal definitions of the roles of social workers, their interrelationships, and patterns of cooperation within social agencies
12. Studies of the values and priority preferences of social groups in the community upon which social welfare practice relies for support and development
13. Studies of the patterns of interaction between the different components in social agency settings and of their influence upon clients and agency staff
14. Studies in the methodology of social work research

[18]Margaret Blenkner et al., *The Function and Practice of Research in Social Work* (New York: Social Work Research Group, 1955), p. 6; Lewis A. Coser, "Functions of Small Group Research," *Social Problems* 3 (July 1955): 1–6; and Neil Gilbert, Armin Rosenkranz, and Harry Specht, "Dialectics of Social Planning," *Social Work* 18, no. 2 (March 1973): 78–86.
[19]Philip M. Hauser, "Demography and Human Ecology in Relation to Social Work," *Social Welfare Forum* (1956), p. 176: Robert C. Angell, "A Research Basis for Welfare Practice," ibid. (1954), pp. 10–11; Greenwood, *Social Science and Social Work*, pp. 24–31; Kahn, "Some Problems Facing Social Work Scholarship," pp. 59–60; Genevieve W. Carter, "Theory Development in Social Work Research," *Social Service Review* 29, no. 1 (March 1955): 34–42; and Fremont J. Lyden and Lawrence K. Lee, "Evaluating Program Change," *Social Work* 18, no. 2 (March 1973): 87–94.
[20]C. E. Schaefer and H. L. Millman, "The Use of Behavior Ratings in Assessing the Effect of Residential Treatment with Latency Age Boys," *Child Psychiatry and Human Development* 3, no. 3 (1973): 157–64.

Recently it has been recognized that social work research needs to develop and define its own conceptual tools, selecting and adapting concepts from the social sciences.[21] Clarification of the definition of social work terms, such as *social adjustment, adaptation to stress, environmental change, milieu and group therapy, social work treatment,* and many others, is necessary. These various concepts require precise definition and delimitation, through analysis and interrelated conceptualization, which is of primary importance for social work research. Such conceptualization may integrate concepts of the social sciences, such as social stratification, social class, social role, transference, perceptions and expectations of clients and social workers, and cultural values, and eliminate serious differences between social scientists and social workers in methodological approach toward research. It will increase the possibility of interdisciplinary studies and allow for the integration of concepts from all areas of social welfare practice. The theory development within such a conceptual framework of social work research will enable social workers to define identical variables, which can be built into research designs and will clarify the multiple relationships among these variables. In this process, social work research will provide the profession with an understanding of its varied relationships and with central concepts that will be refined and interrelated so that a growing, systematically testable practice theory can be developed.

Progress in social work research includes the development of scales for measuring movement in casework and of evaluative criteria for group work practice, devices for interviewing and clinical observations, and application of research methods formulated in the behavioral sciences and human relationships.[22] There still remains the challenge of defining and developing special, appropriate research measures for social work phenomena. This cannot be achieved without the creation of a conceptual framework and research methods that will develop their empirical validation in social work terms.

[21]Henry S. Maas and Martin Wolins, "Concepts and Methods in Social Work Research," in *New Directions in Social Work,* ed. Cora Kasius (New York: Harper, 1954), pp. 215–37. See also: Herbert Marcuse, Robert P. Wolff, and Harrington Moore, Jr., *A Critique of Pure Tolerance* (Boston: Beacon, 1965); Marguerite Pohek, ed., *Teaching and Learning in Social Work Education* (New York: Council on Social Work Education, 1970); Frederick W. Seidl, "Teaching Social Work Research," *Education for Social Work* 9, no. 3 (Fall 1973): 71–77; and J. W. Moore, "Social Constraints on Sociological Knowledge: Academics and Research Concerning Minorities," *Social Problems* 21 (January 1973): 65–77.

[22]Genevieve W. Carter, "Problem Formulation in Social Work Research," *Social Casework* 36 (July 1955): 295–302; Alfred J. Kahn, "Facilitating Social Work Research," *Social Service Review* 30, no. 3 (September 1956): 331–46; Derek L. Phillips, *Abandoning Method* (San Francisco: Jossey-Bass, 1973); and David A. Ward, "Evaluative Research for Corrections," in *Prisoners in America,* ed. Lloyd E. Ohlin (Englewood Cliffs, N.J.: Prentice-Hall, 1973), pp. 184–206.

SELECTED BIBLIOGRAPHY

Social Welfare Administration

ATTWOOD, JULIA C. *Administrative Controls in Welfare—Medical Care Programs.* Chicago: American Public Welfare Association, 1963.

ATWATER, PIERCE. *Problems of Administration in Social Work.* Minneapolis: University of Minnesota Press, 1940.

BLUMENTHAL, S. *Management Information Systems.* Englewood Cliffs, N.J.: Prentice-Hall, 1969.

COLE, GEORGE F., and GREENBERGER, HOWARD L. "Legal Services for Welfare Recipients." *Social Work* 19 (January 1974): 81–87.

DE SCHWEINITZ, KARL. *People and Process in Social Security.* Washington, D.C.: American Council on Education, 1948.

DUBIN, ROBERT. *Human Relations in Administration.* Englewood Cliffs, N.J.: Prentice-Hall, 1951.

GULICK, LUTHER, and URWICK, L. *Papers on the Science of Administration.* New York: Columbia University Press, 1937.

HANCHETTE, HELEN W., et al. *Some Dynamics of Social Agency Administration.* New York: Family Service Association of America, 1946.

KIDNEIGH, JOHN C. "The Quest for Competence in Welfare Administration." *Social Service Review* 24 (June 1950): 173–80.

―――. "Administration of Social Agencies." *Social Work Yearbook* (1957), pp. 75–82.

PAYNE, JAMES E. "Ombudsman Roles for Social Workers." *Social Work* 17 (January 1972): 94–100.

SEARS, JESS B. *The Nature of Administrative Process.* New York: McGraw-Hill, 1950.

SILVER, HAROLD. "Administration of Social Agencies." *Social Work Yearbook* (1954), pp. 19–26.

SORENSEN, ROY. *The Art of Board Membership.* New York: Association Press, 1950.

TRECKER, HARLEIGH B. *Group Process in Administration.* New York: Woman's Press, 1950.

―――. *New Understanding of Administration.* New York: Association Press, 1961.

―――. *Social Work Administration: Principles and Practice.* New York: Association Press, 1971.

TRECKER, HARLEIGH B.; GLICK, FRANK Z.; and KIDNEIGH, JOHN. *Education for Social Work Administration.* New York: American Association of Social Workers, 1953.

WHITE, R. CLYDE. *Administration of Public Welfare.* New York: American Book Co., 1950.

WHYTE, WILLIAM F. *Organizational Behavior.* Homewood, Ill.: Irwin, 1969.

Social Work Research

BLENKNER, MARGARET, et al. *The Function and Practice of Research in Social Work.* New York: Social Work Research Group, 1955.

BROOKS, HARVEY, and LINDZEY, GARDNER. *The Behavioral and Social Science Outlook and Needs.* Englewood Cliffs, N.J.: Prentice-Hall, 1969.

CARTER, GENEVIEVE W. "Theory Development in Social Work Research." *Social Service Review* 29 (March 1955): 32–42.

_____. "The Challenge of Accountability." *Public Welfare* 31 (Fall 1973): 267–77.

CHAPIN, F. STUART. *Social Science Research: Its Expanding Horizons.* Minneapolis: University of Minnesota Press, 1953.

FAIRWEATHER, GEORGE W. *Methods for Experimental Social Innovation.* New York: Wiley & Sons, 1967.

FRANKLIN, BILLY J., and OSBORNE, HAROLD W. *Research Methods and Insights.* Belmont, Calif.: Wadsworth, 1971.

FRENCH, DAVID G. *An Approach to Measuring Results in Social Work.* New York: Columbia University Press, 1952.

GOLDSTEIN, HARRIS K. *Research Standards and Methods for Social Workers.* New Orleans: Hauser, 1963.

GOODE, WILLIAM J., and HATT, PAUL K. *Methods of Social Research.* New York: McGraw-Hill, 1952.

GORDON, WILLIAM E. *Toward Basic Research in Social Work.* St. Louis, Mo.: Washington University Press, 1951.

GREENWOOD, ERNEST. *Toward a Sociology of Social Work.* Los Angeles: Welfare Council of Metropolitan Los Angeles, 1953.

_____. "Social Science and Social Work: A Theory of Their Relationship." *Social Service Review* 29 (March 1955): 20–33.

_____. "Social Work Research: A Decade of Reappraisal." *Social Service Review* 31 (September 1957): 311–20.

HAYES, SAMUEL P., Jr. *Evaluating Development Research.* Brussels, Belgium: UNESCO, 1967.

HECKMAN, A. A. Measuring the Effectiveness of Agency Services." *Journal of Social Casework* 29 (1948): 394–99.

HOFFMAN, ISAAC. *Toward a Logic for Social Work Research.* St. Paul, Minn.: Amherst H. Wilder Foundation, 1952.

HUNT, J. McVICKER, and KOGAN, LEONARD S. *Measuring Results in Social Casework: A Manual on Judging Movement.* New York: Family Service Association of America, 1950.

HUNT, J. McVICKER; BLENKNER, MARGARET; and KOGAN, LEONARD S. *Testing Results in Social Casework: A Field Test of the Movement of Scale.* New York: Family Service Association of America, 1950.

HYMAN, HERBERT H.; WRIGHT, CHARLES R.; and HOPKINS, TERRENCE K. *Applications of Methods of Evaluation.* Berkley: University of California Press, 1962.

JAHODA, MARIE; DEUTSCH, MORTON; and COOK, STUART W. *Research Methods in Social Relations.* New York: Dryden, 1951.

KAHN, ALFRED J. "The Nature of Social Work Knowledge." In *New Directions in Social Work,* ed. Cora Kasius. New York: Harper, 1954, pp. 194–214.

_____. "Some Problems Facing Social Work Scholarship." *Social Work* 2 (April 1957): 54–62.

KAPLAN, A. *The Conduct of Inquiry.* San Francisco: Chancellor, 1964.

KLEIN, PHILIP, and MERIAM, IDA E. *The Contribution of Research to Social Work.* New York: American Association of Social Workers, 1948.

LUNDBERG, GEORGE A. *Social Research: A Study in Methods Gathering Data.* New York: Longmans, 1951.

MAAS, HENRY S. "Collaboration between Social Work and the Social Sciences." *Social Work Journal* 31 (July 1950): 104–9.

———, ed. *Research in the Social Services: A Five-Year Review.* New York: National Association of Social Workers, 1971.

MAAS, HENRY S., and WOLINS, MARTIN. "Concepts and Methods in Social Work Research." In *New Directions in Social Work,* ed. Cora Kasius. New York: Harper, 1954, pp. 215–37.

MACDONALD, MARY E. "Research in Social Work." *Social Work Yearbook* (1957), pp. 489–500.

MORGAN, JOHN S. "Research in Social Work: A Frame of Reference." *Social Work Journal* 30 (October 1949): 148–54.

MOSER, C. A. *Survey Methods in Social Investigation.* London: Heineman, 1965.

MULLEN, EDWARD J., and DUMPSON, JAMES R. *Evaluation of Social Intervention.* San Francisco: Jossey-Bass, 1972.

POLANSKY, NORMAN A. *Social Work Research.* Chicago: University of Chicago Press, 1960.

———. "Research in Social Work." *Encyclopedia of Social Work (1971),* pp. 1098–1106.

POWERS, EDWIN, and WITMER, HELEN. *An Experiment in the Prevention of Delinquency: The Cambridge-Somerville Youth Study.* New York: Columbia University Press, 1951.

PRESTON, MALCOLM G., and MUDD, EMILY H. "Research and Service in Social Work: Conditions for a Stable Union." *Social Work* 1 (January 1950): 34–40.

SCHWARTZ, EDWARD E. "Research and Social Work." In *Social Work Yearbook* (1951), pp. 500–12.

STUART, RICHARD B. "Research in Social Work: Social Casework and Social Group Work." *Encyclopedia of Social Work (1971),* pp. 1106–22.

SUCHMAN, EDWARD A. *Evaluative Research: Principles and Practice in Public Service and Social Action Programs.* New York: Russell Sage Foundation, 1967.

TOWLE, CHARLOTTE. "Some Basic Principles of Research in Social Casework." *Social Service Review* 25 (March 1951): 66–80.

TRIPODI, TONY; FELLIN, PHILIP; and EPSTEIN, IRWIN. *Social Program Evaluation. Guidelines for Health, Education, and Welfare Administration.* Itasca, Ill.: Peacock Publications, 1971.

TRIPODI, TONY; FELLIN, PHILIP; and MEYER, HENRY J. *The Assessment of Social Research.* Itasca, Ill.: Peacock Publications, 1969.

WEISS, CAROL H. *Evaluative Research.* Englewood Cliffs, N.J.: Prentice-Hall, 1972.

WITMER, HELEN L. "Basic Conceptions in Social Work Research." *Mental Hygiene* 33 (January 1949): 108–14.

YOUNG, PAULINE V. *Scientific Social Surveys and Research: An Introduction to the Background, Content, Methods, and Analysis of Social Studies.* Rev. ed. Englewood Cliffs, N.J.: Prentice-Hall, 1949.

AUTHOR INDEX

A

Ackerman, Nathan, 91
Addams, Jane, 89
Angell, Robert C., 226
Aplin, G., 106
Apte, Robert Z., 82, 190, 216
Aram, J.S., 221
Attwood, Julia C., 228
Atwater, Pierce, 228

B

Back, Kurt W., 117, 156
Balgopal, Pallassana, 115
Bandura, Albert, 106
Barcal, Ayner, 95
Barish, Herbert, 116
Bartlett, Harriett M., 2, 6, 82
Benstock, Robert, 172

Bernard, Jessie, 3
Bernstein, Saul, 116
Berry, Margaret, 93
Bertalanfy, Ludwig von, 20
Billingsley, Andrew, 83
Bisno, Herbert, 7
Blackey, Eileen, 115
Blau, Peter M., 214
Blenkner, Margaret, 226, 228, 229
Bloch, Marc, 85
Bloksberg, Leonard M., 153
Blumenthal, S., 221, 228
Blumer, Herbert, 225
Boehm, Werner W., 1
Borgman, Robert D., 83
Bornemann, Ernst, 154
Brandon, Arlene C., 109
Briar, Scott, 3, 82, 146
Brooks, Harvey, 229
Brown, Bertram S., 10
Bugenthal, James F., 113
Burke, Peter J., 87

C

Caldwell, Bettye M., 83
Campbell, Angus, 3, 83, 215
Cannon, Walter B., 20
Carson, Robert C., 83
Carter, Genevieve W., 226, 227, 229
Carter, Robert D., 203
Cartwright, Dorwin, 154
Chapin, F. Stuart, 229
Cohen, Nathan E., 216, 219
Cole, George F., 228
Converse, Philip E., 3, 83, 215
Cook, Stuart W., 229
Coser, Lewis A., 87, 226
Coyle, Grace, 156
Crawford, Paul L., 148

D

Davis, Fred, 83
Day, Peter, 215
Dentler,Robert A., 214
Deutsch, Morton, 229
Dimock, Helley S., 156
Dubin, Robert, 228
Dubos, René, 83
Dumpson, James R., 148, 224, 230
Dunn, Edgar S., Jr., 214

E

Ecklein, Joan L., 173
Ehrlich, George E., 10
Engler, Richard E., 83
Epstein, Irwin, 230
Epstein, Laura, 3
Erikson, Erik H., 101

F

Falk, Hans, 86
Faurweather, George W., 229
Fax, N., 103
Feldman, Robert A., 103
Feldman, Ronald, 105, 106
Fellin, Philip, 230
Finney, Joseph C., 83
Follett, Mary Parker, 99

Forman, Robert E., 11
Frankel, Arthur J., 93, 100
Frankel, Charles, 217
Franklin, Billy J., 224, 229
French, David G., 229
Friedlander, Walter A., 82, 190, 216

G

Gamber, R., 106
Gambrill, Eileen D., 103, 106
Garrett, Annette Marie, 83
Garvin, Charles, 148
Gilbert, Neil, 226
Gilbert, Gwendolyn C., 10
Ginsburg, Saul, 85
Glasser, Paul H., 86, 93, 99, 100, 146
Glick, Franz Z., 228
Goffman, Erving, 84
Goldberg, Carl, 105
Goldberg, Merle C., 105
Goldstein, Harris K., 229
Goode, William J., 229
Gordon, William E., 229
Greenberg, Martin, 12
Greenberger, Howard L., 228
Greenwood, Ernest, 224, 226, 229
Gronseth, Eric, 10
Grosser, Charles F., 168, 169
Gulick, Luther, 228
Gurin, Arnold, 8, 173, 174

H

Haas, J. Eugene, 274
Hadden, Jeffrey K., 214
Hage, Jerald, 215
Hamilton, Gordon, 154, 155
Hanchette, Helen W., 228
Hartford, Margaret E., 156
Hatt, Paul K., 229
Hauser, Philip M., 226
Hausman, M., 151
Hayes, Samuel P., Jr., 229
Heckman, A. A., 229
Hendry, Charles E., 156, 222
Hensch, James M., 10
Herman, Mary W., 10
Hill, Michael J., 220
Hirshfield, Daniel, 218

Hofferbert, Richard I., 215
Hoffman, Isaac, 229
Holland, Thomas P., 12
Hollis, Florence, 3, 12
Hopkins, Terrance K., 229
Horowitz, Irving L., 225
Hoshino, George, 9
Hunt, J. McVicker, 229
Hyman, Herbert H., 229

J

Jackson, Robert C., 218
Jacobs, Alfred, 151, 154
Jahoda, Marie, 91, 229
Jameş, Dorothy E., 12
Jehu, Derek, 95
Johnson, Arline, 2, 220
Johnson, V. E., 113
Jones, Charles O., 215

K

Kadushin, Alfred, 83, 95, 109
Kahn, Alfred J., 8, 79, 86, 171, 218, 224
227, 229
Kaiser, Clara, 156
Kaplan, A., 229
Kaplan, Harold I., 113
Kasius, Cora, 2, 72, 155, 227, 229
Katz, Alfred H., 139
Kaufman, Herbert, 215
Kelman, Herbert C., 14, 84
Kidneigh, John C., 220
Klein, Philip, 229
Klenk, Robert W., 88, 89
Kluckhohn, Clyde, 58, 59
Knoll, Robert E., 148
Kogan, Leonard S., 229
Konopka, Gisela, 2, 4, 5, 92, 93
Kramer, Ralph M., 4, 172, 220
Kuypers, Joseph A., 84

L

Lane, Robert F., 166
Lappin, Ben, 165
Larson, Calvin J., 214
Laruder, Mehrene, 12

Laufer, Armand, 173
Lee, Lawrence K., 226
Leighton, Alexander, 222
Levine, Sol, 84
Lewin, Kurt, 148
Lichtenberg, Philip, 219
Liebert, Robert M., 225
Lindblom, Charles E., 215
Lindemann, Edward C., 150, 155
Lindzey, Gardner, 229
Linton, Ralph, 43
Lippit, Ronald, 151, 215
Lowenstein, Edward E., 3
Lowy, Louis, 153
Lundberg, George A., 230
Lurie, Walter A., 99, 104
Lyden, Fremont J., 214, 226

M

Maas, Henry S., 2, 5, 82, 83, 84, 104,
191, 227, 230
Macdonald, Mary E., 230
Malamud, Daniel I., 148
Maluccio, Anthony N., 85
Marcuse, Herbert, 227
Marion, Ida C., 9
Marlow, Wilma D., 85
Marshall, James A., 170
Masotti, Louis H., 214
Masters, W. H., 113
Maxwell, Jean M., 149
Mayer, Robert R., 215
Mechanic, David, 10
Meriam, Ida E., 229
Merl, Lawrence F., 156
Merton, Robert K., 43
Meyer, Henry J., 216, 230
Middleman, Ruth R., 156
Miller, Ernest G., 214
Miller, Henry, 3
Miller, Walter B., 148
Millman, H.L., 226
Mogulaf, Melvin, 219, 223
Moore, Harrington, Jr., 227
Moore, J.W., 227
Moore, Wilbert E., 3
Morgan, John S., 230
Morris, Robert, 4, 172, 215
Moser, C.A., 230
Mudd, Emily H., 230

Mullen, Edward J., 218, 230

N

Neale, John E., 225
Nee, Robert H., 83
Newman, Edward, 219
Nisbet, Robert A., 4
Northern, Helen, 156

O

O'Connor, Gerald, 10
Ohlin, Lloyd E., 227
Osborne, Harold W., 224, 229

P

Payne, James E., 228
Perlman, Helen Harris, 3, 83, 218
Perlman, Robert, 173, 174
Perrucci, Robert, 8, 12
Philips, Helen, 156
Phillips, Derek L., 227
Piliavin, Irving, 146
Pilisuk, Marc, 8, 10, 12
Pilisuk, Phyllis, 10
Pins, Arnulf M., 7
Pohek, Marguerite, 227
Polansky, Norman A., 79, 83, 218, 230
Pool, I. de Sola, 223
Powers, Edwin, 230
Praag, Philip H., van, 219
Preston, Malcolm G., 230
Prigmore, Charles S., 223
Pressman, Jeffrey L., 214

R

Rainman, Eva Schindler, 151
Redl, Fritz, 156
Reid, William J., 3, 83
Rein, Martin, 4, 172
Reynolds, Bertha, 115
Reynolds, Larry T., 10
Ricciuti, Henry N., 83
Riessman, Frank, 97, 98
Ripple, Lilian, 153

Roberts, Robert W., 83
Rogers, Carl, 113
Rogers, Everett M., 215
Romanshyn, John M., x
Rose, Sheldon D., 90, 154
Rosenkranz, Armin, 226
Ross, Murray G., 165
Ross, Sheldon D., 156
Rothman, Jack, 174, 175, 176, 188, 189
Rubin, David M., 223
Ryan, Robert M., 88, 89
Ryland, Gladys, 4, 106, 157

S

Sachsman, David B., 223
Sadock, Benjamin J., 113
Sagarin, Eduard, 225
Saix, Christine, 83
Sample, William C., 154
Sampson, Edward E., 109
Sandman, Peter M., 223
Saroyan, William, 156
Sarri, Rosemary C., 86, 146, 220
Schaefer, C. E., 226
Schwartz, Edward E., 154, 230
Schwartz, William, 4, 148, 150, 156
Schweinitz, Elizabeth de, 82
Schweinitz, Karl de, 82, 228
Scotch, Norman A., 84
Sears, Jess B., 228
Seidl, Frederick W., 227
Sheldon, Eleanor B., 3
Shoemaker, F. Floyd, 215
Shostak, Arthur B., 214
Shyne, Ann W., 83
Silver, Harold, 228
Simon, H. A., 223
Simpson, George E., 91
Sorensen, Roy, 228
Specht, Harry, 172, 226
Spergel, Irving, 98, 148
Spradlin, Wilford, 151, 154
Stein, Herman D., 10
Steinmetz, Suzanne K., 106
Stratton, W. E., 221
Strauss, Anselm M., 10
Strauss, Murray A., 106
Stuart, Richard B., 230
Suchman, Edward A., 230
Sussman, Marvin B., 3

Swack, Lois G., 90

T

Thomas, Edwin J., 103, 218
Thurst, Daniel, 93, 218
Titmuss, Richard M., 79, 171
Toffler, Alvin, 158
Towle, Charlotte, 217, 218, 220, 230
Townsend, Peter, 84
Trecker, Harleigh B., 156, 228
Tripodi, Tony, 230
Tropp, Emanuel, 103, 113, 117, 224
Turek, Melvin, 219

U

Urwick, L. 228

V

Vasey, Wayne, 220
Vintner, Robert D., 86, 146, 157

W

Wade, Alan D., 223
Walberg, Herbert J., 153
Walker, T.G., 105
Ward, David A., 227
Warren, Roland L., 4, 11, 218
Warwick, Donald P., 14, 84

Waters, Miriam van, 85
Watson, Jeanne, 215
Wechsler, Henry, 139
Weiss, Carol H., 230
Weiss, Paul, 20
Weissman, Harold, 116
Westley, Bruce, 215
Wheelis, Allen, 84
White, R. Clyde, 228
Whyte, William F., 228
Wickenden, Elizabeth, x, 172
Wilcox, Clair L., 218
Wildavsky, Aaron, 214
Wilensky, Harold, 221
Wilson, Gertrude, 4, 103, 106, 157
Wineman, David, 156
Witmaer, Helen L., 230
Wodarski, N. A., 103, 106
Wolff, Robert F., 227
Wolins, Martin, 2, 151, 157, 227, 230
Woods, Thomas L., 151
Wright, Charles R., 229

Y

Yablonsky, Lewis, 146
Yinger, J.M., 91
Young, Pauline V., 230
Younghusband, Eileen, x

Z

Zalba, Serapio, 4
Zaltman, Gerald, 14
Zander, Alvin, 154

SUBJECT INDEX

A

Acceptance, 38, 64-66, 94, 95, 98, 115, 116
Accountability, 219, 224
Adaption to stress, 18, 37, 43, 53-59
Advocacy, 168
Aged (*see* Older persons' services)
Auspices of social services, 198

B

Behavioral modification, 75ff., 95, 100, 106, 218, 226

C

Causation of problems, 8
Child welfare, 10, 13, 16, 47, 58, 79, 112, 156
Communications, 38, 66-67, 90, 112, 215

Community Development, x, 214
Community Welfare, 11, 12
Confidentiality, 16, 64, 70
Correctional Services, 10, 49, 148
Crisis Intervention, 183

D

Delinquency, 98, 146, 148 (*See also* Correctional Services)
Democratic principles, 1, 150, 158
Differential principles, 38, 63, 71, 72, 103, 198, 212, 216
Dignity of client, 2, 21, 112
Drug addiction, 109
Dualistic approach, 7

E

Education for social work, 7, 21, 81, 115, 153, 191, 218, 227

Ego psychology, 32, 37, 59-63, 78
Employment services, 11, 46, 74
Encounter groups, 113, 117
Environment, 3, 8, 20, 72, 73, 113
Epileptic patients, 117 ff.
Equal opportunity, 5
Evaluative research, 194, 203, 218, 227

F

Family services, 9, 22-30, 46, 99
Field of social work, 9ff.
Financing social services, 165ff., 219, 223
Function of social work, 116, 165, 174

G

Generic principles, 1, 80, 89
Goal of social work, 7
Group conflicts, 106
Group intervention, 105
Group process, 103, 104
Group therapy, 91, 95, 97, 98, 103, 105

H

Health Services, 10, 50, 51, 148-49
Homeostasis, 20
Housing, 11

I

Individualization, 38, 67, 68, 97, 101, 144
Integration of Services, 193, 206, 221
Interagency Cooperation, 221
International aspects, x, 6, 11, 163, 172
Intervention, 13, 82, 87, 95, 104, 136, 218

K

Knowledge base of social work, 83, 84, 187

L

Limitation of service, 115, 145, 146

M

Marital counseling, 109, 113
Mental hygiene, 10, 51-53, 117ff.
Moral values, 4, 9, 14, 114, 217

O

Objectives of social work, 6ff., 154, 180, 185
Older persons' services, 149, 150, 199, 200ff.

P

Participation, 68, 85, 167, 180, 214
Principles of practice, 1, 85, 175
Processes of social work, 1
Public assistance, 8, 44-47

R

Racism, 12, 108, 147ff.
Recreation, 10, 108, 127
Red Cross service, 49, 50
Reference service, 141
Religious discrimination, 91, 93, 105, 147
Research elements, 189, 202, 224, 225, 226, 227 (see also Evaluative research)
Right of self-determination, 2-4
Role functions, 37, 40-53, 73, 75, 109

S

School social work, 48, 49, 156
Self-awareness, 70, 71, 116
Self-help principle, 2, 3, 8, 104, 139
Sensitivity groups, 113, 115, 117, 156
Settlement movement, 84, 169, 192

Small groups, 86, 150, 154
Social action, 159 (*see also* Intervention)
Social change, 14, 102, 161, 168, 215, 219
Social diagnosis, 20, 23, 31, 100, 107, 111
Social insurance, 9
Social planning, 8, 11, 159, 162, 166, 170, 185, 194, 226
Social policy, 219, 222, 224
Social problems, 177-179, 214
Social reform, 214
Social responsibility, 5, 14, 104
Strategies of social work, 182
Stressful situations, 14ff.
Supervision, 150, 152, 153

T

Testing, 110
Training, 150, 152, 153, 191
Travelers' aid, 49, 50
Types of social services, 9-12, 175, 192

U

Understanding human behavior, 37ff.

V

Veterans' services, 11
Volunteers, 11, 150ff.